Praise for *In Search of the Tiger:*

'Stafford's greatness (and he really is a great writer) is that he has found a way to combine perfectly modulated, gentle whimsy with an innocently artless yet compelling storyline, to produce considered expertise and seemingly endless insights into his subject. The result is magical. Imagine Jerome K. Jerome writing about golf, or recall P. G. Wodehouse doing so, and you have a pretty accurate picture of Stafford's style. Like Wodehouse's, and unlike that of modern comic writers like Bill Bryson and Pete McCarthy, his humour appears entirely natural and effortless. This is a beautifully written and genuinely funny book.'

—*Sydney Morning Herald*

'Stafford's indomitability, his chutzpah, his lunatic hubris, inspires a kind of incredulous sympathy.'

—*The Times*

'Poignant, amusing and entertaining . . . a must for anyone who has ever dreamed of making it big.'

—*National Club Golfer*

'Golf is evil but Stafford makes a persuasive advocate.'

—*The Mail on Sunday*

'A very funny book.'

—*Brisbane Courier & News*

'Only a writer who is really skilled at putting his foot in the door could dream up a book about learning to play golf and meeting all the top players at the same time. An enjoyable read.'

—*Daily Mail*

In Search of the Tiger

How a Chance Taxi Conversation Leads to a Golfing Odyssey

Ian Stafford

THE LYONS PRESS
Guilford, Connecticut
An imprint of The Globe Pequot Press

The Lyons Press is an imprint of The Globe Pequot Press.

10 9 8 7 6 5 4 3 2 1

Photographs © Ian Stafford 2003
Photographs of Drambuie World Ice Golf Championships © Getty Images

Printed in the United States of America

Text design and typesetting by Textype

ISBN 1-59228-330-6

Library of Congress Cataloging-in-Publication Data is available on file.

Contents

Acknowledgments

A big thank you to the following, without whose help none of what you are about to read would have taken place:

Bill Elliott, Derek Larenson, Bruce Green and Michael Faraone at the Royal Melbourne GC; Bill Exten at the New South Wales GC; Peter Thomson, Jack and Jackie Newton, David Bailey and, especially, David Young at the Jack Nicklaus World of Golf Centre, Sidcup; special thank you to David Rennie at Wentworth GC; Ballybunion GC; Peter Dawson at the R&A; Peter Mason at St Andrews GC; Ernie Jones at the K Club; Portmarnock GC; Brian and Frank O'Driscoll; Dianne Scott and Simon Crawford at Gleneagles; Simon Laird; special thanks to Simon Crane; Nick Faldo; Matt Richards at Infinite Pictures; Ashley Woolfe; Steve Backley; Delphine Chevallier and Morgan Cailleaux at Golf de Saint-Cloud; special thanks to Scott Gorham, also Nicko McBrain and Glyn Johns; Jonathan Brown, Caroline Sutcliffe and Rhiannon Henry at Drambuie; Mark James; Ronnie Gregg and Don McElhone at Cliftonville GC; Natasha Duval at the Glenlivet Office Putting Championships; special thanks to Chip Thomson; Pete Jordan; Fiona Foster at Karen Earl; special thanks to Brendan Taylor at IMG; Michael Jones at IMG; Jos Vanstiphout; Kate Phillips at IMG, Justin Rose, Eric Rogers, special thanks to Fanny Sunesson; Gordon Simpson, Scott

Crockett and David Garland at the European Tour; Georgina Tarrant at IMG; Jack Nicklaus; Scott Tolley; Duncan Wardle at Walt Disney World; Suzie Bills and David Leadbetter; Jim Mandeville; Jaguar Cars; Peter Parr, Tim Davies, Ted McIver, Michael Webb at BMGA; Andy Yamanaka at JGA; Isao Aoki; Penny Thompson at IMG; Mark McCormack; Sir Steve Redgrave; David Williams at the European Tour; Ernie and Liezl Els; Queenwood GC; Christina Caffyn at IMG; Laura Davies; Alan Shearer and SFX; Earl Woods; Tiger Woods.

Also thank you to Robert Kirby, Sugra Zaman, and my editor, Hannah MacDonald, who made me drive those extra yards, and everyone else at Ebury Press involved in the project.

Finally, to my wife, Karen, and my children, Charlotte and Harry, who once more had to put up with the travel, the obsession and, this time, the clothes too. They know the score by now and let me get on with it, but I appreciate their patience, their tolerance and an understanding that allows me to continue to live out a double life. Without them none of this is possible.

Prologue

A cab driver and I were talking golf one spring morning en route to Heathrow Airport. It was early, I was tired and, frankly, not wildly interested in his numbing stack of golfing statistics until he muttered, 'I was nearly killed playing golf last year.'

I jerked awake. 'What happened?'

'I was playing a round of golf in South Carolina,' he began, as if starting a long soliloquy. 'Beautiful course, actually. Lots of water, deep, cavernous bunkers—'

Typical golfer. He's just told me he nearly died playing golf, and then insists on describing every single aspect of the course.

'Yes, yes,' I interrupted impatiently, 'but how were you nearly killed?'

'Oh, right. Well, a bolt of lightning struck the ground a few feet away from me, shot up the iron shaft of my club, and hurled me backwards against a tree trunk, where I fell beside its roots.' His tone was matter of fact.

I imagined a heap with black, static hair sticking upright above his head. A facetious response would lighten the moment, I decided.

'Bet it put you off your next shot.'

'Should have been an easy approach shot to the green, but I sliced it into the woods where the ball had a terrible lie and ended up triple-bogeying the hole. Buggered up the whole round.'

We sat in silence for a few minutes, his an angry one as he clenched his fists noticeably around the steering wheel at the injustice of golf; mine

1

stunned and slightly petrified as I observed a certifiable lunatic taking me at 80mph to the airport.

Any sane human being would be thanking the Lord that after being struck by a fork of lightning his life had been spared. This man was shaking his fist at the heavens for fouling up his round of golf.

This chance conversation was the catalyst to my exploration of the global epidemic commonly referred to as golf. It is to the crazed minicab driver, and to the many millions of other, terminally consumed humans, that I offer the following.

1

Down Under

'Jeez!'

It was an entirely predictable reaction. A ball, which should have travelled high, straight and eventually down the centre of a lush, green fairway, had instead swung violently to the right like a boomerang and disappeared into a small forest of thickset bushes, scattering a throng of exotic-looking birds in the process.

'That's a lost ball,' said Bruce Green, the club professional at the Royal Melbourne Golf Club, without bothering to amble over and investigate. 'A definite lost ball.'

Until now I had been rather enjoying myself in the midst of what the Australians laughingly call winter. The chance to follow the 2001 British and Irish Lions rugby team taking on the Wallabies in a three-test series had meant three weeks of revisiting old friends, drinking myself stupid and, on occasions, writing sports articles, though not always at the same time. I found myself one Wednesday afternoon at the Royal Melbourne, the most prestigious golf course in the country. To be a member means you have arrived in life. Only the very best golfers, or the most successful figures in society Down Under, get the chance to swing their clubs regularly here. Because I had spent a week playing cricket with the Australian test team a few years back, however, the golf club made the mistake of inviting me to pay them a visit. It had been some time since anyone at the Royal Melbourne had witnessed anyone so numbingly bad.

'How often did you say you'd played before?' Bruce enquired, as I reached for another ball, trying to act as if the previous attempt at a tee shot was no more than a figment of everyone's imagination.

It was more of a statement than a question, reminding me of the many times I find myself somewhere like Paris, Berlin or Rome and greet the locals with a less than assured '*Bonjour*' or '*Guten Tag*', only to hear the immediate response: 'Ah, so you're English.' After one appalling shot Bruce Green had me rumbled.

'Not a lot,' I replied to his query. 'In fact, not a lot at all.'

The truth was three rounds of golf in 38 years of life. That's one round every 12.66 years, the last one played some five years ago. Even those three rounds were forced upon me, as I recall, by others who needed a fourth player to fill the required quota. It had been a case of army volunteering, with the end result causing much mirth for my playing partners.

And that's the point of all this. At the age of 38 it dawned on me that I was the only man I knew who did not play golf. At all! All my friends played golf. All my business colleagues played golf. All my sporting contacts played golf. And all of them would talk incessantly on the subject in my presence. In fact, they would only pause when I made some irrelevant or simply embarrassing remark in a vain attempt to partake in the conversation. There would be a short silence, a cough and they'd begin again.

Whether I liked it or not, there was clearly a huge void in my life. In some known circles I might as well have been living on Mars. My non-participation in the game was like standing up in an Alcoholics Anonymous meeting. 'Hello,' I could announce, at a Non-Golfers Rehabilitation Centre. 'My name is Ian, and I do not play golf,' half expecting a small round of applause for my bravery in taking the first crucial step towards golf.

Everyone and his dog would insist on telling me that once you start playing the game it will take a firm grip on you and refuse to let go. Ever. It would become an obsession. I would think about it day and night, find myself taking practice swings in a supermarket or garage or in someone else's living room. The greatest days in your life – becoming a parent, getting married – pale into insignificance compared with scoring your first hole in one or your first below-par round.

This, I could categorically assure you, would not happen to me. I could take golf and most definitely leave it any day. I had this image, you see, of badly dressed people looking like pimps, as Robin Williams once said famously, of ultra-conservative, middle-aged, sexist, racist old custodians of an empire long gone, eyeing people like me up distastefully as if I were something they had just stepped in. In truth I had hardly played golf before because I wanted no part of it. The bank managers and the chartered surveyors could drone on about it until the cows came home, as far as I was concerned. You wouldn't catch me welcoming such suburban, middle-class inanity into my life. No, I was still young in my rose-tinted view, and I stood as much chance of turning my wife into a golf widow as she did of partnering me in the cha-cha-cha for Home Counties North on *Come Dancing*.

Then something happened. Or rather, someone. Tiger Woods appeared on the scene; this young, vibrant, exciting black American who made everyone sit up and take notice as he became a global sporting icon within three years of turning professional. Correction. Not a sporting icon, but *the* sporting icon. He lead the way, and everyone followed. Golfers became younger, fitter, stronger – damn it, even sexier. Suddenly it was no longer embarrassing to me if someone played golf. It was – and this took time for me to accept – cool. The sport had become attractive to everybody, regardless of roots, class or skin colour.

And that everybody included competitive me, the kind of guy who enjoys – really enjoys – firing footballs past his nine-year-old son in the back garden. It had slowly dawned on me that there were other reasons to explain why I had not succumbed to the golfing epidemic, reasons that had nothing to do with my prejudices. You see, I am the sort of person whose attention span is minimal. If you can't do something both well and, more importantly, quickly, then it's not worth doing at all. Others leave this attitude behind with their childhood, but not me. My experiences of golf up to this point had been predictably negative because I had been useless – unsurprising given my non-existent background in the game, but nevertheless an unattractive dose of reality to me. So why bother? Why not go off and write books about an array of sports I knew I could play and, better still, would not each take up more than a week or two's effort. Time enough to achieve my goal of playing with a team, but not enough time to grow bored or offer a more substantial commitment.

The truth was that refusing to turn into the pompous old fart we all think plays golf was just a smokescreen. The man who has happily fought world boxing champions in the past, played in top level rugby matches and partnered Olympic rowing champions, just didn't fancy the challenge of becoming a good golfer because I knew it would take months, probably years, to succeed, if at all.

You can thank Tiger Woods for this realisation. Once I had dug beneath my veneer of excuses, the U-turn I performed was startling.

Golf wasn't going to defeat me, the man who got beat up over 3 rounds by Roy Jones Jr and survived, who withstood 12 minutes of purgatory performing stand-up comedy at the Edinburgh festival and lived, who once fought Kung Fu with a Shaolin Monk and broke his foot with a wooden club. No, I would throw myself into the sport in order to master it. My confidence was such that I convinced myself that 50 rounds of golf over, say, 18 months, would do the trick and that, by the end of this journey, I would have met this latest and biggest challenge full on. Along the way I would be educated too about the whys and wherefores of the game, maybe in the company of some of the greats. Hell, I'd led this kind of Forrest Gump existence before. Maybe I could do it again? My mantra had indeed changed. It's not worth doing it unless it's done thoroughly – ridiculously thoroughly.

I told my wife the good news. She would have much preferred it if she'd found me one afternoon dressed up in her tights and underwear. For years she had put up with my disappearing to other continents to get half killed by angry boxers, humiliated by giant wrestlers and embarrassed in front of thousands and thousands of bewildered spectators in far-flung countries, but anything, just about anything, was better than this latest announcement. The problem, as she recognised wearily, was that my juices had been stirred to the point where arguing against it was pointless.

Then, as all these ideas flooded into my excited mind, came the *pièce de résistance*. I, someone who had never played the game a few months previously, would conclude my quest at the golfing summit by meeting the man to blame for my sudden lobotomy – Tiger Woods. I don't just mean sitting in on one of his press conferences, or even watching him play in a tournament, but actually getting to meet him personally, shake his hand and bore the sponsored logos off him with my stories of woe and joy on the fairways of the world. Never mind if he wasn't in the slightest bit interested. Never mind if he would rather be sticking golf tees into his eyes than listen to me. If I was going to meet the challenge, then he was going to have to provide the climax.

This planned finale would not be easy though. The man who sultans offer millions to for a few holes of golf really is the most inaccessible person on the planet. The demand and interest in him is huge and global, yet interviews with him just don't take place, and have not for five years. Every single move he makes at any given time is planned and polished to the nth degree. In short, the chances of my meeting him for some 'quality time' were equivalent to duetting with Elvis while riding Shergar, or playing poker with Lord Lucan at a resort on the Lost City of Atlantis. Still, there was no point in worrying myself about this just now. Being able to play golf seemed to be the more pressing matter.

So there I was at the Royal Melbourne, the first harsh lesson of golf sinking in after less than a second of my intended quest. I'd reckoned that being on the other side of the world from where I lived might be a useful kick-off point. That way, not much could come back to haunt me.

What I had failed to realise is that choosing to play a first round at the Royal Melbourne was like asking a pub singer – and a bad one at that – to debut at the Sydney Opera House.

It would prove to be a long day for me and especially for Bruce Green who found some convenient excuse, like wishing to live, in order to leave me behind for half the round with his assistant professional, Michael Faraone. Michael's spirits remained remarkably high given the amount of time we spent hunting for my ball as the Southern Hemisphere winter light descended into gloom.

The ball travelled to every far corner of the impressive golf course, from bunker to water, and from the deep rough to most of the copses littering the sides of the fairways. Huge divots of mud flew violently skyward from the ground, and sometimes beyond even the distance the ball had ventured. Indeed, the various animals that inhabited the golf course must have quickly come to the conclusion that the safest place to stand would be either in the middle of the fairway or by the pin on the green.

I may as well just come straight out with it. I scored 122 on the west course of Australia's oldest golf course, a number the English cricket team would be proud of in Melbourne, but not an English, blind or even dead golfer. I'm not sure whether 122 or 50 over par sounds worse, but either way it was a sorry collection of wayward drives, fluffed chips and badly judged putts. Still, among the eucalyptus, acacias and cypress trees, it was at least a start. It showed me what stage I was at – namely rock bottom.

And although it is not the kind of scoreline that encourages drinks all round back in the Royal Melbourne clubhouse – well, not in celebration, although Bruce Green and Michael Faraone may have required a few stiff ones – there were a couple of lifelines, even at this early juncture, that left me curiously content as I bade my farewells to Bruce and Michael. Never mind the four holes in which I scored a nine, and the four others in which I notched up an eight on each. Never mind the air shots and repeated attempts to escape from bunkers that made the round feel like Groundhog Day. Somehow, amid the mayhem, I made a par on the par three 5th. Don't ask me how I achieved this. I thought I had swung my club in the same manner I had each and every time before and after, but this time the ball landed on the green, some 150 yards away, from where I putted to a foot from the hole, and then sunk the ball home.

'In the President's Cup last year [a bi-annual match between the USA and the Southern Hemisphere], Greg Norman couldn't even hit the green,' Bruce remarked in encouragement. 'He managed a par only by holing from the bunker. And I'll tell you something else as well. In the same match Tiger Woods could only manage a par on this hole. So you know what that means? You're as good as Tiger already, at least at this hole!'

My God, Bruce was right. If Tiger and I had been playing together during my round of 122, and assuming he had not committed suicide by then, he would have turned round to me after I had teed off at the 5th, seen the ball plop on to the green, and said: 'Ian, I'll take that shot.' How many sports can truly boast the fact that in every round, no matter how bad a player you may be, there will be a time when you are equal to, if not better than, the best in the world?

A taxi took me back to my hotel downtown, past battered old trams, gleaming modern tower blocks on the banks of the Yarra River, and the impressive Colonial Stadium with its sliding roof. I conveniently forgot my nightmare display of golf and imagined instead a threesome of Woods, Norman and Stafford on the 5th, with the latter more than holding his own. One terrible round, maybe three decent shots, and already I was daydreaming like a demented, like a demented . . . what's the word? Ah yes. Golfer!

In the cold light of morning I figured the man I was visiting would not be wholly impressed with a score of 122.

Peter Thomson is five times winner of the British Open (or, as the

British somewhat arrogantly refer to it as, 'The Open'), and one of the greatest players ever to have graced our greens. I was on a fleeting visit but one well worth the effort. After all, my quest meant meeting the best, and in his heyday Thomson was one of the best. We met at his home and set off down the Victorian coast to a course he had designed close to completion.

'It suited me playing links golf,' the 72-year-old explained. 'Back in the 1960s most recognised the Open as the world championship. I thought the Masters was a pissy little tournament in comparison. Maybe winning my first and last Opens were my best moments but, in truth, winning Opens are like having children. You love them all the same.'

He retired at 50. 'I was losing my powers and I wasn't leading a normal life. I wanted to go to cricket and football. I tried to represent Toorak in the Victoria State Parliament, but my bid coincided with a landslide away from the party that had been in power for 26 years beforehand. So instead I became one of the founding members of the Seniors Tour.

'Then, having won a good few senior tournaments, my eyesight seemed to go overnight. I looked down at the ball one morning and I just couldn't focus on it at all. I thought I'd go on for ever. So I turned to course design. I'm behind a fair few now, including four in China, and I'm working on one in Iran.' (Is there anywhere golf isn't played these days?)

Back at the Moonah Links course, on Cape Schank, two State ministers, John Pandazopolous (Tourism) and Justin Madden (Sport, Recreation and Youth) were preparing to begin their round. Madden is a well-known figure in these parts, a former Aussie Rules player of some distinction, and now a popular local politician.

'Don't mind me,' he announced, as he dropped his pants and emptied his bladder beside his car, before hitching up his golfing trousers with a hefty tug.

'You wouldn't catch Tony Blair doing that in public,' I told him.

Madden's reply was short and spot on. 'Welcome to Australia, mate,' he answered, with a beaming smile and a slap on my back.

He then proceeded to tee off, in front of Thomson, myself, his colleague in the Victorian State Parliament, and a few interested observers, with a drive at least as bad as my first (or second, or third, fourth, fifth . . .) at the Royal Melbourne. Maybe I wasn't the worst golfer Down Under, after all? I quietly thanked Justin Madden for this as Thomson drove me back to Melbourne, parting with a few other opinions en route.

'Ben Hogan's my all-time player. I must have partnered him twenty times, and on every occasion I was in awe of him. I'd put him above anyone, and that includes your Tiger Woods. Mind you, I wouldn't mind seeing him down at Moonah. We're staging the Australian Open there, you know. Might have to bribe him to come down.'

I didn't say anything at this point, but felt a strange, warm sensation at the pit of my stomach when he used the phrase 'your Tiger Woods'. He was right, without realising it. Like a mountaineer who starts out dreaming of one day conquering Everest, Woods truly depicted a summit found only at my furthest horizon. In that sense I had already become personally attached to the man.

Thomson left me with one piece of advice. 'The only person you ever have to beat in golf is yourself,' he said. 'In the process you'll find out all your weaknesses, and all your strengths. You are always your toughest opponent.'

Which, on initial evidence, suggested that I was proving far too tough for myself.

Nicky, the female club assistant professional inside the shop at the New South Wales Golf Club, would never make a good sports psychologist. 'You sure you don't want a few more?' she asked from over the counter, when I took down a packet of five balls from a shelf and fumbled in my pocket for some dollars.

'How many do you suggest I have?' I asked, slightly indignantly.

'Oh, I'd say you should take ten balls with you,' she replied. 'It's that hard out there.' For all she knew I might have been a seasoned golfer. After all, that's what everyone else who played at the NSW GC was, for heaven's sake! What chance, then, for me?

I had taken the two-hour flight northeast to Sydney – a city I had grown to like very much, partly for the obvious sights such as the harbour, its bridge and the opera house, but mainly for its vibrancy. But on this, my fourth visit, I detected something else, too. There was a confidence about the place like never before, and this came from the glowing success from the Olympics staged one year earlier. Up until then Australians, due to their geographical location, had been forced to go out to the rest of the world, but now the rest of the world were coming to Sydney and liked what they saw.

Just a few miles south of the city centre I was experiencing *déja vu* at the NSW GC. Bill Exten's reaction to my first tee shot was identical to Bruce Green's at the Royal Melbourne – hardly surprising when you consider that the tee shot was also identical to that produced in Melbourne. 'Lost ball,' he announced, with deadpan delivery. Two first drives at the top two golf courses in Australia, and two lost balls. At least no one could accuse me of being inconsistent.

Ranked 43rd in the world, the course is sited on the northern headland of Botany Bay, on the outskirts of Sydney. Set among hills and valleys that lead to the Pacific coastline, the golfer has uninterrupted ocean panoramas from many points of the course – providing he or she is not spending much of the time hunting for their ball.

My confidence was hardly aided by the fact that apart from Exten my other playing partner was the state amateur champion, a young man whose patience during a torturous round of golf only buckled twice: first, and in true, matter-of-fact Australian style, when he pointed out that a few lessons would not go amiss, and then when he whispered in my ear that one should not really walk straight across the line of someone else's putt. Hitting a ball in its intentioned direction was proving to be difficult enough for me at this early juncture. Etiquette had not even come into the equation.

At one point Bill and I were discussing the dangerous reptiles and insects found lurking round here. 'The brown and black snakes are the worst,' Bill insisted. 'You don't want to meet one of those fellers.'

'Where do they hang out?' I asked, as I sliced an approach shot with an iron smack into a clump of bushes.

'Bushes,' Bill replied, his now haggard gaze following the direction of my shot. 'Now I suppose I've got to help you find the bloody ball.'

Despite a score of 114, and six lost balls that made Nicky's advice appropriate after all, I left Botany Bay that evening clutching at a number of straws. Once again, I had gone against the rest of my round by scoring a par on the par four tenth, the result of a mishit approach shot that saw my ball fly across the ground instead of the intended loft through the air, and settle a couple of feet from the flag. Ludicrously, I pretended this had always been my intended shot, something very obviously not the case to the eye of any seasoned golfer.

But one of Bill's stories gave me hope. 'We had Bill Clinton here last year,' he recalled, sounding like a London taxi driver. 'Played a round with Greg Norman. It took him hours and hours to complete the course. I remember messages were being relayed back to the First Lady, and to Air Force One. "There's going to be a one-hour delay," said the first one. "There's another hour's delay," said the second. It was pretty dark when they finally came in.'

In Sydney I had improved my score from Melbourne by eight strokes in just one round. At this rate, I'd be scoring 66 in just six rounds' time!

Jack Newton used to score 66 for fun. He won his fair share of tournaments along the way, too, although he just missed out on a major when finishing as runner-up to Tom Watson in the 1975 British Open, and then again to Severiano Ballesteros in the 1980 US Masters. These disappointments would seem largely insignificant compared to the accident with a moving aeroplane propeller in 1983 that left him without an eye and an arm, and his career in tatters.

I made the two-hour drive north from Sydney through the heart of Australia's wine country and along mainly deserted freeways to meet Newton at his Newcastle home. I was a little nervous about the state of mind I would find him in, a sportsman cut off in his prime by the most horrific sequence of events. Incredibly, 18 years on, he boasts a 12 handicap, a mark that I, with my two hands and two eyes, would be astonished to achieve in my 15 months. I was told over the telephone that he could spare me an hour's conversation at most. What followed was an extraordinary half-day of self-reflection as frank and brutal as Newton's physical condition.

'I'd still be playing now. I'm competitive, you see. I don't accept mediocrity, whether it's golf or marbles.' He smiled wryly and shrugged his shoulders. 'My expectations on myself shouldn't be so high. After all these years I should accept it more.'

We took a walk around his house, which was christened Augusta, with Jack pointing out his various prized exhibits displayed on the walls. A marlin's head; the aluminium cricket bat Dennis Lillee, the Australian fast bowler, once used and threw famously at an umpire; a signed bat from Sir Garfield Sobers. Various scorecards were dotted around the house, and in the corner of one of the living rooms stood a trophy cabinet with the Stonehaven Cup inside, for winning the Australian Open, and a silver bowl for placing second in the British Open.

He'd won 20 tournaments around the world, and pushed the greatest to the limits during his time. After a blip in his career, Jack felt he was coming back strong when his life was changed irrevocably in the summer of 1983. A night out watching the Sydney Swans Aussie Rules football team ended with a collision with a light aircraft's propeller. For ongoing legal reasons he could not discuss the actual accident but was more than willing to describe the aftermath.

'I found myself in intensive care, knowing that this was a very serious room to be in,' Jack recalled. 'I didn't need to see a priest standing over me to know I was in trouble. Things weren't looking too good.

'I remember, in the midst of all this, seeing a 21-year-old blonde girl being wheeled by on a bed. She had just tried to kill herself. Even in the state I was in, I thought to myself: "I'm trying desperately to cling on to life, and she's tried to end it all.'"

Jackie, his English-born wife, joined us with a coffee. 'Two girlfriends of mine rushed round to tell me,' she said. 'I rang the hospital and was told to get down there as quickly as I could. They told me he was fighting for his life, and that he would most probably die. I kissed the kids goodbye and endured the longest 90 minutes of my life as I was driven to Sydney.

'Jack was in a terrible state. The worst of it was not that he had lost an arm and an eye. The whole of his right side had been torn to shreds, and his stomach had been split wide open. I had to hold Jack tight to help stem the flow of blood. At the hospital they told me his survival chances were forty per cent at best. But you want to know something? I always knew he'd pull through. I never doubted it for a moment.'

Jack pulled through all right, although the battle was long yet won. 'Initially I was in a state of real shock,' he continued. 'My thought process was irrational. I've just lost an arm and an eye. What would my mates think down the pub? What would people think of me in the street? Would everyone be looking at me, talking about me?'

The golfing fraternity rallied round: he was even sent a tape with encouraging words from Jack Nicklaus and Seve Ballesteros among others, as well as thousands of letters and faxes from all over the world, not just from the best golfers on the circuit, but from amateurs hacking their way around municipal courses.

He would spend the next 12 months in and out of hospital. At home his mother proved to be the driving force. 'My mum was a battler. She's where I got my determination from. At first I didn't really feel like doing anything. She kept on urging me to hit a few balls with my remaining arm. I didn't see the point, but in the end I did it for her. She teed up a few balls, and I hit them with a seven iron. I kept on doing this for a few days and as I did so some of the old juices began to flow again. I realised I could still hit a golf ball, and that I wasn't as handicapped as I first believed.'

15

18 years on, Jack Newton has subsequently led a full and fulfilling life. Bob Hawke, former Australian prime minister, launched a Jack Newton Junior Golf Foundation for 6,000 children to learn golf. Jack commentates for Australia's Channel 7 television network, designs golf courses, watches his beloved Newcastle Knights Rugby League team and plays golf.

'I don't find it easy as I used to,' he understated. 'I'd love to get my handicap down to single figures again. It's still a good feeling when you hit a pure shot. I guess having hit millions of golf balls before the accident meant I had a good idea of the game. I had always possessed a strong, left arm, too, so I can still club a ball 220 yards. Where it gets difficult is with certain shots that require a right-handed attack on the ball, in thick rough, or in a bunker. Also, one eye impairs your vision. I used to pour tea, for example, on to the side of a cup. It can make putting hard sometimes.'

We moved outside. Budgerigars and macaws squawked and fluttered around the Newton garden as if we were sitting in the middle of an aviary, a sight very common for the Newtons, but incredibly novel for an Englishman a long way from home. 'You know what the biggest problem is,' Jack asked, his booming laugh making a couple of birds leap from their branches. 'I can't hold a cigarette and a beer at the same time any more. You know, people are guilty of giving handicapped people a wide berth. I'd never come across it before, but then again I would probably not have noticed. Maybe I was guilty of it as well? I don't really know. But I do know that every 17-year-old should spend a day at a rehab centre. That would give them a fresh perspective on life.'

His time at the top was an interesting era. He felt doomed to lose his 1975 Open defeat to Tom Watson – 'The shot that finished me off was when he holed a 30 foot putt' – and at the 1980 Masters, Jack found himself up against a brilliant young Spaniard named Ballesteros. 'He had been nine shots ahead of me, but in the final round I made three birdies as he made three bogeys. On the 14th, I drove straight down the middle of the fairway, and he sliced his drive over some pine trees. I thought I had him at that moment, but he knocked the ball over the trees and on to the green to par the hole. It was a miracle shot, and it won him the Masters. We've been friends ever since.'

A month before, my eyes would have glazed over at such tales but I was already finding them supremely interesting.

That night I would be flying home to England. News had just filtered down to Australia that Tiger Woods had revealed his human side by tying a mere twentieth in a tournament in Wisconsin. Woods would have no way of knowing it, of course, but on the other side of the planet someone had begun a long journey that could end – with a large slice of luck and after a golfing transformation – beside his famous frame.

It was early days. But I was inspired. Inspired beyond belief. Golf had just about saved Jack Newton's life.

2

An unfortunate thump

Four days back from Australia and still struggling with jet lag, I decided to take up the New South Wales amateur state champion's advice. I fixed up the first of a regular series of lessons and a few rounds of golf at some prestigious courses over the coming weeks. After all, if I really was going to 'master' this game and appear alongside some of the very best in the business I had no option but to play. And play. And play.

David Bailey, at the Jack Nicklaus Golf Centre in Sidcup, had come across a few diverse characters in his time as a teacher, but never before had he heard such an introductory statement. 'I've just started this golfing quest, have played two proper rounds, I'll be playing at Wentworth next week and in just over a year's time I'm hoping to have played with some of the best, become a good golfer and meet Tiger Woods. Can you help?'

He didn't say a word as he digested this preposterous notion, instead looked me up and down in my brown and white golf shoes which would not have been out of place in a Harlem tap-dancing joint.

'Well, we'd better take a look at you, then,' he eventually said, beckoning me towards a mat and placing a ball on a tee. I struck the ball with my five iron fairly sweetly and watched as it soared into the distance. It could easily have scuffed along the ground, such was my good shot to bad shot ratio, but luck was on my side – or at least I thought it was.

'That was down wholly to your good eye-to-hand co-ordination,' Bailey surmised. 'You clearly possess that, which is good news. I have to say that your actual technique was lousy, though. Absolutely lousy. Come over here and take a look at this.'

I watched on video screen as Bailey first called up my recorded swing and then, splitting the screen into two, produced footage of Tiger Woods. I was excited just to see the two of us – Woods and Stafford – teeing off at the same time, that is until comparisons were made. While Woods remained tall and upright, with a swing natural and free-flowing, I stood hunched over the ball, feet far too wide apart, back rounded, head moving wildly, and my swing so vertical I looked like an executioner using an axe to behead someone.

'Hmm,' Bailey said. 'Looks like we've got a bit of work to do, then.' He sounded like Professor Higgins out of *My Fair Lady*, although Bailey's task was clearly the harder of the two.

Half an hour later I was teeing off with a straight back, my knees locking. It didn't look too good, but was an instant improvement. It also felt completely unnatural and uncomfortable, but this would be the way I would be striking the ball from now on.

David Rennie was suitably impressed when watching my little pre-shot routine as we stood on the first tee at Wentworth a week later. Behind us, the turreted roof of the resplendent, cream clubhouse resembled Bart Simpson's head. The man who had taken over from the former Ryder Cup captain, Bernard Gallacher, as club professional at the home of the World Matchplay tournament, reckoned he had been out with all kinds of golfers, from the very good to the ludicrously bad, but few went through the highly personalised straight-back, bending-knees, club-swaying, wriggling-toes, cheek-puffing routine that I enacted.

Rennie, a fervent football supporter sporting a signed Glasgow Rangers jersey on his office wall inside the Wentworth clubhouse, made no attempt to hide his thoughts as we traipsed round the east course of the plush Surrey establishment. On the sixth hole, I drove my tee shot straight into the woods. My attempt at a second drive saw the ball follow its predecessor into the dark depths of late autumn foliage.

'Did you say you wanted to meet Woods or merely play in the woods?' David asked, with a mischievous grin. I went on to score a ten there, a mark which would have been even worse had I not somehow landed my best putt of the round, a 12-foot downhill putt to avoid an 11. That typified the round, and the way golf can be at this level. Nine shots of dross and then a putt that anyone would have been proud of. Where did that last shot come from? It was the ultimate tease.

Despite this, and the fact that I secured just the one par at the par four 15th, I ended the day with a score of 109, which improved my score from Sydney by five strokes. Rennie was frank in his summing up. 'Your putting was terrible,' he announced. 'Quite appalling. On another day, if only your putting had been bad, as opposed to terrible, you would have broken one hundred. Just remember one thing. You're never going to sink a putt that's hit short.' With that, he presented me with a book commemorating Wentworth, signed by Gallacher, and wished me well.

One hundred was fast becoming the Holy Grail for me. To score a round of double figures would be my first major goal, my four-minute mile. It seemed, on this evidence, to be just around the corner, but a combination of the most testing golf courses and the onset of winter would stave off this magical moment for many a round to come.

Such objectives had not concerned Tiger Woods since the age of four when, unbelievably, he first broke one hundred. I'll just repeat that fact for those who assume that this is a misprint. He was four when he achieved what I was failing to do. While I was misdirecting putts all over the Wentworth greens, Tiger was busy returning to form, after a disappointing Open at Royal Lytham, by winning the million-dollar WGC-NEC Invitational tournament on the US PGA tour, with a total score after 4 rounds of twelve under par.

*

Ballybunion, County Kerry, is one of the most beautiful though demanding golf courses in the world. 'A man would think the game of golf originated here,' was Tom Watson's verdict. Bill Clinton had been there too. I asked Sean, my caddie for the day, what the former president had scored at Ballybunion. 'I could tell you the score,' Sean replied, fixing me with a long and mysterious stare. 'But then I'd have to shoot you.'

I was still trying to work out that last comment when my first drive of the round saw the ball fade sharply and bounce into a small cemetery situated on the other side of a stone wall, to the right of the fairway. 'Take a mulligan,' said Mark Hoffman, a New York real estate agent who was on a week's golfing holiday in Ireland.

'Thanks,' I replied, not knowing quite what a 'mulligan' was. I placed a fresh ball on my tee and drove my second effort down the fairway. That evening a phone call to a golfing friend confirmed the mulligan to be a free, second shot from the tee, with no questions asked.

Hoffman was an excitable chap, to say the least. At the 11th hole, he could not contain his pleasure any longer. 'This, my friend, is why we play golf,' he announced, giving me an impromptu high five. On the 17th he went even further. Somehow I produced one of those occasional shots we're all capable of (and of which Tiger would have been proud), a five iron second shot that landed within six feet of the pin. Naturally, I missed the eminently gettable birdie putt, but that wasn't the point. Hoffman was beside himself on my behalf. 'Baby, you're beautiful,' he declared.

'Er, thanks,' I replied, avoiding eye contact and shuffling my feet awkwardly in response.

My score of 103 was achieved after I decided to swallow my pride and revert to teeing off using my trusty but slightly girlie five iron, rather than slice and fade the ball into the deep rough and, therefore, into deep shit, with a three wood. 'That's sensible golf,' as Hoffman put it. 'Sensible golf.'

It was all coming together nicely, I felt. This verdict would prove to be incorrect for quite some time, but as I drove back to Shannon Airport that night I felt confident and happy. I still didn't have the experience to realise that golf had merely been kind to me during my formative stages. As far as I was concerned, my natural sporting prowess was already forging me ahead in my quest. Better still, in a week's time, I would be playing at St Andrews, the home of golf. Where better to score double, and not treble figures, in a round for the first time in my life?

Peter Dawson was surprisingly welcoming when I tapped on his office door and was ushered in. I had imagined the Secretary of the Royal & Ancient, the very bastion of golf as we know it, to be a little stuffy. Nothing could have been further from the truth.

Take, for example, his admission about his job. 'Never dreamt I'd get it,' he said. 'I'm passionate about it. I wake up every morning and pinch myself. I look out over the Holy Ground, as I like to call it, and get a buzz every single day.'

You could see what he meant. Dawson's office sported a balcony overlooking the 18th green, site of so many famous British Open conclusions over the years, including the year 2000 in which Woods was crowned champion. To the left stood the historic town of St Andrews, with its dark stone buildings and spires, to the centre the old course of St Andrews Golf Club, and to the right the coastline and the North Sea. 'It's where it all began,' Dawson added. 'Sometimes, when I'm having a bad day and I'm pacing up and down this room, I go out on to the balcony and then things never seem quite so bad.'

En route to Dawson's wood-panelled office, I had passed a members' lounge which seemed full of elderly gentlemen from a distant age when the empire was still going strong. It made me wonder what exactly was the point of the R&A. The Secretary soon put me straight on this.

'Firstly, we're a members' club, with 2,400 overall, of whom 800 come from overseas,' he explained. 'A hopeful member has to be proposed and seconded by existing members who would have needed to have known the individual for at least five years. Secondly, we run championships, the most famous being the Open, but also the Walker Cup and the amateur championships. Third, we're the governing body for the rules of the game, in conjunction with the US Golf Association who do the same sort of thing in America, and fourthly, through our commercial activities we finance the development of the game around the world.'

Having been in the engineering industry all his life, Dawson was in no hurry to relinquish his newly acquired position, either. 'I'm here for life, or until I'm sacked,' he explained. 'Replacing secretaries at the Royal & Ancient is like announcing a new pope. Really, they ought to have white smoke appearing from our chimney like they do at the Vatican.'

I'm not sure if the Pope has a large telescope in his office, though. I'd been itching to ask Dawson throughout what the telescope was there for. As our meeting ended I pointed towards it with an inquisitive glance.

'Oh, that, well now,' he began. 'There's no practical reason for it, really. You can see anywhere, and virtually anyone on the golf course, mind you.' He swung the telescope round, took a peek and laughed. 'You can even look into the adjacent hotels, if you like. Never seen a lady undressing yet, but I'll keep on looking.'

For all I knew, one of those hotels was the Rusacks, where I spent the night overlooking the 18th fairway. Every single room in the grand old Rusacks was named after a golfer. I could have stayed in 'Nick Faldo' or 'Arnold Palmer' (they ought to make 'Fred Couples' a double room) but was instead given the keys to Freddie Tate, the British amateur champion back in 1896 and again in 1898. He was killed in action at the age of 30, leading a battalion of the Black Watch during the Boer War in 1900, but is remembered to this day by St Andrews with the 'Freddie Tate gold medal', the town's major matchplay competition played annually on the New Course. On the wall hung an old, sepia-brown photograph of the man himself, looking resplendent in his golfing plus fours and moustache. A man like Tate would have not had too many problems playing the New Course. A man like me, however, would be finding out for himself in the morning.

It was an early start – 7.44 a.m to be precise – when I met Peter

Mason, the external relations manager for the St Andrews Golf Links, at the first tee of the New Course. The Old Course only allowed players with a handicap to walk its hallowed turf, so it and I would have to wait until I possessed a more impressive handicap than the one I possessed at the time – the handicap, if I was being honest, of not being very good.

The New Course is in fact the oldest 'New Course' in the world. When it was constructed 106 years ago it was named 'New' simply because the 'Old Course' had already been built. Like Ballybunion, St Andrews is a links course, but the rough here is knee deep and damp, and the gorse treacherous to escape from. Every now and again, the tranquillity of an early St Andrews morning was shattered by the booming noise of jet fighter planes darting across the coastline from nearby RAF Leuchars.

On this day, the white stewards' hut, which stood proudly beside the edge of the 18th green and is thus renowned the world over, had just been sold in an Internet auction. According to Mason, a two-horse race developed between an American and a Danish bidder before the American won the day with an accepted offer of a mere $90,000. Oh, and that's not including the cost of actually transporting the damn thing to California, where it will sit, no doubt, in his back garden like a British red telephone box. This story serves to prove that there is a Californian not just slightly smitten with the golfing bug, but ravaged from head to foot.

The Japanese golfer Mason told me about might have bid for the hut if he had known about it. A couple of years back, Mason went out for a round with a businessman from Tokyo. As they stood poised to begin their round at the first tee on the Old Course, the businessman broke down in tears. 'He was overcome with emotion to be playing at St Andrews.'

The businessman had claimed beforehand that he played off a 7 handicap, and then proceeded, despite the various breakdowns, to shoot a score of 7 over. Then came an amazing admission as he shook Mason's hands on the 18th green. 'He told me he'd never actually played a round of golf before in his life. All he had ever done was use a driving range.'

I felt like breaking down in tears myself as we waded through the long grass and the gorse bushes looking for my ball. Although I went desperately close to sinking a 15-foot birdie putt on the 13th, the rest of my highly forgettable round of 112 was highlighted by an inability to drive the ball. For some inexplicable reason, my driving, which had been pretty acceptable at Ballybunion a week before, had deserted me, while my putting, which was poor on the Irish course, was reasonably good. Now, why had my game been turned upside-down in the space of a week?

Mason didn't have it all his own way either. Although the words 'damn' and 'bugger' would be uttered often by my playing partner throughout the round, his favourite word – and one not frequently heard these days anywhere in the world – was 'buggeration'. I haven't heard anyone use the term since. His methods of psychology were interesting too. 'This one's a really hard par four,' he'd say, for example, as we'd stand on a tee preparing to drive. 'Now you're really going to be in trouble.'

A little perturbed by my poor showing that day, I vowed to myself that I would return to the home of golf before my journey's end, play the more renowned Old Course next time and play it well. One little setback, after all, was hardly going to knock me off my confident stride. That said, my plan to play at Carnoustie the following week was, in the circumstances, probably not the best. As Mason put it: 'You're a real glutton for punishment, aren't you?'

Circumstances across the Atlantic, the day I first played St Andrews, soon removed any displeasure I felt and placed even the increasingly major matter of golf in my life into some perspective. The date was September 11th, and Edinburgh Airport was in mayhem by the time I arrived and heard the shocking news. All flights had been delayed and airport officials had switched off all television screens in the rather naive hope that it would help prevent alarm inside the terminal. Instead, a minor revolt took place among the commuters, a set was turned on again and we all crowded round transfixed at the horrors befalling New York. I arrived home consequently much later than I had envisaged but, in the light of that day's events, relieved to be home at all. The American golfers, particularly Woods, felt the need to be at home too in the immediate aftermath, hence the postponement of the 2001 Ryder Cup for 12 months.

It was empty at Carnoustie a week later, just 24 hours before my round, something unheard of pre-September 11th. Gary Player described Carnoustie as 'the toughest course in the world', and he knows a thing or two about golf. Player won the Open championship there, as well as Henry Cotton, Ben Hogan and Tom Watson, but none of them ever found it easy.

Stewart Harper had been a caddie at the club for 15 years and knew Carnoustie back to front. It seemed a good move to employ his services for the day, but before we ventured out into the wind, we sat down for a drink and a pre-round conversation which did nothing to increase my confidence.

In 15 years of caddying Harper had seen only 15 punters beat a score of 80 on the championship course. Once, he went round with a woman golfer, on a day he has never forgotten. 'She scored 265,' he recalled. 'That's right, 265. It took us just under 6 hours to complete the course. During another round an American scored 27 on the par four 9th, including 19 shots just to get out of a bunker.'

Then there was Jean Van der Velde, the hapless French golfer, who approached the 18th hole on the final day of the 1999 Open three shots ahead of the field, only to throw away the lead in the burn beside the green, eventually losing the championship in the resulting play-off to the Scot, Paul Lawrie. The sight of Van der Velde, with his trousers rolled halfway up his legs, knee deep in the stream, remains one of the lasting images of Open golf history.

'I was in charge of the bag store at the Carnoustie Hotel for the Open that year,' Harper explained. 'The day after the Open had finished, Mr Van der Velde came into the store looking for his black golf bag. "Where are my clubs?" he asked me.

'"Right here," I answered, producing a bag with his name on the side.

'"Throw all my clubs into the water exactly where I was yesterday," Mr Van der Velde ordered, before giving me his white visor as a souvenir. I didn't, and later I discovered he'd taken them. At the time, though, I think he was serious.'

In which case, Harper could have thrown my clubs into the water too, or over a cliff, into a good number of the cavernous bunkers, or into any of the thick gorse bushes that scatter the fairways. My round of 118 – and my scores were now worsening at an alarming rate of knots – was only bearable because Harper insisted that on that course, on that day, when the wind was so strong, it was almost an acceptable figure. To strengthen his case he produced a number of examples – Greg Norman took 7 on the 17th, Sergio Garcia shot 89 on the first day of the Open, and so on – designed to make me feel better. He failed because Messrs Garcia and Norman have not, and will never score two 11s in a round – at the 'Railway' 9th hole and 'South America' 10th hole, and most definitely will never record a 12 as I did at the 'Lucky Slap' 15th. There wasn't too much of the 'lucky' here, and 'slap' is something of an understatement. In my case, the hole should be renamed 'Unfortunate Thump'.

I had become so disorientated by the challenge of Carnoustie that I drove all the way back to Edinburgh before discovering that I had left my golf clubs behind at the Carnoustie Hotel. How ridiculous is that? Leaving behind a towel, perhaps, a pair of socks or even your golf shoes is just about explainable. But your whole set of clubs? Would Lennox Lewis walk out of the ring, job done and opponent floored, without his gloves? Would Sachin Tendulkar depart from the wicket without his bat?

As I sat on the plane heading back to London that night the reasons why I had avoided golf for so long came flooding back to me. The scorecard from Carnoustie didn't lie. It read 118, a numerical way of saying crap. I didn't like being crap. After all, I'd played five rounds now and a combination of my naivety and stupidity had convinced me that my steady progress down to the low hundreds and beyond would continue unabated. Instead, I was going backwards. It was, as I would come to realise, golf's way of reminding you just who was boss in the relationship, but just then I wasn't too sure whether I wanted this relationship to continue. Like some teenage lover – maybe it was better to chuck golf before it chucked me?

3

Joy to despair

My despondency lifted when I was asked to appear on Channel 4's now defunct *The Big Breakfast*, to be interviewed about a sports book I'd recently written and published. After the interview, unbeknownst to me until it was announced live on air, I was invited to meet Tim Davis, Britain's miniature golf champion. A mini-golf hole had been set up, complete with windmill and dog-leg that made a hole in one difficult but not impossible. Davis and I were asked to play off against each other in a one-hole challenge. This, due to lack of time, was reduced to one shot each.

My putt cannoned off the side of the wall opposite the windmill, leaving the ball a couple of inches away from the hole. (A tip – always use the walls in miniature golf; don't try and be brave by putting the ball in between the sails of a windmill!) When Davis followed, he could only send his ball to within six inches of the hole. I was declared winner and was driven home happy in the knowledge that I had defeated a British champion.

Two weeks and two lessons later, as the October leaves began to brown and the horse chestnuts were full and ripe, I travelled to Dublin to play the K Club, a 40-minute drive south in the picture-postcard village of Straffan. This is horse-racing country, and especially horse-breeding country, with numerous studs littered around the nearby environs, but on the edge of Straffan village the magnificent Kildare Golf and Country Club can be found.

The K Club, venue for the 2006 Ryder Cup, is owned by Dr Michael Smurfit, a Monte Carlo tax exile who is chairman and chief executive of Jefferson Smurfit, the Irish paper and packaging group. In 1989, Smurfit founded the K Club after spending £30 million building an Arnold Palmer-designed, 18-hole golf course on its 300 acres. His splendid office inside the clubhouse sports a framed thank-you letter from Bill Clinton (he's kind of desperate to be in this book), as well as numerous photos of Smurfit with various golfing luminaries; and outside, beside the more modest collection of golf buggies, stands the Rolls-Royce of buggies, complete with windscreen wipers and doors that enclose you completely from the elements. This, so I was informed, belonged to Dr Smurfit.

Ernie Jones would be my partner for much of the day, although we were joined for nine holes by Brian O'Driscoll, the Irish rugby union player who became something of a sporting superstar after his performances for the British and Irish Lions in Australia the previous summer. Brian's father, Frank, made up the foursome, and while the O'Driscolls tore up the fairways, I had time to listen to one of the great raconteurs of the game.

At 69 years of age, Ernie has seen it all in a career that has included 50 years as a golf professional, two Irish PGA titles, and 11 tournament wins in total. In 1961 he beat Bobby Locke and Peter Alliss to win £1,000 first prize – only the second time such an amount had ever been awarded in golf. 'Christy O'Connor had won the first, and when I picked up the winner's cheque most of the lads in the tournament wanted to look at it,' Ernie recalled. 'Neither they nor I had ever seen a four-figure cheque before in our lives. You could buy a house in Dublin for that sum back then.'

Ernie went on to captain the Professional Golfers Association, in charge of some 5,000 members, and became a founder of the seniors tour, too, both as player and board member. The most sporting gesture he reckons in golf and, indeed, in sport took place when Ernie was the 1969 Ryder Cup referee at Royal Birkdale. It is a well-chronicled tale for those who know their golf, but one worth repeating if only because Ernie was closer to the incident than anyone else in the world.

'It was the final match between Jack Nicklaus and Tony Jacklin, and to give full value to the event, we have to go back to the 17th hole,' Ernie began, falling just short of sitting me on his knee to tell the story. 'Both had found the green in two shots and Jacklin holed a 30-foot putt for an unlikely eagle. The whole place erupted. For a good minute, the huge crowd roared their appreciation until I announced: "Quiet, please." Jack turned around to me and said: "Leave them at it. They're enjoying themselves." He then missed his 10-foot eagle putt to lose the hole and leave the match all square, with one hole remaining.

'On the 18th Jack made his par and Tony faced a nasty little two-and-a-half-foot putt downhill to halve the hole and draw the Ryder Cup. It was the kind of tricky putt you wouldn't fancy playing for half a crown on a Sunday morning, but Jack conceded the putt, thereby drawing the Ryder Cup, and preventing the possibility of Jacklin making a missed putt that would be remembered for the rest of his life. It really was the most sporting gesture you are ever likely to see.'

Bizarrely, two events took place in my round of 104 that Ernie insisted he had never witnessed since the day he joined the K Club in 1989 as the resident golf professional. At the 10th, I drove my ball straight and reasonably far down the fairway off the tee. We had all seen the flight of the ball and expected to find it right in the centre of the fairway. Instead, it was nowhere to be seen. All four of us hunted for the ball for some while, refusing to concede that it was gone. As that part of the fairway was close to a lake, and the morning rain had made the course damp in any case, Ernie suggested the only explanation was that the ground had swallowed the ball up. 'Either that or a squirrel's playing games,' he added. It cost me two strokes.

Then, after the O'Driscolls had headed off back home, came my first real experience of golfing ecstasy. For much of the round Ernie had been commenting on how poor my putting had been. He was correct. Many a hole had been spoiled by my unnerving ability to take three putts when on the green. On the par three 17th, my drive directed the ball off the green and into some light rough – a good 40 feet from the hole.

My initial fear when I struck the ball with my putter for my second shot was that I had hit it far too hard. Nineteen times out of twenty the ball would have zipped right across the green and deposited itself in the rough opposite to where I had just played my previous shot. On this occasion, however, the ball slammed against the pin with a resounding clang and dropped straight into the hole.

Ernie and I whooped with joy and enacted a small jig on the green to celebrate my first ever birdie, before shaking hands and slapping backs. Anyone observing from afar would have thought I'd just scored a hole in one. 'I've never seen anyone sink a putt from off the green at the 17th before,' Ernie announced. Later, he would stop people in the clubhouse and tell them how his partner had conquered the 17th. 'Now, you see, anyone in the history of golf would have been proud of that shot, from Jones to Nicklaus, even your Tiger Woods.'

'My' Tiger Woods, incidentally, would fleetingly prove himself to be human with a 23rd finish, a 16th and a 13th in his next three tournaments in America, but just when questions were being asked about a young man who had, after all, already won five tournaments in the year, Woods ended 2001 with two consecutive runners-up places, and then another victory, this time in the Williams World Challenge. Any other professional golfer would have given their right arm to have secured six titles in one year, but for Woods it represented, in comparison to the previous two years, only an average return.

None of which could dent my mood after the K Club success. Oh, how wonderful the game of golf appeared to me that night as I flew back to London, reliving that birdie putt over and over again. I couldn't decide which was the more beautiful noise: the sound of the ball hitting the pin, or when it dropped into the hole and circled round and round before coming to a stop. Never mind the other 103 strokes of wavering quality. The second on the 17th had made it all worthwhile. Of course, all that had really happened was that I had managed to hit a small, white ball with an iron stick into a hole in the ground. But it made me extremely happy.

Like any love affair in its initial stages it can work both ways. Emotions were already swinging violently as I struggled to keep the game of golf in perspective. The dark mood of Carnoustie had been replaced by sheer, unadulterated joy in Ireland, and all because of one, lucky putt. No matter, my next round would see me burst into double figures and kiss 100-plus scores farewell for ever. Birdies would plop into holes on a regular basis, no putt would faze me, and I would soon become the toast of clubhouses all over the world. Which was all well and good, if it were not for the fact that my next 3 rounds, in close succession, would witness a drastic downward spiral of fortunes once again.

Aspirations had clearly become misplaced, something not untypical when it comes to me. When I was a boy, a furtive smile from a girl at the high school clearly meant she fancied me rotten. When I discovered the hard way that I had exaggerated her message, it was normally embarrassing, and public.

This self-deluding tendency was already a key element in my game: on a windy day at Portmarnock GC, near Dublin, I chased three 20-Euro notes that had flown out of my pocket on the 1st green and finally came to a halt on the very tee I had driven off 5 minutes earlier. 'That's a 95 in decent conditions,' I convinced myself, even though I had just shot a 104.

Eight days later I was in Edinburgh to watch the Calcutta Cup rugby international between Scotland and England, which meant, of course, in my now golf-dominated mind, another opportunity to play a renowned Scottish course. Gleneagles, an hour's drive north from the capital city, is due to host the Ryder Cup in 2014. Described by Jack Nicklaus as 'a playable monster', on this day Gleneagles was Godzilla and King Kong rolled into one. Britain had been battered by gales for the past couple of days, and on this morning Gleneagles would take the full brunt. My playing partner for the round at the Nicklaus-built PGA Championship course was Simon Crawford, a young greenkeeper so diminutive in stature that you worried whether the winds would blow him away.

It made playing golf nigh on impossible. A straight, well-hit tee shot would see the ball begin its course directly down the middle of the fairway and end up thrown wildly into the rough by a wind borne down from the nearby Grampian Mountains and Ochil Hills. At times, when caught full on by the force of the wind, it made breathing – even standing – difficult. Crawford, who played off three, was scoring 7s and 8s for the first nine holes before his game came together. I was scoring 7s and 8s throughout, save for my par four at the 7th, named 'Larch Gait', and my par three at the 'Sleekit Howe' 10th.

At least Crawford made interesting company. Unlike most playing partners, especially those who represented their golf club, Simon said it how it was. 'That was crap', for example, was one of his more favoured responses to my intended five iron that dug a huge divot in the centre of the fairway and managed to knock the ball only a few feet forward. I'd become rather accustomed to the 'never minds' and 'you were unlucky' responses elsewhere. 'Don't let me put you off, but there's a huge stream just over the other side of that hill, and there's every chance your ball will end up there', was another offering from my partner.

God only knows what he said to Dan Quayle, the hapless, former American vice-president, when Crawford was charged with the dubious honour of seeing the man around Gleneagles a few years back. His best comment he saved for last, however, when it came to playing with me. Crouched over a 12-foot putt on the 18th green, I was about to strike the ball with my putter when Simon offered one final piece of advice. 'Devour it like a fat man over a bowl of Smarties,' he suggested. I missed.

Afterwards, having conveniently forgotten to admit to Ken McNaught, the former European Cup-winning defender for Aston Villa, now in charge of the Gleneagles bag store, that I'd lost one of the club covers on the course, we both decided there were a number of reasons why I shot 112. The winds were atrocious, the course was hard in any case, and unfamiliar, and I'd also been up since four in the morning to catch my flight north to Scotland. And then Simon had given me a couple of duff pieces of advice when it came to the choice of clubs, and the buggy broke down after three holes. Oh, and it was a Saturday.

That birdie at the K Club had left a remarkable effect on me because here I was, notching up three-figure totals at Portmarnock and particularly Gleneagles, convincing myself that it wasn't me but a series of unfortunate circumstances that resulted in such derisory scores. The truth was that my new-found lover was about to deliver another slap in the face and these previous rounds had merely served as a prelude.

So immersed had I become in golf, so rapidly insatiable my hunger to play, that three days after my Gleneagles debacle I was back behind the wheel of a rental car driving around the southern tip of Edinburgh and onwards to the Fife coastal course of Muirfield, the venue of the 2002 Open. Playing with PR consultant Simon Laird, a newly registered club member who had waited a mere 16 years for the privilege, I shot 118 in near-perfect conditions. In hindsight it would have helped if I'd driven a few balls on the practice range beforehand, and had not made another early-morning flight north. The golf course is recognised globally, too, as one of the stiffest tests a golfer can face. And the rough, long and damp, was totally unforgiving.

None of which, though, can explain why for almost the complete round, save for a couple of rare rays of sunshine, I was unable even to drive the ball cleanly and straight off the tee. It was as if I'd forgotten how to ride a bike. The embarrassment I felt in the company of Laird was acute. We had spent some weeks beforehand arranging this round at one of the most famous and inaccessible golf clubs in the world and, to make matters worse, my partner was playing like a dream.

By the end no part of my game was functioning. The driving was the first to fall apart, but the irons off the fairways, the chips and finally the putts – the latter having been reasonably solid in the past few weeks – nosedived into chaos. In the process my mood sank. By the final hole, I resembled an eight-year-old boy stomping around the house after being ticked off by his parents.

A late luncheon was served in the wood-panelled dining room inside the old, Muirfield clubhouse. I had been pre-warned to bring a jacket and tie with me in order to be permitted inside, but this only served to darken my mood and intensify all my previous prejudices about the game. As with the members' lounge at the R&A, Muirfield possessed its fair share of middle-aged and elderly gentlemen who lived on a different planet to mine. If I had been honest with myself, none of this would have bothered me a jot if I had shot 95 and not embarrassed myself in front of my playing partner. Indeed, I would have enjoyed the experience of ordering my starter from the traditionally dressed clubhouse waitress, content in the knowledge that I had just made a good account of myself at Muirfield. As it was, I couldn't wait to get out of the place and back to my world.

Throughout the flight home to London I tried to figure out how my game, seemingly about to break below the hundred barrier, had spiralled so dramatically downwards. My mood was as low as it was high after my birdie at the K Club. The game that I was growing to love could not have been despised more that day. In fact, on reaching home, the thought occurred to me for the second time since I had began my quest that it might be better just to pack the whole damn thing in.

A message was flashing on my voicemail machine as I entered the house and threw my golf clubs down on to the hall floor with a resounding crash. Simon Crane, group director of a sports marketing company called WSM, was informing me that his client, Nick Faldo, had invited me over to his house for half a day, to chat and undergo a coaching session. This would be taking place in a week's time.

I sat down in the nearest chair and examined the situation. I faced three options: to cry off sick; to find a decent golfer masquerading as me to visit Faldo; or to hope that whatever game I possessed, embraced me in time. Otherwise a new dose of humiliation, greater still because of the company I would be in, was waiting for me.

The next morning I headed straight to the driving range and started hitting balls. The first few were a re-enactment of my pathetic attempts at Muirfield, but after a while, and a conscious effort to slow my swing, raise my arms up straight and high and ensure that my torso swung fully from left to right and then back to left again, the drives began to reappear. Oh, how sweet this felt, and how frustrating too. As I watched the ball shoot straight and far down the range, I wondered why it was that this simple act was not produced at Muirfield.

'It happens,' explained David Young, my new coach at World of Golf. David Bailey had left by then, although the fact that he had been teaching me should not necessarily be linked to this. 'It happens to very good golfers, too. There are some inexplicable days when nothing goes right and you play appallingly bad. It's one of the frustrating facts of golf. But the bad experiences are outweighed by the good ones. Or they should be.'

Three further visits to the range, and a purposeful avoidance of any golf course designed to erase my confidence, meant that when I arrived at Nick Faldo's house early on a Tuesday morning, I felt there was just a chance I might not be completely wasting the man's time.

4

Faldo

We'd been sitting at the kitchen table for barely 5 minutes and already the greatest conspiracy of all time had been mooted. Nick Faldo, having recently watched a documentary on television, raised the theory that man had never landed on the moon. Instead, the Americans, conscious of the need to beat the Russians in the battle for space supremacy when the Cold War was still raging and the Cuban missile crisis was still very much in everyone's thoughts, filmed the whole event in one of those remote, cordoned-off sections of the Arizona desert that resembled, with clever photography and lighting, the moon. Like Roswell, he argued, the truth may yet emerge.

We could have gone the whole hog and ventured into UFOs and the world of the supernatural but, instead, he jumped up to make some cappuccinos from his swanky machine on the kitchen surface, then led us into a room sporting a large cabinet. His teenage daughter, Natalie, was slumped on a sofa watching a video, singularly unimpressed (as teenagers would be) by the vast array of silverware glinting from inside the wall-size cabinet. Faldo began to present a guided tour of his trophies: three silver Augusta clubhouses, the result of three US Masters wins, together with three replica claret jugs, albeit half the size of the genuine trophies, denoting his three British Open triumphs; seven Ryder Cup trophies, handed out each time to anyone competing in the bi-annual, transatlantic competition. Faldo's attempting to get his hands on four more to mark his first four Ryder Cup appearances when such trophies were not awarded, merely to complete his full complement of a quite remarkable eleven Ryder Cup outings. Various other trinkets and cups, shields, jugs and medals included his first-ever cup won at Royston Golf Club, Hertfordshire.

I'd been a little unsure how the day would pan out, given Faldo's hitherto reputation for being, shall we say, intense, but as we retired to a living room it soon became clear that the man who had struggled during the past four years, and who was desperately trying to rediscover his old form, was keen to make a few confessions and rid himself of a few demons in the process.

'It's a funny thing, but people seem to respect me now for what I've achieved and the way I went about achieving it,' he said, with a sardonic smile. 'When I was winning those majors, people hated me, not just because for a time I was the most dominant golfer in the world but because of the way I went about it. All the things I was knocked for – commitment, dedication, single-mindedness – I'm now praised for. Back then I was seen as the loner who was aloof and stand-offish. People wanted me to be everything: the best competitor, the nicest guy, a fantastic husband and father, but for ten years the only thing that mattered to me was playing golf and being the best. Looking back, there were times when I was too hard on others, when I pushed people aside, when I was blinkered. That's where my reputation for being unfriendly came from, but I was a professional sportsman and it was my business to compete. I didn't want to give people an inch. To me it was just great when my competitors saw the name Faldo on top of the leaderboard and thought: "Shit, it's that bastard Faldo again." It was the only way I could become the world's number one.'

He was saying this to a man who had yet to break 100 and had given serious thought to packing in the game seven days before. It didn't seem quite appropriate to show my sympathy for him by equating it to my own struggles on the golf course. 'Never mind the fact that people didn't like you for the way you won your six majors, I couldn't even hit the bloody ball at Muirfield' was probably not the way I, who Faldo had sought after to confess, should respond. Besides, he had only just started.

He'd won his last Masters title in 1996, but in the ensuing six years Faldo's life had tumbled almost out of control. A messy divorce, broken relationships, business splits, and a major loss of form saw the man spiral downwards on and off the golf course. The Faldo of old would have been the last human on the planet to make such an admission. The new Faldo appeared eager to come clean.

'It wasn't long after winning the '96 Masters that I found myself at a low ebb,' he explained. 'I started to lose my concentration, I couldn't sleep at night, and on the golf course I'd let my frustrations get the better of me. When it started to go wrong, it went very wrong. I tried to shut things out, but I couldn't. I remember saying to Fanny [Sunesson, his Swedish caddie] in Germany one day: "Fanny, I'm standing here today with my chin up a little higher."

'She said: "Why?"

'And I replied: "Because the crap is right up to my neck now." And it was, with businessmen, lawyers and girlfriends. I felt hurt and embarrassed when I started to miss cuts on a regular basis. It was getting to the stage when I couldn't see me ever winning a golf tournament again.'

Faldo began to feel that whatever he had achieved in the game was on the verge of being forgotten by the new breed who were passing him at an alarming rate of knots. 'Players have gone past me who should not have. I don't think there's a great deal of respect for me in the game, right now, for what I'm doing, especially from the young players bursting on to the scene. Some of the young stars have wondered who the hell I am. They certainly haven't feared me as a competitor. When Tiger Woods walks, say, from the clubhouse to the practice range, the sea parts in front of him. It got to the stage with me where nobody even batted an eyelid.'

The very worst moment of all, the time when Faldo had sunk to the very depths, came about during the 1999 British Open at Carnoustie. 'I was in the bunker at the third hole in the first round,' he recalled. 'I'd just pulled a horrible shot into the bunker, and proceeded to duff the ball up the fairway to score a five or a six. That's when I felt that the game had gone from me completely. I remember actually saying to myself: "That's it. I can't play any more. It's gone." I pulled myself together to complete the round, but that night I realised that by playing golf I was damaging myself.'

I nodded my head in complete understanding. 'I felt like that the other week, Nick,' I told him, wishing immediately that I had just kept my mouth shut. He looked at me blankly and said nothing.

It is an incredible sequence of events to take in, given his success story prior to this downfall. As a boy growing up in Welwyn Garden City he was a sportsman looking for a sport. 'I tried tennis but was told I was too tall, which is ridiculous now when you look at the size of the best players.' Faldo was a decent cricketer, a committed cyclist, especially on the track, a goalkeeper in the school soccer side, and a particularly fast swimmer. In 1972, at the age of 13, he happened to come across Jack Nicklaus on television and took note. 'I went down to my local club in Welwyn the next day and booked up six lessons. All I wanted to do was to hit some balls, but my first lesson was an early instalment on discipline. All my teacher and I did was work on my grip. Lesson two was swing. It was only midway through my third lesson that I hit my first golf ball. From then on I used to practise my golf every day after school, hitting a ball with my wedge into the long-jump pit at the side of the school playing fields.'

In relating this, Faldo reminded me of one of the first, life-enhancing lessons of golf that I was struggling to come to terms with. Practice and patience, time and a belief that it will come together but not immediately. All these ingredients were against my impatient nature, but slowly the game was forcing me to reappraise my approach.

At 15 Faldo was hooked on the game, spending all his spare time playing golf and deciding that he would become a professional golfer. At

16 he left school and benefited from an unusual show of faith from his parents. They could sense his dedication. 'I suggested one day to my father that I should get an assistant's job at Knebworth Golf Club for £4 per week. He said he'd lose the same amount in child allowance and it just wasn't worth it. Instead, we agreed that I should practise every day.'

That's precisely what he did, riding his bike to Knebworth, with his lunch in a Tupperware container and clubs strapped on to a plank of wood, through woods and steep, muddy banks that often resulted in crashes and falls. He'd hit balls until midday, eat his lunch and return to the fairways for another four hours of golf. 'My parents must have held a great deal of trust in me because they never came to the club to check up on me.'

His approach to the game even back then was revealing. Take, for example, his stories of visiting Open Championships. 'I went to the 1973 and 1974 Opens with my father,' he recalled. 'We stayed in a tent and it was so cold that I'd wear my pyjamas underneath my clothes during the day. I'd only spend around twenty per cent of the time watching the players on the course. My main interest was at the practice area. I was fascinated by the various idiosyncrasies of the players. I sucked in the tempo and developed a photographic knowledge of the way they played their game. Then I'd go back to Knebworth and announce to myself: "Today I'm Jack Nicklaus in a threesome with Johnny Miller and Tom Weiskopf," and take turns trying to copy their styles.'

In 1975 it all began to happen for Faldo. 'I went from a three handicap (he says this as if having a three handicap is derisory) to plus one and started to win everything, from the Berkshire trophy to the English Amateurs.' A short spell on a golf scholarship at the University of Houston followed, before a girlfriend's father suggested he should turn pro. On 14 April 1976 Nick Faldo joined the ranks of the golfing professionals and made rapid progress, from winning £50 at his first professional tournament, the French Open, £2,000 in total prize money for the season and a standing of 58th in the European Order of Merit to, a couple of years later, finishing eighth in the money list and qualifying for the first of his eleven Ryder Cups at the age of just 20. To complete a sensational season he beat Nicklaus and Raymond Floyd in partnership with Peter Oosterhuis, and then defeated the current Open champion, Tom Watson, in the Ryder Cup singles. Perhaps most telling of all, however, was his performance in that '78 Open. 'I finished four shots behind Nicklaus and that was the moment when I told myself that one day I would win the Open,' Faldo admitted.

Despite my previous aversion to golf I had always been a sucker for against-all-odds success stories, and here was another one. It is easy to look at a successful, famous and, above all, wealthy sports star and question whether the fame and the money is deserved, while forgetting conveniently the sacrifices made and the belief held that it would all come good at an age when the odds were heavily stacked against you.

It would take another nine years for Faldo to fulfil his prophecy, a spell in which he first became the most dominant golfer in Europe and then, inexplicably at the time, had reconstructed his game totally in a move that almost backfired on him. The events of the 1983 Open proved to be the catalyst for this dramatic decision. 'I was tying for the lead with just nine holes to go, but blew up and finished well down the field,' he recalled. 'Within a year of this I realised that although I was good, I didn't quite have the game to be the best.'

He turned to David Leadbetter, a coach who has since become recognised as the guru of the world's finest golfers, and spent two years rebuilding his game. 'I thought it would take two months,' Faldo admitted. 'I started to shoot high scores because I was using a style alien to me. People thought I'd lost it. I was the number one in Europe 1 minute, and then way down in the seventies the next. Deals were lost because of this and it scared the hell out of me at the time.'

In spring 1987 it clicked. He was at Atlanta Airport meeting his wife as all the players arrived for the Masters at Augusta. They all turned left at the airport to catch the connecting flight, and Faldo turned right to travel on to Hattysberg. 'It had got to the stage when I had not been invited to play in the Masters. I remember how much that hurt me at the time, watching the other players disappear as they made their way down towards the Augusta gate. I shot four 67s at Hattysberg and came second in the tournament, returned to Europe and won the Spanish Open a fortnight later. That's when I had a vision that I would win the Open. Nobody fancied me to do it, of course, but I never doubted it for a moment.'

Muirfield 1987 initiated nine years at the top, including a second Open win at St Andrews sandwiching a third back at Muirfield, and those three Masters titles. 'It gives me a tremendous amount of pride to have my name up there alongside Arnold Palmer and Gary Player with six Opens and Masters, with only Nicklaus and Tom Watson above us,' he declared.

As the number one player in Europe, Faldo realised he did not possess the armoury necessary to become the best in the world. He thus took an extraordinary risk in starting out all over again, incorporating a totally new style. To put this into some kind of perspective, imagine David Beckham deciding he wanted to become a goalkeeper and ending up playing for England. Small ponds and comfort zones suit most of us just fine, but what makes winners amongst winners is the hunger to reach the very top. We may be talking about golf here, but the very same virtues can so obviously be applied to life.

'Do you know, for everything I've done in golf I can't help thinking that I've underachieved,' he explained, which took some believing. 'I'd like to think there's still one more major left in me. My passion for the game has returned, and my motivation to prove all those who wrote me off, or have not respected me in recent years, wrong is immense. It's not an impossible dream. Far from it. I'll have to be as dedicated as I was before, but I must also have my smiley face with me at all times. My view on people has changed, and for the better.'

When I first decided to throw myself head on into embracing golf I had planned to meet some of the world's better golfers, but had not prepared myself for the rather obvious fact that these people happen to be emotional human beings, just like the rest of us. Jack Newton had already blown away this preconception, but this was mainly down to the fact that a personal tragedy had befallen him. But Nick Faldo, the robot of the fairways? To the watching millions of golf fans, the likes of Faldo represent untouchable and unbreakable sporting gods, but the reality, of course, is that they have the same inequalities and insecurities as the rest of us.

At this point Faldo, the human being, reverted to Faldo, the golfer, when he suggested we ventured outside to hold a practice session in his back garden. This was the moment I had been looking forward to and dreading in equal measure, especially after my harrowing experience at Muirfield. Any repeat of my driving there and Faldo would conclude that he had just wasted a whole morning in his over-busy and complicated life.

We changed our clothing in a small, wooden shed where he keeps his clubs, balls and other golfing paraphernalia. Ambling over to his tee-off mat, Faldo suggested I take a couple of swings and then drive a ball using my nine iron. Straight ahead of me I saw 130 yards of back garden. To my left was a fine view of Windsor Castle; to my right stood my car, a selection of Nick's various vehicles, and the Faldo house behind them. His pink mansion was testament to the money he had earned during his illustrious career. Elton John lives just over the wall from Faldo, which means either the singer-songwriter must have to throw back a good number of golf balls, or the golfer's two teenage children are forever knocking on Elton's front door.

Please God, if ever I needed a clean hit and a straight drive this was the time. Shuffling and waggling for an eternity, I finally got round to striking the ball. It was a terrible connection, shooting off at almost a 90-degree angle to the right and no more than knee height directly towards one of Faldo's cars, before hitting a small mound of grass and careering off into the corner of the garden. It is not an exaggeration to say that the mound of grass may well have saved one of Faldo's headlamps. To break my own would have been bad news. To have broken his would have been catastrophic.

Nick recognised the potential immediately and asked the watching Simon Crane if he could move a couple of his cars for him. It was a perfectly understandable reaction on Faldo's part, but one not designed to improve my fragile confidence. Mercifully, my second drive was better. The ball soared high and straight in the air in front of me before landing close to the fence. Although a perfectly decent shot had just been played out, the man who knew a little more about the game than me spotted some immediate deficiencies. I was moving my legs and my torso too much, my arms weren't locked straight enough, and I was attempting to help the ball to its intended destination – all common traits, apparently, of the rookie golfer.

With a little physical help from Faldo, and a few rotational exercises using the club, the resulting nine irons were sent down the golfer's garden at a surprisingly consistent rate, with good length, height and direction. Easy game this, if your coach just happens to be a six times major winner. Moving on to chips using my wedge, Faldo soon halted my tendency to top or scuff the ball by moving my feet and my body position, and ensuring that the distance my wedge ended up after the stroke from my body was the same as it was when it began its downward movement. Again, things were happening that had never occurred in my embryonic game. Chip after chip flew neatly into the air, some for a good distance, others for just a couple of yards or so, depending on my intentions.

Faldo also took the opportunity to take a few drives himself. 'I'm often in my garden practising,' he explained, as he sent the ball over a tree, beyond the fence and into the field behind. 'Matthew, my son, and I will regularly have a competition here.' It was all rather difficult to take in. There I was, in the back garden of Nick Faldo's house, hitting balls with the man himself, and hitting them rather well. Or at least by my dubious standards.

I left the Faldo home in the afternoon possessing a totally new and positive mindset. For a man who considered throwing his clubs away only a week before, I had just undergone something of a golfing lobotomy – again. I would become fitter, I would explore all possible ways to improve my play, and I would venture out on to the next golf course convinced that never again would I return to the humiliation of Muirfield. It would help, of course, if I had Nick Faldo standing over me at all times when I played, but when I enquired of such availability, he informed me that this would be impossible, that is unless I had a few million bucks to spare.

5

Sex and drugs and rock and golf

'There are four typical stages in a golfer's cycle.' I was standing in the middle of an empty athletics track, close to my home in the south-eastern outskirts of London, with Steve Backley, the double Olympic and world javelin silver medallist. The man who has also won four successive European titles was waxing lyrical about golf on a cold, blustery morning.

'The first stage is unconscious incompetence,' he explained. 'The second is conscious incompetence. The third is conscious competence. And the one we're all aiming for is unconscious competence. In other words, when you're doing things correctly without even thinking about it.'

Backley, who plays off seven and has an ambition to reach scratch when his javelin career comes to an end in three or four years' time, has started a sideline in fitness training specifically for golfers, and already has a number of European Tour professionals seeking his expert advice.

I reckoned I had left unconscious incompetence behind and was shuttling between conscious incompetence and conscious competence. As Tiger Woods had set the tone in modern golf with his higher levels of fitness and strength, I figured I should follow suit. Reinforced by Nick Faldo's recommendation that I should work on my rotational muscles, keeping my spine and legs straight as my hips twisted round, rather like those characters in that recent television advert promoting Levis, I sought out the help from a man who uses similar muscles and movements when unleashing a javelin.

Strangely enough, Steve Backley the golfer has made something of an impact, at least with Colin Montgomerie, who once wrote in a British golf magazine that Backley's swing was one of the finest he had ever seen. 'He went on to say that my short game must be pretty crap because otherwise I'd be a top golfer,' the big, strapping athlete added. 'Actually, my short game is my biggest strength on the golf course. My problem is threefold: the power muscles I've built up for javelin throwing can hamper my golf, I have a tendency to try and drive the ball as far as I can, losing accuracy for distance, and I just don't play enough to become seriously good.'

He knew a thing or two about golf fitness, though. We began an hour-long session with four laps of the track, not just jogging but using foot drills designed to link the mind and the body towards balance, co-ordination and agility. Quite what a casual observer would have made of two guys at times waddling on the insides and then outsides of their feet, before stumbling around on their heels and toes, and then finally goose-stepping like a couple of right-wing extremists, I will never know, but I felt slightly less stupid when we started to hop and skip from foot to foot, controlling the centre of gravity in the process.

The warm-up completed, Backley produced a couple of medicine balls, one distinctly heavier than the other, and soon had me enacting a number of exercises designed to increase the stability of my legs and improve my rotational plane. Now this made a lot of sense because in attempting to keep my legs and spine relatively still, while my shoulders swung from side to side, even I could recognise the similarities with a golf swing. 'We're working on your rotation,' Backley explained, when he saw my pained expression. 'It's making your legs fixed and stable, but at the same time generating enough mobility in the spine to turn the shoulders for maximum impact. By not swaying around when you're swinging the club you'll generate consistency.' It was more or less what

Nick Faldo had said, in an albeit different way, the week before.

The session concluded with some work on the wrists. 'They play a huge part on the golf swing,' my new fitness coach insisted. Backley had me standing rigid, with a golf club held out directly in front of me on a horizontal plane, as I moved it from my right to my left using my wrists and not my arms. After a while it began to feel distinctly uncomfortable but, seeing as he had made this exercise look ridiculously easy, I kept my discomfort to myself.

'One day I'd like to find out how good I can be as a golfer,' he admitted afterwards, as we sat in the warmth of my car and gazed out at the athletics track. 'I'm not saying I'd be good. I have a great deal of respect for professional golfers so I'm not saying I could match them, but I would like to find out. Certainly there's a physical connection between striking a golf ball and unleashing a javelin. Every javelin thrower I know can hit a golf ball for miles, even if they don't play the game.'

'It's Tiger Woods, of course,' who can take the credit for the trend among professional golfers to improve their fitness. Tiger is at the same time supple and powerful; he whips through the ball when he drives it but still remains graceful.

As for me, after the nightmare of Muirfield it was important I returned to at least a semi-consistent round of golf, but becoming fitter was also a means to a particular end: to break the 100 barrier. The number '99' was starting to become my holy grail.

My next round was at the plush St-Cloud Golf and Country Club, near Paris. I had taken the short trip across the Channel to watch the France versus England rugby international, fancying that a change in nationality might make a difference on a golf course. No logic was applied to this theory, of course, but it was a straw I was more than happy to clutch.

Although only the first day of March, the finest day of the year developed, with an early spring sunshine and a full bloom of flowers scattering the 'Jaune' course at St-Cloud. A private members' club, frequented by a 'who's who' of Parisien society and the venue of the French Open on 11 occasions, the course offers stunning views of Paris from various vantage points on the fairways and greens. Built by British architect Henry Colt in 1923, the 'Jaune' complements the 'Vert' course constructed some 10 years earlier.

My playing partner for the day was one of the club's assistant professionals, Morgan Caillaux, a laconic 24-year-old who once played in the same British amateur tournament as Sergio Garcia. 'I beat him by three strokes in the first round,' Morgan recalled with pride, as we ambled over to the first tee.

Despite this fond recollection, and the first signs of spring, Morgan was not a happy chap that day. At first his explanation was simple: he was merely not feeling too good. As the round continued, however, and he continued to play with his shoulders drooped, not even mustering a smile when he holed a long putt, the truth came out. Morgan had split with his girlfriend the week before. 'Four years we were together,' he admitted, with a doleful expression. 'Four years! Now I am very sad.'

Over the subsequent couple of hours I became, without much qualification, something of an agony uncle. In between drives, chips and putts I offered the following snippets of careworn advice: France is full of beautiful women; better for it to have happened now than if you were married; everyone goes through this kind of heartbreak; there is always a reason why relationships don't work out; it's a test of your strength of character; you'll feel a lot happier in a few days' time; and so on. Paris in the springtime is a time for love, of course, which only highlighted Morgan's problem more.

What made this all rather more bizarre is that in the process I was putting together a decent round. No, I mean a really decent score. I was concentrating so hard on trying to cheer up my playing partner that I hardly gave my game any thought at all. There was no time to stare at the ball on the fairway and think to myself: 'I'm useless at approach shots using irons off the fairway,' or eye up a 40-foot putt from the edge of the green and say: 'Well, there's no way I'll hole this.' I just played.

And so it came to pass that on 1 March 2002, I not only managed to score my first sub-hundred round, but obliterate the mark with an orgasmic 93. The 'Jaune' is, according to the St-Cloud information booklet, 'a short, narrow course which requires skill', with a par of 68, but a 93 is a 93. And to me, who eight months previously considered golf to be a sport for the elderly, and just a couple of months back was on the brink of giving up, breaking 100 constituted one of the finest days of my life.

It could have been even better, too, although you can make that argument, I suppose, if you shoot 59. It began with a par on the first, 'Les Genets' (Broom), and although I double bogeyed the next three, I would drop only three more shots in the next five holes, five to nine. This purple patch included another couple of pars, with a 20-foot putt sunk on the 'Terre Haute' (High Land) 5th – definitely my second best putt of all time after the K Club birdie putt – and a bunker shot on the 'La Haie' (The Hedge) 8th which ended on the lip of the hole. Moreover, the golfing gods seemed at last to be smiling on me. Twice, balls heading for the trees took ridiculous rebounds from the branches and ended up back on the fairways. After nine holes I was only 9 over, with a score of 44.

My joy contrasted with Morgan's gloom. Mindful of my partner's broken heart I tried my best not to celebrate too much. I tried, but often I failed. Morgan had been halfway through explaining why there was no chance of a reunion after just a week away from his ex-girlfriend, when he stopped talking to allow me to concentrate on my 20-foot putt. When the ball plopped beautifully into the hole I shouted out 'Yesssss!!' and punched the air like a soccer player having just scored a goal. Eventually I remembered what stage we had reached in the conversation. 'Sorry, Morgan,' I said. 'You were just saying how there's no chance you will ever get back together again.'

The inward 9 was not quite so clever. The 44 had gone to my head and I was ruminating over the possibility that I was not only going to beat 100 for the first time, I was going to record a sub-90 score in one fell swoop. Predictably, the pars disappeared and an inward 49 resulted in a final round of 93.

Even Morgan's sorrowful face broke out into a half-smile when I slapped his back, shook his hand and thanked the great gods of the fairway that at last I could report an acceptable score. I considered telling him that perhaps I should always play with a lovesick partner to help me with my game, but thought better of it. Poor Delphine Chevallier, the lovely assistant at St-Cloud who had been so helpful in arranging my round, ended up being hugged, and anyone else who was passing soon knew of my glad tidings.

It did not end there either. Nick Faldo, Ernie Jones at the K Club, Simon Laird, who had witnessed my sorry 118 at Muirfield, David Young at World of Golf, Steve Backley, even Bruce Green, who had witnessed that truly dreadful 122 at Royal Melbourne, all received notification of my 93. The way I was treating this it should have been the top story on the nightly news bulletin throughout the world, when in reality I had recorded a score that all the above, plus any half-decent golfer, could achieve with ease. Naturally, everyone was very nice and complimentary on hearing the news. 'Well done,' they said. 'Congratulations.' On replacing the telephone receiver, or on putting down the fax paper, they probably muttered: 'Sad bastard.'

I'd like to think that my wife did not share this thought, but she clearly wondered what all the fuss was about when I told her the news from Paris. 'Great,' she said, her tone revealing her disinterest. 'What time are you home again?'

Things were looking up for Tiger Woods too. Although beaten by Ernie Els, he still recorded a second place in the Genuity Championship, over on the US Tour, at the same time I was hitting 93.

For the first time since beginning this long golfing quest, I had been presented with some evidence that I just might be able to play this damn game. With luck, I would never again venture back into three figures.

*

Here are the temporary rules issued by Richmond Golf Club in 1940 as the Luftwaffe began to rain down:

1 Players are asked to collect Bomb and Shrapnel splinters to save these causing damage to the Mowing Machines.
2 In Competitions, during gunfire or while bombs are falling, players may take cover without penalty for ceasing play.
3 The position of known delayed action bombs are marked by red flags at a reasonably, but not guaranteed, safe distance therefrom.
4 Shrapnel and/or bomb splinters on the Fairways or in Bunkers within a club's length of ball may be moved without penalty, and no penalty shall be incurred if a ball is caused to be moved accidentally.
5 A ball moved by enemy action may be replaced, and if lost or destroyed, a ball may be dropped, not nearer the hole, without penalty.
6 A ball lying in a crater may be lifted and dropped, not nearer the hole, preserving the line to the hole, without penalty.
7 A player whose stroke is affected by the simultaneous explosion of a bomb may play another ball from the same place. One penalty stroke.

Having heard of these particular rules administered by the Richmond GC committee, Dr Joseph Goebbels, the minister for Nazi propaganda, announced on German radio: 'By means of these ridiculous reforms, the English snobs try to impress the people with a kind of pretend heroism.'

You couldn't make it up, could you?

Scott Gorham has a true story that also underlines the way golf can result in the loss of all perception and reality. The lead guitarist of the rock group Thin Lizzy is a member at Richmond GC and met up with myself, Nicko McBrain, Iron Maiden's drummer, and Glyn Johns, record producer of the likes of Eric Clapton, Led Zeppelin, The Eagles and The Who, for a round at the south-west London course.

'I was playing in a foursome when one of the players suddenly collapsed in the middle of the green,' Scott related. 'Nobody else seemed perturbed by this but I certainly was. I asked what had happened and one of my playing partners explained that this was a minor epileptic fit, it occurred on a fairly regular basis and that it would be over in a minute or so.'

Scott shook his head as he recounted this tale and shrugged his shoulders by way of introducing the punchline. 'We all stood there for a few seconds watching this poor fellow in an obviously uncomfortable state,' he continued. 'Eventually I asked if there was anything we could do.

'My playing partner considered this for a few moments and replied: "Well, I suppose we could all putt around him."'

The reason why I had arranged a round of golf with these three characters is because I could not imagine a more contrasting image than heavy metal rockers who have spent most of their lives trashing hotel rooms and instruments, and having indulged in every excess going, suddenly becoming besotted with golf. As far as they were concerned you can take exotic substances, you can be a hotel manager's worse nightmare, but you can never, ever, walk across someone's putting line. It just goes to show how golf can immerse absolutely anyone.

'I remember when I first played with Nicko and the boys from Maiden,' Scott continued. 'I was engrossed in my round when, suddenly, I looked up at the boys and saw nothing but a mass of tattoos and hair blowing in the wind. I said to them: "Who'd have thought ten years ago that we'd be out here now playing golf?"'

'The funny thing is for years I kept it quiet. I was happier to admit to taking drugs and alcohol in stupid amounts than to playing golf. It just appeared to me to be the most taboo thing a rock musician could do. You know, with all those God-awful checked pants and diamond-patterned sweaters. When I did finally come out of the closet – and that's how it felt, coming out of the closet – it was a huge relief. And your friend Tiger Woods has played a huge part in this. Hey, now that Tiger's made it cool, it's acceptable for anyone to play this game. Even rock musicians.'

No matter where I went, no matter what I did, you just couldn't keep the name Tiger Woods out of the conversation for long. Whether it's former major winners, Olympic medallists or rock musicians, they all seem to have hoisted the man up on to his own high pedestal. Scott's use of the word 'your', when he mentioned Woods, also reminded me that day once more how Tiger represented my personal journey's end.

Despite the new-found coolness of golf it still made a strange sight, the long-haired Scott Gorham, the pony-tailed, tattooed Nicko McBrain and Glyn Johns traipsing along the fairways. Glyn, who plays off 18, is as sick with golf as Scott. He only took up the game four and a half years ago but has become obsessed. He even admits to having had a driving range built in his back garden. It was Ian Stewart, late keyboard player with the Rolling Stones, who introduced him to the game, and it turned out to be the only way they could spend any time together doing something they mutually enjoyed.

Nicko, whose golf bag and golf balls are emblazoned with the words 'Iron Maiden', used to caddie and occasionally play at Muswell Hill Golf Club in north London as a boy. He already loved playing the game, but he became even more besotted with drumming and for the next twenty years or so golf was put on the back burner.

'I remember the day I decided to start it up again very clearly. The band were in the Bahamas recording. We had a habit of coming in after a night out – which was every night – at 7 o'clock in the morning, just as the golfers would be emerging to begin their rounds. We used to laugh at them, in their dreadful clothes, but on that day I said to the other band members: "Wouldn't it be good to be able to play a round of golf in the day, then play a gig at night?" That's when I started to play again, over in the Bahamas.

'It's fair to say that as a result the game of golf saved me from total self-destruction. The way I and the rest of the band were going we couldn't have gone on forever behaving like we were, and abusing ourselves to the degree we were.'

Scott's story, though, is the most dramatic. Originally from Los Angeles, Scott co-fronted Thin Lizzy with the late Phil Lynott, who died from heroin abuse in the 1980s. Scott, but for the game of golf, would almost certainly have followed suit.

'There was nothing I didn't try,' he admitted, as we ambled along the fairways. 'There are periods of my life which to this day remain empty. I have no idea what I did. My biggest problem was smack. It took my wife to explain to me one day that everyone else could see I had a problem. This came as a complete shock. In my drug-ridden self-delusion, I thought I was the only person who knew.

'I'd tried to give up a few times, but after my wife's statement I became more determined than ever. Within days of quitting drugs for the nth time I was in a terrible state. It was real cold turkey. I was going out of my mind thinking about taking some more smack. My doctor suggested we should go out and hit some golf balls in Richmond Park. I thought it a crazy idea but went along with it. As soon as I started driving something happened: I stopped thinking about drugs and concentrated fully on hitting the ball. For half an hour my mind was transfixed on striking a little white ball.

'The next day I went out again to hit some more. Then the next day and the day after. Before I knew it I was hooked on golf, and not drugs. This was in the early 1980s. I haven't taken any drugs since. Golf has become my obsession now. I'm clearly an addictive personality. Before it was an addiction to heroin. Now it's golf. It's a sport I'm greatly indebted to.'

It's not just the actual process of hitting the ball with a club into a hole that has Scott, Nicko and Glyn living, eating and breathing the game. It is the manner in which golf is played, too. 'It's the only thing I've ever done in my whole life where I've been required to play by the rules,' Scott explained. 'Maybe I want to impress my friends. I want to show them how I can conduct myself sometimes. And I enjoy the sanity about golf in a life I lead that is chaotic in almost every other aspect.'

It was beginning to dawn on me just how wrong I'd been in some of my presumptions about golf. First Jack Newton, now Scott Gorham. But when Scott turned to golf, after a life of self-destruction, he became consumed by an addiction that required nothing more than long walks in the countryside, a mental challenge and a little sporting talent as well.

Yet it was the statement about enjoying playing by the rules that got me really thinking. You see, even up to this point, I had always assumed that although you require rules in all sports, many of golf's regulations were petty in the extreme. Did it really matter if you accidentally kicked your ball, or touched it with your club before playing it? What difference did it make if you mistakenly carried one too many clubs in your bag? No one really minded if you half-heartedly tapped in a close-range putt one-handed, missed but claimed the putt in any case because you had not really tried.

Well, actually, it matters a great deal. All those golfing clichés you hear about cheats only cheating themselves, about having to deal with whatever problems the round conjures up, about knowing the correct way to behave in the company of others, are all true to golf and to life. I used to believe the way golfers behaved with their stupid rules was worth the contempt I gave them. Now I saw this in a totally different light. There was something almost noble about the fairest of sports. It took a long-haired rock star to point this out to me.

Unintentionally, Scott provided further proof of his infatuation with golf on the 13th green. Nicko was talking about a forthcoming Iron Maiden gig in Frankfurt and then his immediate plans afterwards. 'Hey, Scott, why don't we get together and play some time?' he suggested.

'Yeah, good idea,' his friend replied. 'Do you want to come back here to the Richmond Golf Club, or try somewhere else?'

Nicko stared at Scott for a few seconds, shook his head and then burst into laughter. 'I was talking about jamming. You know, me on the drums, you on the guitar?'

I had wanted to slip into the conversation that I played guitar and used to be a student busker in London. Fortunately my preoccupation with playing half-decent golf took over, which is just well. Consider the following conversation.

'Wembley's a pretty good venue, but I like the Monsters of Rock at Donnington.' – Nicko.

'Candlestick Park in San Francisco and the Pasadena Rosebowl, LA, are great places to play, too.' – Scott.

'We should get together the next time I'm at the studios in Monterrey.' – Glyn.

'I always found Elephant & Castle underground station the best. I'd earn twenty pounds in an afternoon, plus some half-drunk cans of Stella Artois and a few gobstoppers from schoolchildren.' – Ian.

Instead, despite the calibre of the company, I found myself willingly sucked into almost total golf conversation. Nicko, for example, has homes in north London and Florida, where he plays at a club that insists that if you wear shorts you must also wear knee-length socks. 'Can you imagine how stupid I must look?' he asked, as we all tried to envisage this middle-aged rocker looking like some colonial army officer.

My performance at Richmond in this relaxed, enjoyable company almost exactly mirrored that of St-Cloud. Consequently, my new-found rock friends were not convinced about my golfing incompetence. When Scott and I took on Nicko and Glyn, we triumphed four and three, with an extra stroke put aside for the weakest player – who, in case you were wondering, was deemed to be me. 'We're going to have to stop this extra stroke rule with you,' Nicko would mutter. I felt proud and relieved to have held my own and to have actually won, even if it was just a friendly game between two pairs.

When it was all over, and a couple of drinks had been consumed in the Richmond clubhouse, Nicko gave me a huge hug, swapped numbers and invited me to play over in Florida with him whenever I was visiting. Glyn would be returning to his home in Aix-en-Provence the following day and Scott, the reformed drug addict who owed his life to golf, drove back to his home in Putney. 'And you know what I'll be thinking about tonight?' he asked me, as he departed. 'When's the next round of golf? Where will it be? And with whom will I be playing?' He laughed in a self-deprecating manner. 'And guess what? I'm already getting excited just thinking about it.'

6

Ice and a slice

By anyone's standards it was a difficult shot. The ball was still some distance from the flag, the group of golfers behind were growing impatient with my slow play and the round, which had started reasonably well, was beginning to disintegrate. The main problem, though, was the iceberg.

It was one week later and while my new rock 'n' roll chums were hitting the fairways in springtime England, France and America, I was attempting to play golf on the frozen Arctic Ocean, just off the island settlement of Uummannaq, midway up the west coast of Greenland.

As first golf tournaments go, I had chosen a strange one. The Drambuie World Ice Golf Championships were being staged for the fourth time here in the middle of absolutely nowhere and I, in a moment of madness, had persuaded the organisers to let me enter, hoping that the ice and the cold might disguise my deficiencies.

The journey alone was something of an epic: flight to Copenhagen (where I played a quick two holes against Jeff Louwman, a competitor from New Zealand, on a golfing simulator game at Copenhagen Airport), a long flight to Kangerlussuaq in Greenland where we drank horrendous blue and green Greenlandic vodkas inside an igloo bar, shorter flight to Qaarsut in a dodgy-looking Dash-7 and finally a bumpy 45 minutes in a jeep across – that's right, across – the Arctic Ocean. A welcoming dinner and a deep sleep prepared us for the following day's practice round, 370 miles north of the Arctic Circle, which is where the iceberg comes in.

Icebergs, quite naturally, are major obstacles when found in the middle of a fairway, especially big, glistening, blue and white ones jutting out of the frozen sea. The weather, -25° plummeting to -40° whenever even a slight breeze hit our faces, had produced embryonic signs of frostbite on my fingertips and toes, and the walk down the 'fairway' had already posed the potential dangers of crevasses and thinly concealed seal holes that could result in a dip in seawater so cold that I would not survive for longer than fifteen minutes.

Some of the many thousands of husky dogs used as working animals in these parts lay on the ice in packs, looking on quizzically, while groups of local Inuit children gathered round, not fully understanding my sporting predicament but interested, nevertheless, to watch this strange man with his strange stick thrashing about on the ice.

The particular attire required to keep out the cold hardly helped matters. Underneath my fleece I wore a thick, thermal vest, T-shirt, sweatshirt and jumper. Below the waist I sported thermal leggings, tracksuit bottoms and thick, ski salopettes. A warm headband, neckband that rose as high as my chin and a woolly Tyrolean hat bought in Innsbruck during the Christmas break protected much of my head (together with copious amounts of lipgloss and sun cream), while two pairs of gloves, two pairs of socks and thick, ski boots completed the outfit. Pretty useful for temperatures as cold as was being experienced in Uummannaq. Pretty useless when it came to swinging a golf club. It was an achievement merely to lift the club above your head.

I struck the ball (orange, of course, so that it could be seen in the ice and snow) and watched as it rebounded off a slab of 10,000-year-old iceberg and fell fortuitously close to where the flag fluttered in the centre of the green – or rather the 'white' – leaving me with a simple putt to complete the practice round.

The nine-hole course, with its pack ice making it the only moving golf course in the world, was carved out of the frozen landscape only a couple of days before the start of the championships. Nowhere else on the planet can a golf course truly lay claim that on no single day does it remain the same. Overnight, new juts of ice emerge from the sea and the 'fairways' – consisting of a thin layer of compact snow over ice – can flatten out in a totally different place from the day before. Moreover, the seabed, some 1,200 feet below, will be littered with orange golf balls, claimed by the ice but released to the bottom during the warmer weather of the summer.

For 51 weeks of the year life carries on as it has always done in Uummannaq, named after its heart-shaped mountain that dominates the island and the bay. Time, and the way the Inuits go about their business, have stood relatively still for centuries. The recent efforts to modernise this massive outcrop of Denmark (Greenland is the world's largest island but is governed by the Danes) has resulted in an influx of technology in contrast to the surrounding environment.

The Internet may be used here like anywhere else in the world, the one local bar provides a disco throbbing to the latest dance sounds and the youngsters, judging by the posters donning the bedroom walls of the local orphanage, were into Britney Spears and Westlife at the time. Yet the Greenlandic people still fish and hunt for halibut and seal, with the occasional polar bear thrown in for good measure, while the rest of the world goes on in its troubled ways almost unnoticed.

For one week only, however, something utterly implausible comes to town. The Drambuie World Ice Golf Championships have now become a permanent fixture on the island of Uummannaq, luring the 1,700 local inhabitants to observe with genuine curiosity as Scots and Americans, Spaniards and Australians, Danes and New Zealanders, English and Irish men and women battle it out on the ice.

The tournament was the brainchild of local hotelier Arne Neiman, who came up with the creditable notion that holding such an event would attract guests who would require a room for a week at the one hotel in town. Given that mid-March still represents the last few weeks of winter in one of the most inhospitable environments on Earth, tourists had not exactly been the norm.

All that changed with Neiman's introduction of golf, especially when the Edinburgh-based Drambuie Liqueur Company Ltd came in after a year to sponsor the event. It has progressed to the extent that some seriously good golfers abandon their usual pastures of Florida and South Africa for the frozen wastes of the Arctic. From America, we had the likes of Jack O'Keefe, who made the cut in the US Open in 1996 and now plays on the Buy.Com Tour, and Chip Thomson, a former US PGA tour player who now coaches and broadcasts on golf, as well as South African-born Roy Wegerle, former Premiership and World Cup footballer for the United States, who successfully turned his hand to golf and almost instantly qualified for the South African Open.

Challenge tour professionals such as Austria's Rudi Sailer and Scotland's Roger Beames also fancied their chances, as did twice defending champion, Annika Ostberg, who was back for a third time of sporting lunacy. Oddly, Annika, a schoolteacher and many times former Danish women's golf champion, disliked playing in the cold. 'Give me a warm day when I can wear shorts any time,' she admitted. 'But it's different in Greenland. The scenery is so beautiful, the wilderness so awesome, and the actual tournament so much fun that the temperature doesn't come into it.'

Maybe not to Annika, but to the majority of the golfers the climate presented severe problems. 'I've never known anything like it,' Roy Wegerle admitted, suntanned from his life in Florida, but shivering in the freezing Greenland air as he fought a losing battle to prevent his fingers turning blue during the practice round.

I was one of the few outsiders in Uummannaq who knew what was going to hit us. A few days spent trekking in Arctic Spitzbergen, with polar explorer David Hempleman-Adams, for a participatory article in *Esquire* magazine the year before had introduced me to the niceties of -25°, but it was still a shock to the system. There's a cold winter's day in England, and then there's a cold day in Greenland. Add the wind-chill factor and it's like sticking your head into a freezer that is twice as cold as normal.

The locals, proud Greenlandics with a few Danes thrown in, are used to this. Their sealskin coats and polar-bear fur trousers keep everything the Arctic throws at them out, but to the golfers the extreme cold was a new phenomenon. This coupled with a strenuous walk around the nine-hole course that meant each round took over three hours to complete, because of the icebergs and lumpy surface of the sea ice, made it so arduous that world championship regulations insisted you played no more than nine holes in a morning before returning to the warmth of the hotel for recovery.

As if these hurdles were not enough, the snow and the ice-covered landscape created a brilliant white that threatened to give you snow-blindness unless precautions were taken. Silence – save for the occasional whine from one of the huskies tied to the sledges on the sea ice or curse from a frustrated golfer – reminded you that Greenland is a very unique part of the world.

Some of the local Inuits volunteered to become caddies for the top golfers, while others had been to the golf schools set up each year in the area prior to the first day of the tournament. You won't find a driving range here, a professional golf shop or a putting green. But the sight of Uummannaq residents coming out in their hordes to follow the golf championships is as unlikely as seeing people scuba-diving in the middle of the Sahara Desert.

I'd struck a deal with a local Inuit, Fleming Nicolaisen, that if he taught me some Inuit words, I would teach him golf. On reflection this was hardly a fair arrangement. Fleming, on the basis that he was a Greenlandic, had taken up the language from around the age of one, when he uttered his first words. I, in contrast, had taken up golf seven months ago. To Fleming, though, a man who had no knowledge of golf whatsoever, I might as well have been Tiger himself.

We ventured out from the hotel in the afternoon and on to the sea ice, where we took turns hitting balls. Because of the temperature the ball did not travel as far and even a loss of a ball meant little. The organisers had provided us with hundreds of the orange things. Fleming played and missed, and missed, but it was worth it to see his face light up when he finally connected and sent the ball scuttling along the ice and out further to sea. 'Maybe I can become Greenland's golf champion?' he asked, as he pondered a change in career. On the basis of one, clean connection, he had already, most probably, become the finest Inuit golfer in Greenland.

My new friend remembered his side of the bargain as we trudged back across the ice. After twenty minutes I had just about come to grips with *qujanaq* (pronounced 'cayannak') meaning 'thank you'; *naamik* meant 'no' and *aap* meant 'yes'. *Illillu* (pronounced 'ichichu') stood for 'you're welcome', *komorn* (pronounced 'come on') was translated as 'good morning', while *baajat marluuk* meant the all-important, universal request of 'two beers'.

Fleming and I were very pleased with ourselves. Both of us thought we were very good at something we had just been taught, whereas the truth was that both us were unbelievably crap. I would spend the rest of the week uttering these Inuit phrases, occasionally receiving a friendly acknowledgement from a local, but mainly initiating confused expressions as if wondering which planet I had arrived from. When I first visited Greece twenty years earlier as a student, I greeted everyone for the first few days with a friendly *'kalamari'*, and wondered why people replied with a glower and the word *malaka*. When I enquired what *malaka* meant and was told it was Greek for 'wanker', I asked why the locals should be so unfriendly. The taverna owner explained that if I was trying to say 'good morning' I should have used the phrase *kali mera*, and not *kalimari*, which meant squid. So whether I was really saying 'Thank you, you're welcome and two beers, please,' in Uummannaq or 'Your wife smells like a husky and looks like a seal's bottom,' I shall never really know.

On the evening before my first-ever tournament, as I lay exhausted on my bed, I flicked on the one channel available on the small television set in my room. There, before me, was Tiger Woods, on a global sports cable channel, claiming the Bay Hill Invitational title for a third straight year. In doing so he became the first player to win 30 US Tour victories before the age of 30 (he was only 26, for goodness sake!), a mark achieved in just 115 starts. Now that's a win ratio that is simply unheard of. One other fact stood out from all this – Woods was currently averaging prize money of £180,000 per tournament.

Even here, in just about the remotest place imaginable on the whole planet, a television screen was broadcasting pictures of Tiger Woods. So that ruled out Uummannaq for a getting-away-from-it-all holiday for the man.

It was an early start the following morning and, after a few too many alcoholic beverages the night before courtesy of the sponsors, I discovered one of the positives of playing golf in -25°. Extreme cold does wonders for your hangover. The Drambuie World Ice Golf Championships were formally opened by a slightly bemused deputy mayor of Uummannaq, and the beginning of two days and four rounds of competition was signalled by the sound of a shotgun punctuating the Arctic tranquillity.

I was teamed up with Roger Beames, touring professional from Skibo Castle in Scotland (where Madonna married Guy Ritchie) and the local doctor, Poul Lauridsen, who had just arrived from his native Denmark. It was good to play with someone as good as Roger, just as it was good to play with someone as bad as Poul. After his first couple of strokes I knew I would achieve my first ambition, namely, to avoid finishing last.

The trick about ice golf is not to hit your drives too long (Roger did and lost quite a few balls in the white wilderness), and to go for the holes with your chips because the 'whites' were so unpredictable. This suited my game because my very average driving was not so badly penalised on this course as it would be under normal circumstances. It meant that the difference between scratch golfers like Roger and newcomers such as me, barely able to claim a handicap, was significantly less noticeable. After two rounds of nine holes each I had scored a 48 and a 43, and discovered that in the separate net championship over Stableford points, I held a healthy midway lead thanks to my generous handicap of 28. At the top of the leaderboard proper, Jack O'Keefe led the way at the halfway stage, his clear ability managing to overcome most but not all of the icy obstacles. Roger, despite spending most of the day cursing the cold or his lost balls, still ended up in second place overnight, some four strokes behind Jack, with Rudi Sailer third, Annika Ostberg fourth and Chip Thomson fifth.

After dinner a presentation was made. There was an extra purpose to the practice round. Two teams – a much larger Europe versus a rather small America – played for the Neiman Cup, named after the hotel owner, Arne. Europe emerged the winners, but as Chip received the losers' medal as America's captain he was on the receiving end of some friendly heckling based around the controversial scenes of the 1999 Ryder Cup, when American players, wives and officials stormed the 17th green following Justin Leonard's winning putt from long distance. Later on I mentioned to Chip a heckling story Ed Byrne, the Irish comedian, had told me once concerning one of his stand-up colleagues who began his act with the statement: "I'm a chronic schizophrenic." Some wag from the audience shouted back: "Then why don't you both fuck off, then?" Chip liked this tale so much he spent the rest of the week greeting me thus: "How are you guys today?"

The next morning I found my playing partners to be Roy Wegerle and Ed Rice, an Irish website expert who was ever so slightly mad, but wonderfully entertaining company. Roy, despite his obvious prowess as a golfer, had not found this trip to the high Arctic quite to his liking, and had long given up hoping to win the tournament.

For much of the round we tried to come up with suitable names for ice golfers. This followed an interview Roy conducted on British radio where the presenter asked if we were playing with Sergio Glacier. The best we came up with was Ernie Ice and Seve Balaclava.

Formerly a professional football player at the highest level, Roy played for Chelsea, Luton, Queens Park Rangers and Blackburn, as well as for the USA in both the 1994 and 1998 World Cups. Indeed, he featured in the US win over Colombia in 1994 that resulted, later, in the murder of the Colombian midfielder, Andrez Escobar, who scored an own goal in that defeat to America, and paid for it with his life back home in Medellin.

'When I retired a couple of years ago I needed to find something to fill my days,' Roy explained. 'It's a major bonus that the something – golf – not only achieves this, but goes a long way to replacing the buzz I felt as a professional footballer. Most players are not so lucky, and spend the bulk of their retirement searching for something to match their days as a sportsman. I've found it in golf, and after qualifying for the South African Open, I really believe I can make it.'

It was during the final round that, for a while, I obtained an entourage of local children. They wanted to know my name. I told them it was Tiger, and was promptly followed for three holes by fifteen children chanting 'Tiger' as I played my strokes. This was probably the only place in the world where I could be mistaken for Tiger Woods by some of the more naive locals. Occasionally I played some decent golf, but more often that not, if not hunting for my golf balls submerged deep into the ice, I was falling thigh deep into soft snow or cracking my kneecaps on slabs of ice.

Jack O'Keefe held on to his lead late into the final day before being first caught and then overtaken by a late and ambitious flurry that paid off from Roger Beames, who emerged as the 2002 Drambuie World Ice Golf champion, with a score of 140 by one stroke from O'Keefe, then Sailer, Thomson and Ostberg, the latter having to bow to an improvement in quality this time after her two previous victories.

Meanwhile I held on to my net leadership, adding two 45s to my previous 48 and 43, for a final score of 181. As a result I can claim an irrefutable title: I am, officially, the world ice golf net champion – and also the 17th best ice golfer in the world. It was not my fault that I was given a 28 handicap. After all, on my previous rounds in golf, that was probably about right. Nevertheless, claims that I am an ice bandit could be justified.

Receiving a statuette made from Greenlandic soapstone and carved by the apparently famous artist Dorthe Kristoffersen, I made a short speech in front of a still bemused town deputy mayor at the gala dinner to celebrate the finish of the tournament, and was referred to as 'Champ' for the rest of the evening by Jack and Rudi, and 'Champs', of course, by Chip.

The real winners, though, after the most bizarre golfing week in one of the remotest corners of the planet, were the good people of Uummannaq. As the closing ceremony was being held – Roger Beames was lofted on board the traditional winners' sledge after standing on a podium made of ice – local youngsters were practising their golf shots in the snow. Arne Neiman was looking forward to a particularly good night's business back at the hotel, and the mayor of this frozen outlet was already planning his opening ceremony speech for next year, when the solid Arctic Ocean becomes once more the most demanding, coldest and yet most beautiful golf course in the world.

7

Mark James

A few days after my return to the relative warmth of England, I found myself doing something I vowed I never, ever, would.

I was in my friend Gareth's kitchen, after a visit to the theatre with some friends, for a few drinks which were rapidly turning into a full-blown party. As I was in the midst of talking to a small group I started to play out some imaginary golf swings with my hands, keeping my back straight and swivelling my arms. Having seen others enact this in the past, I'd always concluded that they appeared to be extremely sad. Now, like a nervous twitch, I was doing the same thing. Perhaps even worse, I'd started to wear some of the clothes I sported on the golf course at home. The good news was that despite my worsening golf condition, I was still able to recognise these flaws in my character. The bad news was that there seemed little I could do to stop the rot. It was beginning to look as if my disease was terminal.

My wife viewed all this with growing disdain. One of the reasons why I appealed to her in the first place was because I used to be the last person to be found swinging an imaginary golf club in someone else's kitchen, let alone start wearing polo shirts with logos and blue socks with the words 'Ping' emblazoned on them. Now, in a little more than 7 months, a golfing lobotomy was taking place. At first, showing willing, she encouraged my new-found crusade. Now it was beginning to wear a bit thin. As we made our way home that night she murmured: 'You'll be wearing plus fours next and banning me from certain parts of the house because I'm a woman.'

I mentioned all this to Mark James the following morning, as we stood on the first tee at Ilkley Golf Club in West Yorkshire preparing to begin our round. The seven times Ryder Cup player, and European captain during that controversial match at Brookline in 1999, nodded his head at my sorry tale like a psychiatrist who had heard it all before. 'There's nothing anyone can do for you,' he said by way of diagnosis.

There can't be too many more beautiful courses in England than Ilkley, just a couple of miles from the James' family home. Designed in 1898 and improved by the famous golf architect, Dr Alister MacKenzie, the course is dominated by Ilkley Moor looming large and high and the River Wharfe, the latter a constant companion for much of the outward nine holes. The great Harry Vardon won his first prize as a professional player at Ilkley, while his brother, Tom, was one of the club's early professionals.

Although I did not admit it to James, I was pretty nervous striding up to the first tee because he represented the first high-profile professional I had ever played with. The seven months of learning the ropes previous to this moment, from Royal Melbourne to St Andrews, the K Club to Muirfield, were designed to turn a complete no-hoper into someone who would not completely embarrass himself in the company of a professional. Now the moment of truth had come. Could I justify sharing a round with a man who had won eighteen titles on the PGA European Tour?

James, ever the competitor, suggested we should play for money, an idea that alarmed me greatly until he came up with the sum of £5. He awarded me a 24 handicap based on my previous two rounds at St-Cloud and Richmond, which meant a stroke per hole, plus an extra shot on six of the holes. On that basis I should have given him a run for his money, but initially this did not quite work out.

While James hit his first drive straight down the centre of the fairway, mine swung violently left and into the River Wharfe, an inaugural shot that resulted in a triple bogey at the first. One hole completed, one up to James. Although a bogey at the second par three maintained the status quo, a triple, two doubles and then another triple bogey from holes three to six, thanks largely to the presence of the river, meant that James, who was hitting the ball sweetly, found himself five up. At this point the sledging began. 'Looks to me as if it's all over,' he muttered, as we trudged along the fairway. 'The writing's well and truly on the wall.'

My partner then had minor apoplexy when I picked up the ball up in the rough to check it belonged to me. 'You can't do that,' he said, indignantly. 'Hasn't anyone ever told you before?' They hadn't, and although in the back of my mind something told me you should not really do that kind of thing, carefree rounds in Greenland and with my rock chums at Richmond had slackened my discipline.

'Tiger Woods would have you for that if he ever saw you,' James warned. Later, he asked me if I was trying it on. 'I wasn't sure if you'd thrown it into the game just to test me out,' he admitted. 'I thought maybe you were seeing how I'd react. Perhaps you were looking to throw me out of my groove.' He chuckled and added: 'Obviously I attributed too much cunning on your behalf.'

At the turn I found myself seven holes down. Seven down after just nine holes! They'd warned me over in Greenland that my next round would be difficult simply because of the readjustment required to play on green grass again after pack ice. The short game, in particular, would suffer, because the holes in regular golf were smaller. Even so, I was heading for a three-figure round and a humiliating defeat at the hands of Europe's previous Ryder Cup captain.

Then, mercifully, my luck changed. I had warned James, with some rather obvious bravado, that his ill-advised words would motivate me, and that I would launch one of the greatest comebacks of all time. For a while, this unlikely scenario was taking shape.

I dropped just two shots in the next four holes, managing two pars and two bogeys from holes 10 to 14 not only to prevent James from taking an unassailable lead, but also reduce the advantage to five holes. 'You're beginning to get me worried,' he confessed, as I strode confidently to the 14th tee. With the handicap I had outplayed one of Europe's finest golfers for four holes. Even without the handicap I had played only two more shots than him in four holes.

There was one other significant highlight during this temporary impression of being someone who could play this game reasonably well. At the par three 13th (named 'Willow Garth') I sank a 15-foot putt to par the hole. Now, by my reckoning, that was my third greatest putt of all time, behind the K Club birdie and the St-Cloud par. On reflection, this was a rather sad state of affairs. I could list my best putts in order and, no doubt, my best birdies, if it was not for the sorry fact that up to this point I had only achieved one of them.

The other aspect that caught my attention was that James, at 48 some ten years older than me, could direct me to the nearest clover leaf to my ball, even if it was some 200 yards away. Now I happen to have particularly good eyesight, but I was damned if I could see exactly where the ball had flown. He explained that it was all to do with starting the game at the age of 10 and playing it seriously not long afterwards. 'You can't afford to lose golf balls at the age of 10. They cost far too much money. And then, once you have become a professional golfer, a lost ball can cost you serious money. It hits you where it hurts the most. That's why a pro rarely loses a ball.'

My purple patch came to an abrupt end. Four double bogeys followed, and with James winning two of those last four holes, the round ended with a resounding victory by seven holes to my partner, which was the lead he held at the halfway stage. In the process he scored an impressive 63 – or six under – an achievement even he was pleased about. 'I'm happy with that,' he announced. 'I hit it well and putted consistently.' Even his one bad shot in the whole round – a misdirected drive at the 12th – ended up with an outrageous bounce right out of the rough and on to the fairway. As if Mark James needed any luck against me?

In contrast I ended the day with 97. After two previous rounds of 93 you might think I would have been disappointed with this score, but all things considered I was reasonably satisfied. At least I had scored my third, consecutive sub-100 round, and after the very different conditions experienced in Greenland, I reckoned it could have been a great deal worse. James, very kindly, was positive about my play, declaring that it wasn't at all bad as we made our way to the clubhouse. 'Let's face it, you've only been playing for seven and a half months. This course can be pretty intimidating, especially those first five holes beside the river, and you were playing with a well-established professional who found a bit of form today. You didn't have much luck either in terms of the rub of the green.'

I felt a lot better after that and handed over my £5 to him happily once we had found a corner in the clubhouse bar and sat down for a well-earned drink. James pointed out how he had lobbed a number of 'psychological grenades' at me over the first few holes, using every weapon available in his armoury after many years of playing golf at the highest level. 'Every psychological nick-nack I had at my disposal was thrown in your direction.' He seemed genuinely delighted by all this. 'There's no question about it, for nine holes it worked.'

'Maybe, but what about the next five, then?'

James conceded this, before sinking a final, winning verbal putt. 'Fair play, you started to turn it on for a while. It wasn't that I was playing badly. I didn't drop a shot, but you really played well. Let me draw your attention to the final score, though. I said the writing was on the wall after two holes, and I wasn't far wrong, was I?'

It was good to see the man in such high spirits. He had been in the wars, professionally and privately over the past couple of years, a time which had tested his resolve to the very limits. As captain of the European Ryder Cup team he had witnessed the sorry scenes at Brookline, which led to accusations and counter-accusations criss-crossing the Atlantic. He spoke his mind at the time, and shortly afterwards, on his return to Britain, providing a field day for the world's media. Worse, in a book recounting the match, lurid headlines and carefully selected passages appeared in the world's newspapers, creating an unbalanced review of what he had to say, and a sorry mess. Ultimately, once some personal criticisms of Nick Faldo appeared all over the press, James found himself in hot water. Asked to be Sam Torrance's deputy for the 2001 Ryder Cup that was subsequently postponed for a year following the September 11th attack, James was forced to quit by the Ryder Cup committee. It seemed an ignominious end to a Ryder Cup story that for James spanned seven appearances as a player, a crucial assistant's role to Seve Ballesteros when Europe won the trophy at Valderrama in 1997, and then the captaincy itself two years later.

The reaction to his book had genuinely surprised him. 'If more people had bothered to read it, they would have seen that I used a balanced argument in everything I said, but when only one side of an argument is presented, like the Faldo stuff which appeared in all the newspapers, then wrong impressions are made.'

He actually said a lot of nice things about Faldo, too, and wasn't as one-eyed about the Ryder Cup as was made out. People who knew him understood this, he believed. They were aware of the true story. Ultimately, it went before the Ryder Cup committee who made it plain that if he didn't resign they would take action, which didn't bother him. If anything, it affected Sam Torrance, the present Ryder Cup captain more, because he valued James's judgement and advice and wanted this out on the course.

'As for the Ryder Cup committee,' he said, 'we're talking about people out of touch with the tour whose opinion has no great input into golf.'

It was, of course, the unprecedented scenes at Brookline that prompted most of this. Contrary to popular belief, it was not actually the mad stampede on to the 17th green that angered him the most. 'You know, I can just about accept that what happened on the 17th was spontaneous,' he admitted. 'Even the Americans said afterwards it shouldn't have happened. I don't have any problem with that. We all know it shouldn't have happened, but sometimes things get out of control.'

What wasn't spontaneous, though, was the premeditated heckling designed to give America an advantage. In all his time involved in the Ryder Cup James had never known anything like the behaviour of some elements of the spectators and of people inside the ropes inciting the crowd. 'I still have great memories that will live with me for the rest of my life, but there's no doubt that Samuel Ryder would have been turning in his grave at the events of Brookline.'

I have a Brookline story of my own. Every 2 years I am asked by *Sky*, the Delta Airlines in-flight magazine, to write an article explaining why the Europeans will win the Ryder Cup. An American colleague produces a similar piece at the same time backing the USA. After the American win in 1999 I began to receive a series of emails, first in their twos and threes, and then in a torrent, from various backwaters in the States. A few were complimentary of my writing skills, but the majority expressed in no uncertain terms how much they enjoyed shoving my words right up a place you wouldn't want a golf ball to be hit. I read the pick of the bunch first thing one morning. The gist of it told me how I – the writer of the email had not quite grasped the fact that I had not actually played for the European team that year – had shown no bottle in allowing the Americans to come back in such dramatic fashion on the final day. But it was his final flourish that had me reading the message over and over again. According to my new friend, if it was not for America, I and the rest of Britain would now be under Nazi rule! This, remember, was an email concerning the Ryder Cup. Here we had another example of how the game of golf can dominate one's personality to the extent that all sense of reality is lost.

All of which paled into insignificance compared to the far stiffer challenge James has had to overcome in the past couple of years. In October 2000, after suffering from pains in his back during his past four tournaments, James was diagnosed with cancer. 'It was lymphoma, to be precise,' he explained. 'After a course of chemotherapy it seems to have been cleared up. I'm now seeing the doctor every four months for scans and there's no reason to suppose anything nasty will happen now.'

He said all this in a very matter of fact kind of way, but this is how James views life. 'I did the best I can, of course, but ultimately it's down to the doctors putting the chemicals inside you, and luck.' James doesn't subscribe to all the talk of bravery. In fact, it irritates him. 'People who beat cancer are always described as brave, as if people who don't are not. When put to the test you'll find that everyone has much more fight in them than they ever imagined. People commented at the time on how so together I came across. My wife, Jane, made a huge difference. She looked after me non-stop. We're both realistic, level-headed people, and so we just got on with it.'

Typically, the world of golf rallied round. He received thousands of letters both from the many friends he'd made playing golf on tour over the years, and from people he'd never met. 'You can't help but be galvanised by that. I know there is this perception that I've fallen out with a few in my time, but in truth I've made very few enemies, probably less than most involved in the game. And that includes in America.'

As a professional golfer, though, cancer may well have ended his career. 'The funny thing is, when I first heard the diagnosis my initial reaction was that it had buggered up my plans to go skiing that winter.' He revealed this with a self-conscious grin and a raising of his eyebrows. 'As it turned out, I was skiing in America six weeks after my second operation.'

After that, at least for a while, it was difficult to get away from the fact that he had an illness that could kill him. This was when he didn't fully comprehend how bad his condition might be. Obviously, it was a terrifying thought to know that he could die from it at a very young age.

The golf hardly came into it. Once he knew his chances were good, he reckoned that losing six or seven months of golf would not be the end of the world. 'I've played for 27 years on the tour, most of which I've earned well and picked up a fair number of tournament wins along the way. The cancer set me back in terms of my career, but I'm not complaining. And I'm not finished yet, either.'

James thinks he never quite had the putting game to challenge for the majors or win a money list, but he was beginning to hit the ball as well as ever – as today's round proved – and he was interested to see whether he could return to something like his best form, or whether those days had gone.

Whether they can be rediscovered or not, James was prepared to admit that when it came to Tiger Woods, the man I was hoping to meet in the future, the American had left him trailing behind.

'Tiger's another Jack Nicklaus,' James said. 'There's no doubt about that. He's pushed back the boundaries that much further. No one's hit the ball so far, with such accuracy and control as he does, and no one's undergone such physical work as Tiger. In the early days of my career I was told it was dangerous to pump the weights and work on certain muscles. Tiger's raised the profile of the sport immeasurably and, ethnically speaking, he's also introduced a lot of new people to the game. Of this, we should be thankful.'

James, it emerged, was a great *Star Trek* fan and I mentioned that as part of my stand-up routine the year before at the Edinburgh Festival, I drew the audience's attention to the fact that aliens always seemed to fall in love with Captain Kirk. The crux of the joke was that most men are unable to find certain parts of the female human anatomy, whereas Kirk had no difficulty locating them on an alien. Now how clever was that?

James appreciated this point. 'Why do all aliens fall in love with Kirk? And have you noticed that all of them are strikingly beautiful, even though they're aliens from another planet from another galaxy? I mean, they have a few extra wrinkles on their forehead, or a purple smudge on their face or something to denote that they aren't human, but never five eyes, no teeth, or an antenna sticking out of their heads.'

A few weeks earlier I had Nick Faldo making cappuccino in his kitchen, expounding the theory that man never walked on the moon and that the whole event was an *X-Files*-type cover-up. Now Mark James had sat in a golf club bar discussing aliens. And I'd thought golfers were unimaginative.

8

A sea of sanity

Two rounds of golf followed in quick succession, both on testing golf courses, and both springing up a few surprises along the way. Playing with Gareth Hale (actor, comedian) and a mutual friend, Anthony Smith, at the west course at Sundridge Park in Kent (a difficult course which has been used as a qualifying venue for the Open), I produced a couple of shots which I doubt shall be repeated again throughout my journey from tee to hole.

First, a chip from around eighty feet from the bunker left me with a putt of no more than three feet for a par. Nothing wrong in that, you may think, save for the fact that it was obviously a good shot. Well, yes, I suppose it was, except it was neither a nicely lofted chip that plummeted down from the sky and plopped next to the pin, nor a little, jabbed chip that forced the ball to run along the ground before grinding to a perfect halt beside the hole. No, I plumped for the misdirected shot, through the bouncing out of the bunker route some distance from the pin on the left-hand side of the green, via the rough that slowed down a shot that would otherwise have careered off the far side of the green, before then rolling down the hill using the right to left slope. Any attempt to claim intention was shot down by a torrent of friendly abuse.

The second shot was equally bizarre. Attempting a putt quite close to the pin but from the edge of the green, the ball trickled its way towards the hole and was on the verge of dropping in when a gust of wind blew the pin sideways, forcing the ball to become lodged over the hole by the flag-stick. Anthony had returned home by then, having played nine holes, but Gareth and I scratched our heads and tried to figure out whether this constituted a holed putt or not. After a good twenty seconds a second gust of wind blew the flag-stick in the other direction, allowing my ball to complete its journey. A later examination of the rules confirmed that even if the ball had remained stuck over the hole it would have counted as a putt, on the basis that the removal of the pin would have resulted in the ball falling to the bottom of the hole in any case. 'I started to clap before the ball got lodged by the flag,' Gareth said. 'Then I realised it was a case of premature congratulation.'

The next round, at the Royal West Norfolk Golf Club on the Norfolk coast at Brancaster, reintroduced me to the questionable pleasures of links golf. It had been a while since I had come across the treacherous winds of a links course, and the horrors of St Andrews, Carnoustie and particularly Muirfield had almost been conveniently buried into the depths of my memory banks.

On past evidence a round of 98 was just about acceptable, a scoreline explained by a typical mixed bag of holes most save the better golfers experience on a links course. The double and triple bogeys vied for pre-eminence with the bogeys and pars, but the one hole that made the whole day worth the trip was my second – yes, in twenty rounds of golf – my second birdie. What was especially pleasing about rattling in a three on the par four 13th was that every shot was planned, and every shot seemed to find its intended mark. The drive found the centre of the fairway some 220 yards from the tee; the second approach shot hit with a seven iron dropped short of the green and rolled up a slight hill before depositing the ball six feet from the hole; and finally the putt, slightly overhit I felt, rattled into the hole with some aplomb. There, now there's a prime example of how, not just for one shot, but maybe for three, I had transformed myself into Tiger Woods. Except that Tiger, no doubt, would have holed in two!

Needless to say, I fell asleep that night reliving that hole over and over again in my mind, counting drives, irons and putts (as opposed to sheep) and listening to that beautiful sound of the ball hitting and then circling round the bottom of the hole. In Rio de Janeiro, where I once spent a week playing soccer with the city's top team, Flamengo, they used to say that the most beautiful noise in the world was the sound of the ball hitting the back of the net. Well, although the Brazilians would disagree, the sound of the golf ball dropping into a hole comes pretty close.

You will have taken on board by now that I am coming out with statements (as well as the wearing of certain items of clothing and imaginary golf swings) that would have been impossible just a few months ago. A few rather stupid superstitions had come along as well.

Why, for example, did it make the remotest difference whether you used the same tee over and over again? As long as it is the same make, or style, how can a yellow-coloured tee ensure that your drive will hit the centre of the fairway some 200-plus yards away, whereas a nasty blue one will initiate a fluffed drive that sends the ball skimming into a bush 30 feet from where it was hit? Why, for that matter, especially at my level, did I have to use the same ball because I'd hit a few good shots with it, and when I was forced to use a second one of similar quality it threw me? And why, while we're on the subject, had my white polo neck golfing jersey become my 'lucky' item of clothing? My dark blue, light blue and white polo shirts lay redundant and unwanted in my wardrobe at home because I had to wear my 'lucky' white polo neck. All this had reared up in my life, and I was only hoping it didn't invade my home, where my wife could not come into a particular room because it might affect my next round, or my cat had to be locked out because the last time it happened I played well.

Even Tiger Woods has his superstitions, like his lucky red top he always wears on the day of the final round in a golf tournament, a final round, incidentally, that he usually completes with another win notched up. Apparently, he wears the red shirt on the advice of his superstitious mother, Kultilda, who believes red is her son's 'power colour'. I'll buy that theory. In fact, I'd wear a dress and high heels if it resulted in becoming a multiple majors' winner.

The red top was in evidence at Augusta where Woods notched up his third green jacket with a near nerveless display of golf that not only saw off his hottest pursuers in the form of Retief Goosen, Ernie Els, Phil Mickelson and Jose-Maria Olazabal, but also erased the mental exhaustion that had plagued, by his standards, his game since pulling off the Masters a year before. Everything about Tiger's performance told us that not only are the opposition not catching up, as had been previously assumed, but that Woods simply needed a little rest before careering on towards Jack Nicklaus's record mark of 18 majors. By beating nearest challenger Goosen by three strokes Woods bided his time until the cut, like an athlete on the shoulder of the race leader as they turn the final bend, before putting into force his notorious 'A' game that blew everyone away. Tucked away in joint 14th place was Nick Faldo with a score of one under par. For a three-time Masters winner this may not appear to be one of his better times at Augusta, but for a man who had been roundly written off this was some achievement. Faldo was the equal best British golfer, alongside Colin Montgomerie, and the highest Englishman. It was early days, but the old Nick Faldo, at least on the golf course, was beginning to stir again.

Meanwhile, down a few rungs of the golfing ladder, I fixed up a round at Cliftonville Golf Club. After my recent experiences with the likes of Faldo and James, I thought it was time to discover some dedicated real-life golfers who make up the world's millions of players. Situated in one of the more troubled areas of North Belfast, you don't get much more real life than at Cliftonville. The day had begun badly. British European Airways had dumped me in Belfast over an hour late, and then left my golf clubs behind at Gatwick Airport. 'It's because he was on standby (which I was not) and never got on the plane,' explained BEA from Gatwick to the baggage lady in Belfast, which seemed a trifle odd as I was standing in front of her at Belfast Airport.

The taxi drive to Cliftonville introduced me to some of the everyday scenes of North Belfast. Huge murals depicting balaclavared Loyalist gunmen adorned the walls, with the letters UFF or UDA, or in the case of the Mount Vernon Volunteers: 'Prepared for Peace, Ready for War'. The Holy Cross primary school, that caught the glare of the world's television cameras when its pupils had to run the gauntlet of blinkered hate, was nearby, and the street lamps were painted the red, white and blue of the Union Jack.

Yet across the same street, similar lampposts were daubed with the orange, white and green of the Irish tricolour, and to one side of the golf club began the notorious area of North Belfast known as the Ardoyne, where helicopters hover and armoured army cars patrol.

Arriving at the club over an hour late I was met by a small reception committee, led by former captain Don McElhone and treasurer Ronnie Gregg, who dismissed my profuse apologies with a friendly smile and dragged me straight up to the clubhouse. 'You'll have a whisky before you start,' Ronnie suggested, not waiting for an answer. 'And you'll have lunch with us afterwards, won't you?'

The club, formed in 1911, moved to its present site in 1924, just as partition in Ireland was in its throes. Sepia photographs cover the walls, depicting a different time when the members appeared very grand in their suits and waistcoats. Now the clientele is a little less exclusive, and the club has no problems filling its membership. You may wonder how this can be, especially when you hear some of the stories Ronnie and Don had to tell.

Ronnie remembered playing a round of golf when a full-blown riot began in the surrounding streets and eventually poured on to the fairway. They tried to carry on playing, but it became impossible and they had to run for cover. Although the Troubles were a lot worse than they are now, they would still hear the odd explosion, try and work out where it came from, and plot a different car journey home as a result while playing out on the course.

Don, who worked for the nearby waterworks, predicted that our forthcoming round would be continually punctuated with the noise of helicopters hovering above. They'd got used to it now. In fact, it sounded strange when the helicopters weren't there.

Both have had their horror stories away from the club, too. Ronnie may have appeared avuncular in his maroon 'Past Captain' sweater, but behind the conveyor belt of jokes and laughs is the realisation that he is very lucky still to be around to tell his tales. He was walking along a street in Belfast, back in the 1970s, alongside two other people. Although he wasn't with them, he seemed to be walking at the same pace. At a junction he turned off and they carried on walking straight. A few seconds later they were hit by a car bomb and blown to pieces. Obviously, if he'd carried on walking in the same direction as the couple his fate would have been the same.

Don's equally horrific story happened a couple of years ago. As he got out of his van three IRA gunmen ran up, placed a bomb wrapped up in a black bin liner inside the vehicle, and ordered him to drive to the city centre with them behind him. A police block prevented him from reaching the intended destination, and while the others got away he was held overnight in a police cell until it was realised he was the victim. At the time it was as nerve-wracking an experience as you can get. He really believed his number was up. Don, ironically, is a Catholic.

And this is the point of Cliftonville GC. The members are 'mixed,' a term used in Belfast to mean both Protestant and Catholic, and proud of it too. Don's one of Ronnie's best friends – and Ronnie is a Protestant. 'We don't care a jot what religious persuasion you have in this club. Teams are picked on ability. The question of religion is never asked, never even considered.'

What a strange animal the human being is. Here we have an example where it is not the golfer that appears insane, but some of the people living outside the confines of the course. Having already witnessed and indeed played a part in ice golf in Greenland, I was now in North Belfast taking stock of gun-clad army officers patrolling the streets, provocative slogans daubing the walls and still the odd outbreak of violence and death, and yet sheer tranquillity within the Cliftonville Golf Club, where the worst offence would be a breakdown of golfing etiquette.

Ronnie insisted that religious persuasion' was not a problem at the club. The violence in North Belfast these days is to do with drugs and protection rackets. It's a form of entertainment to the people involved. 'Some people take exception to us leading a normal, peaceful life when we're at the golf club. But the way I see it, the answer to our problems can be found right here, in the clubhouse, and out there, on the fairways.'

I walked out on to the first tee to join Don, who would be my team partner. Against us were two other former captains, Lee Whiteside and Ronnie's brother-in-law, Maurice Harrison. 'I don't give a damn what religion you follow,' Maurice declared, by way of an introduction. 'It's your money I'm after.'

We decided on a pound bet per person, and Don, who played off seven and was quite clearly the best golfer of the four, started the proceedings. Cliftonville is hardly St Andrews when it comes to space. There are just 50 acres there, sandwiched between the waterworks where Don worked and the intimidating estates below the Ballysillian Road, but the nine holes are testing, and long. The second hole, in particular, a 455-yard par four known as 'Squires Gap', is as difficult as any par four you're likely to find, with a misdirected drive off the tee resulting in a lost ball in one of the two school playgrounds, or in the Water Commission over on the other side.

After three holes I had recorded two double bogeys and a triple, and although Don was playing reasonably well we found ourselves two down. Since I had started to hit consistent scores in the 90s, I had found that I would have patches of poor play followed by a few holes which even a low handicapper would accept, and this took place once again at Cliftonville, although my little run of form was initiated by an outrageous slice of luck.

Having bogeyed the par three fourth, I found the middle of the fairway with my drive on the fifth, named 'River'. Preparing for a four iron which, I hoped, would elude the small river running across the fairway in front of the green, I was delayed by an interesting anecdote from Maurice. Pointing to a strangely shaped hill that dominates much of the Belfast skyline, Maurice explained how the hill, known as 'Cave Hill', inspired Jonathan Swift. Living in nearby Carrickfergus at the time, the author best-known for *Gulliver's Travels* believed that the shape of the hill resembled the sight of a giant lying on his back, with his head pointing upwards. With a modicum of imagination you could see what Swift was going on about. Locals today have another name for the hill. 'Napoleon's Nose,' informed Maurice. 'You'll see the shape of a Roman nose there on the hill, which we think looks a lot like Napoleon.'

When I finally got round to using the four iron, I sent a firmly driven approach shot well wide of the green. It looked as if my ball would either plop into the river, or fall well wide, but instead it smacked against the branch of a tree and rebounded to within six feet of the hole. Although I missed the subsequent birdie putt, a par four won the hole for us and reduced our deficit to just one hole.

A second par at the fifth par four followed, even though my drive was disturbed by the sound of a helicopter hovering above, looking like a kestrel high above a motorway searching for some prey. On the hill to the west of Belfast, a gorse fire seemed to have developed from a few flickers to raging flames. 'Kids like to set the gorse on fire and then go home and watch it from their bedroom windows,' said Don, with a weary shrug of his shoulders. His tired expression changed to delight when I, without any previous hint of such a shot, sunk a 35-foot putt that rolled up a hill and turned from left to right. In my pathetic lists of all-time great shots, that overtook my K Club effort in the putting stakes, knocking the 20-footer at St-Cloud back into third place.

With bogeys at the 7th and 8th as well, it meant that I dropped three shots in just five holes, by which stage Don and I had won the match and collected our pound coins from Maurice and Lee, who were both making good-natured mutterings about golf bandits.

A double bogey spoilt the final hole for me, but not the day. As Ronnie drove me back to the airport, he had one question he had been wanting to ask me since the moment I had arrived at Cliftonville Golf Club.

'Seeing that you've already played at places such as Muirfield and Wentworth, the K Club, even Royal Melbourne, for goodness sake, why would you want to come to Cliftonville?' he asked. 'After all, they're all great golf clubs, and as proud as I am of our place, you can hardly describe it as great, can you?'

It was typical of the unassuming way the members at Cliftonville went about their lives, and heart-warming to hear. As long as there are people such as Ronnie, Don and the others at Cliftonville, then there is reason for continued hope in North Belfast. 'It all depends on what your definition of great is, Ronnie,' I replied.

Eight months previously I had considered golf, in all its pomposity, with disdain. Now, I had just witnessed first hand how the very merits of the game have created a sea of sanity amid such destructive forces. At Cliftonville GC the game of golf takes on a whole new dimension for being played.

9

Fun with 'The Guys'

For Chip Thomson, New Orleans represented a homecoming. He now lives in Austin, Texas but was born in the 'Big Easy'. He and I were there for the Compaq Classic Tournament on the PGA circuit, where Chip was to coach and I would have the chance to meet one or two stars as well as some of the lesser- known mortals who spend their lives on courses or in hotel rooms, but who have mostly all enjoyed a rare moment of glory that keeps their hopes alive and their dreams intact.

On the first evening of my stay, Chip was keen for me to sample the city's famous Cajun cuisine in the company of one those golfing gladiators. Pete Jordan who Chip coached, is a Chicago-born professional golfer now living in Tampa, Florida. A man with evident talent who, despite never actually having won a tournament on the PGA tour, had twice come close, Pete might have troubled the leaderboard more if he possessed greater dedication and was not affected quite so much by the rigours of the tour. 'Right now, I'm feeling all burnt out,' he explained, once Chip had driven us to the Sidmar seafood restaurant on the banks of Lake Pontchartrain for a plate of crawfish and amberjack.

The lake, incidentally, possessed just enough seawater to accommodate sharks, and just enough freshwater to house alligators as well. We all ventured close to its waves as they lapped against the shore and peered over nervously into the black. The air was hot, and the cool water looked momentarily inviting, but somehow the thought of its lodgers dissuaded any thoughts of a dip.

A waitress appeared with a clutch of cold Dixie beers, the local brew that was swallowed eagerly by us all as the humid heat of the Deep South still beat down despite it being the middle of the evening.

Pete's problem was the same as many on the tour. This week it was New Orleans, next week Dallas. Another week, another city, another few dollars. 'I've been a pro now for 16 years,' he said, as he took a swig from his bottle. 'I've got three kids – ten, seven and a half, and four – and I'm missing them grow up. If I shoot a 78 it doesn't bother me. Missing my kids does. Last year I played in 37 tournaments. My family came out for three of them, which means I was away from home for 34 weeks. Everyone thinks it's a great life, but my buddies back home are in softball and basketball teams and see their families. OK, so I get paid more than them, but at a price.'

This is a chicken and egg situation. Jordan needs to finish inside the top 125 each season to secure his card for the following year's circuit. Even to achieve this takes some doing. Pete usually succeeds, but only just. He is, in terms of professional golf on the US PGA circuit, a journeyman golfer, but to the likes of the rest of us an exceptionally fine golfer nonetheless. A few big wins would ensure his card, and mean that he would not play anywhere near as many tournaments. 'And believe me, I wouldn't play one more tournament over the required 15 if I had my way,' he admitted. 'The rest of the time I'd be at home.'

Once, just once, the 38-year-old came close to pulling off a tournament victory. Tying for the lead with compatriot Fred Funk in New York six years ago, Jordan found himself in a play-off situation which went disastrously wrong even before the first shot had been played. 'I was being driven down to the tee in a buggy and stood up to take a look,' he recalled. 'Just at that moment the buggy's wheels locked on some wet leaves as we went downhill and I flew out of the back, landed crouched on my feet, and slid down the rest of the hill like a downhill skier.'

It wasn't the best way to prepare for a play-off. He was already pumped up due to the occasion, and this made him feel much worse. He was trembling, as if he'd just been in a fight. Somehow he managed to find the fairway with his drive and so did Funk. After Jordan's approach shot left him on the edge of the green, Fred's approach dropped inches from the hole. Jordan needed to chip in just to halve the hole. He didn't, of course, and that was that. It was all over after just one hole.

'At the time it didn't hurt too much,' he said. 'I was excited that I'd finished second, having almost won my first tournament. But now I just feel sick thinking about it.'

Like the average hacker on the golf course – in fact, like me – Jordan experiences the same frustrations, albeit on a much higher level. 'Sometimes it doesn't matter what you try, it never pays off in a tournament,' he explained. 'When that happens, when you're playing bad, you feel as if it will never come good again.

'Then, without any prior suggestion, the game comes back to you. Suddenly, it's so incredibly easy. The ball does exactly what you want it to do, goes precisely where you have planned it to go. Then you feel as if you'll always have it. When you've played reasonably well and still missed the cut, it hurts big time. But when the game deserts you for the first two rounds of a tournament, you just want to catch the first flight out of there. Missing the cut almost becomes a relief.'

Hardly the picture most avid followers of golf have in their mind, but this was reality for the majority of professional golfers, entrapped within a perennial struggle to sacrifice enough of their lives just to make a living, and teased relentlessly by a game that seemingly toys with anyone who chooses to play. We could have been almost anywhere in the world, with virtually any other of the professional golfers who face a desperate race to make the money lists. As it was we were in New Orleans, the thought of which excited me a great deal, but to Pete meant just another town to try to make a buck. The loneliness of the professional golfer was very evident that night.

Pete could have carried on in this vein all night were it not for the fact that his coach was hungry and not exactly enamoured with this kind of talk from one of his star pupils. Besides, Chip's particular obsession just happened to be crawfish. As the well-travelled man of the world that I believe myself to be, I took a gamble on which half of the crawfish I should suck out of the shell. I chose wrong, much to Chip's consternation and Pete's disgust.

'You've just eaten its ass,' Chip informed me, as Pete shoved his plate away from him across the table in a show of horror. 'You really don't want to do that.'

Bourbon Street was as tawdry and seedy as any red-light district in any European city, maybe more. None of the jazz, Creole or street dancing I'd imagined. As we wandered, the odd syringe could be seen lying on the road, and above, leaning over the various balconies that spilled out from the first-floor bars, hookers offered to reveal their breasts in return for a necklace of multicoloured Mardi Gras beads sported by seemingly half the public wandering along the street. Chip and Pete, whose relationship was so obviously close that they acted like brothers, began to argue over whose idea it was to come to the area, both insisting it was the other's, before deciding that neither wanted to see it, but felt I should experience this rather colourful element of the city. 'Why do people come to New Orleans in order to behave totally different to the way they behave back at home?' Chip said, more as a statement than a question.

'It's all about your state of mind,' Pete said, when we arrived back at the Hotel Fairmont and headed for the elevators at a time later than any of us had planned. 'Anyone on the circuit is good enough to win a tournament, that's if you believe you can. It's just that it's difficult to know what comes first, success or confidence. You kinda need one to have the other, don't you? Normally, before winning a tournament, you've taken a few stepping-stones. You know, a good couple of rounds, maybe then a top ten finish.

'Before the start of every tournament I say to myself that this could be the week when I break my duck and win. I just can't see it this time, though. I haven't stepped out on to any of those stepping-stones recently. The truth is that I'm trying to fool myself into believing that I'm playing well but, as you can see, I'm not making a good job of it.'

He smiled a rather weak, wan smile and headed off to his room, another hotel bedroom in another strange city, on the eve of another golf tournament he would most likely not win.

It was in some contrast that I spoke to Fulton Allem, the following morning, beside the driving range at the English Turn golf course on the outskirts of New Orleans. Allem could have been described as another PGA tour journeyman, albeit a hot-headed one originating from Johannesburg, except that he took everyone by surprise by winning the 1993 NEC World Series of Golf, thus granting him a ten-year exemption from having to qualify for the tour after claiming what many refer to as the 'fifth major'.

'Concentration, composure, commitment, dedication, discipline and determination, my friend,' Allem declared in his unmistakable South African twang, untarnished by 15 years of living in Florida. 'Get those priorities in order, wake up each morning and look long and hard at them, and nothing should stop you from achieving your goals.' It could have been a statement straight out of any of those self-help manuals on sale at American airport bookshops.

The World Series win may have taken some by surprise, but not Allem. 'I always knew I could play this game as well as anyone in the world, especially from 1985 to 1995,' he insisted. 'But I wouldn't want you to think I'm anywhere near the finished article because I'm quite clearly not. Nobody is in this game because nobody can be. Tiger's probably the nearest because he has the mind of Jack Nicklaus, the determination of Gary Player and the tenacity of Tom Watson. As for me, though, my temperament has let me down.'

I'd heard that about the South African, and was wondering how to broach the subject. Thankfully, Allem, drenched in sweat from morning practice in the 90° heat, did it for me. 'I let it go when I shouldn't,' he admitted. 'And it never looks good when it happens. The way you handle it separates the men from the boys and, unfortunately for me, I've fallen into the trap all too often.'

Fulton reckoned golfers have it easy today. 'The courses have become a lot softer, they don't penalise players for a bad shot like they used to, and the game's become easier for the average guys. Personally, I prefer it hard and fast. In fact, I love it when everyone wants to complain about the conditions. That's when the artist emerges, someone like Bobby Jones used to, when touch meant so much.'

At 45 years of age he conceded his best days are probably behind him. 'From 27 to 40 I lived and breathed golf, but I've got kids and enjoy doing other things on top of golf, but the game still pays my wages.'

That's just about the only concession you'll hear from the man, though. Suggest his competitiveness might have lost its edge and be prepared for a firebrand answer befitting his temperament. 'I may be more mellow in some respects, but not when it comes to the killer instinct,' Allem responded. 'I still want to beat your brains to pulp.'

'In golf,' I asked, not unreasonably.

'In anything,' the South African replied.

Chip, who used to manage Tommy Armour III, had made the introductions earlier. When we told Armour that we'd been to Bourbon Street his reaction was, 'did anyone puke on you?' Tommy's grandfather was Tommy Armour (the first), one of the sport's earliest big names. Known as Silver Scot, Grandad Armour won the US and British Open, as well as the PGA back in the 1920s. Armour junior had not benefited from such success, but had made more than a decent living on the circuit. When Chip and I met before practice he was in typical pose, with a cigarette hanging out of his mouth as he eyed up the driving range, the stub clinging desperately to his lips. His now greying mop of hair flopped over his visor, but he still possessed one of the cooler personas on the range that morning.

Tommy came up with an interesting analogy. 'When you shoot something like a 78 in a tournament you may as well have taken your clothes off in public,' he announced. 'That's how it feels. It's as if you're standing there, in front of all those people, naked.

'It's been a little like that over the past couple of years. I haven't played that well and if there's one thing I'd like to change it's the fact that I've only won one tournament in all the years I've been playing on the PGA tour. It's my own fault, though. I haven't been single-minded enough. I've made sure to take care of my family and friends and, purely in a selfish way, at a sacrifice to my game.'

If this sounded like a regret, Tommy was at great pains to point out that he's not complaining. After all, he may have finished 161st on the money list the previous year, but he still raked in nearly $240,000.

'You won't find me regretting anything,' he insisted. 'You can't change what's happened, so there's not much point wasting your time thinking about it. Instead, you should remember how lucky you are. Too many golfers these days are complaining about their lot. Well, I'll tell you about my lot. My worst days are pretty good. Take a look at the whole world. Then you realise that I'm lucky. I'm blessed. I've never had to punch a clock in the morning or wear a name tag. No one's told me what to do throughout my whole working life.'

Tommy invited me to a party he was staging at his house the following Monday night, on the eve of the Byron Nelson Classic Tournament in Dallas. I couldn't make it, which was a great shame because, by all accounts, when Tommy Armour III stages a party it is always quite something. The surprise guests normally turn out to be celebrities such as basketball megastar Charles Barkley or rock star Jon Bon Jovi.

'A good number of the golfers will be there too,' Tommy continued. 'Actually, it's not my big, traditional party. Every Christmas I hold a massive party when everyone comes, but it'll be pretty good on Monday night. If you promise not to tell anyone, I'll let you into a secret. I'm hoping the sushi might poison most of the pros at the party, That way, I might win the Byron Nelson.'

He was still laughing later and shaking his head at the thought of his cunning plan as he set off for his hotel to prepare for the first day of the Compaq Classic the following morning, while Chip and I headed back briefly to the Fairmont. The hotel barman was the embodiment of American over-friendliness. 'Hey, had a good day?' he asked, his face beaming a toothy grin. 'Come and enjoy a beer.' We made our order. 'You gotcha!' he added.

We told him how we were about to head down to the French quarter to buy a ton of crawfish, then call in on a restaurateur friend of Chip's to cook and eat the aforementioned shellfish. 'Hey, you have fun with those guys,' the barman insisted.

Exactly what kind of fun were we going to have with 'the guys?' I wondered. Were we going to hit the town, Chip, me and a hundred crawfish? Maybe go back to their place? And how much fun were 'the guys' going to get out of an evening in which they are first thrown into a boiling vat of water, then torn in half and, at least on my part, have their asses eaten?

It had Pete Jordan going when we told him later that evening. 'In Louisiana food is always one of the great topics of conversation,' he explained. Chip agreed. 'In New Orleans people go to breakfast to discuss lunch. They go to lunch to decide what they'll have for dinner. And then they go to dinner to talk about what they might afterwards, last thing.' Later we strode across the road to take a closer look at the commotion occurring beside the Orpheum Theater on Baronne Street. It emerged that playing live that night were a Grateful Dead tribute band, and those unable to claim a ticket had assembled outside to spread a little peace and love. Beside a psychedelic Volkswagen Beetle, resplendent in its colours of the rainbow and decked out in chains of flowers, were a group of forty-odd hippies, smoking a whole array of exotic substances and parading the peace 'V' sign with their fingers.

It was as if we had just been transported back in time, into the late 1960s in fact, at somewhere like Woodstock. What made this the more surreal is that it was all taking place directly opposite the hotel where half the checked-trousered golfers were sleeping in readiness for day one of the Compaq Classic.

Two extremes of the spectrum, there, in evidence, on either side of Baronne Street. What with a night out with 'the guys' and now the Grateful Dead hippies, it had been quite a night. As I retired to my room I came to the conclusion that there was no way any of our friends across the road would be remotely interested in golf, the complete antithesis of the way they lead their lives.

Then I recalled Scott Gorham and Nicko McBrain walking the Richmond fairways. On second thoughts, I half expected to see a good number of the hippies at English Turn the following morning.

10

Son of Bo

The day before Chip had greeted a couple of NOPD officers like long-lost brothers, a ploy that proved successful when we were waved in and allowed to park near the clubhouse despite not possessing the accreditation. Twenty-four hours' later Chip wound down his car window and, as the full force of the smell of magnolias hit us, began the same patter again.

This time, however, his polished routine fell on the deaf ears of a different cop who was singularly unimpressed. We were forced to park a good deal further back, but at least it gave us more of a chance to take in the famous golf course as we made our way towards the clubhouse and the driving range.

The name of the course derives from historical events some three hundred years earlier. In 1699, war between England and France raged in the New World. The exploration of the Mississippi River and the colonisation of her shores were considered to be of paramount importance to both sides.

A small settlement had already been founded by a couple of Canadian-born brothers, Jean Baptiste (Sieur de Bienville) and Pierre (Sieur d'Iberville), but they knew that the larger British colony nearby could grow and soon drive every other nation from the New World. As feared, the British dispatched an expedition to seek a new location suitable for colonisation along the Mississippi. As the English corvette *Carolina Galley* anchored in the river, Bienville and five Frenchmen paddling two canoes approached the 12-gun warship and demanded that her captain should depart. Refusal to comply, Bienville warned, would compel them to employ force. The bluff, ludicrously, succeeded and the captain of the *Carolina Galley* ordered his crew to retreat.

Such brazen courage from the half-dozen men has been honoured ever since by the name bestowed upon that bend in the Mississippi where they sent the British downriver. 'Détours des Anglais' or, as it is known today in this part of Louisiana, 'English Turn'. In 1986 the golf course was built on this reclaimed land, designed by Jack Nicklaus.

Jesper Parnevik was not beginning his assault on the Compaq Classic until later that day and so had time to talk and take the rays on to his tanned face that his famous, upturned rim of his cap allowed. I'd been wanting to meet the Swede for a long time, even before I had grown interested in the sport. Known for his retro dress, that individual cap, and his general sense of humour that often reveals itself on the course, Parnevik's self-picked list under the title, 'Special Interests' in the official US PGA Tour 2002 handbook reads: 'Magic, vitamins, bridge, backgammon and yoga', among others. That, alone, immediately attracted my attention. Then, of course, there is the fascinating fact that he is the son of Sweden's best-known and most-loved comedian, Bo, which might explain his alternative ways on the golf course.

Parnevik had become one of the major stars of the US Tour, having won well over $1 million in each of the past five years. Before that he was doing pretty well on the European tour and had become a regular in the European Ryder Cup team. There were two reasons for his move to the States. After turning professional in 1986, he would visit a friend in Florida to practise his golf during the European winter. Then, after winning the Scottish Open in 1993, he felt his life and career were becoming too comfortable. There were so many Swedes on the tour who were his friends, and it wasn't hard to be consistently in the top 30 on the European money list. He felt he was falling into a rut and needed a new challenge.

He didn't have any kids or responsibilities and wanted to break loose. For Parnevik, the great thing about coming out to America was that he had to start all over again. It was good to be a nobody again. If he played badly no one cared because nobody knew, but the plan was always to reach the next level.

He has provided a rare splash of colour to a game which has become increasingly dour as the stakes, the pressure and the spotlight have risen inexorably higher.

'I like to listen to everyone. I want to hear what they have to say for themselves, all their theories and all their views. I've met hundreds of interesting people throughout my career and I believe I have benefited from such an experience. As a result I like to experiment with life. I don't just look to improve my game, I'm searching for ways to improve my personality. It's made me very analytical, and very critical, both of myself and others. People have to prove their point to me. I don't swallow anything.'

I pointed out, as a fellow Anglo-Saxon, that as a Swede his stereo-typical characteristic would be cold and unemotional, and certainly not flamboyant. Parnevik gave this generalisation some thought and eventually suggested that he clearly possessed some of his father's genes. 'There must be some of him lurking in me,' he said, with a look up to the heavens. 'You see, even now I cannot quite escape my dad.'

This was not expressed as a complaint, but was an interesting comment to make nonetheless. For much of his life he has had to deal with being the son of Bo Parnevik. 'My dad's incredibly well known back home in Sweden,' he explained. 'He's done most things, from stand-up comedy to television and theatre, and even if I were to win the Grand Slam in golf he'd still be better known than me in Sweden.'

Such a father-son relationship conjured up images of a juvenile adult in the house placing whoopee cushions under young Jesper's backside, or throwing stink bombs around, but in truth, as with most comedians, Bo was a great deal more serious when at home.

'I've met a few comedians in my time and I'd say that ninety-nine per cent of them are pretty serious people,' Jesper insisted. 'Certainly, my father spent most of his time thinking up new stories to tell, most of which he derived from everyday situations and events.

'It was a lot of fun growing up with a father like mine. I saw how much he entertained people, and I wanted to achieve similar things. I didn't think it would be on the golf course. At first I wanted to entertain in some way on stage. I've always enjoyed writing and telling stories, and to this day the whole Parnevik family throws themselves into entertainment. At Christmas, on birthdays or at weddings, we're always performing in little plays we've written and directed ourselves. Sometimes we even sing in them. Dad always does his own thing and then watches the rest of us.'

His move to Florida also had something to do with Bo. 'When I started playing golf professionally, it didn't matter what I did I was front-page news – not because of me but because of my father. So you'd get headlines such as "Bo's son finishes last", which became a bit of a pain. It certainly played a part in my decision eventually to move to America. I wanted to break loose from all that.'

Even today he's still known more as son of Bo in Sweden, although he likes to think that to the younger generation of Swedes Bo is now known as Jesper's father. It taught him to be very cautious and tentative from an early age, though and to distinguish true friends from hangers-on. Parnevik Jr has three children, including youngest son Phoenix named after the state capital of Arizona, where he won his first PGA Tour event in 1998. With such an illustrious father and grandfather, Jesper thinks that maybe Phoenix will become a bit of both – 'a stand-up golfer'.

Although I'd heard the story of Parnevik's famed upturned cap secondhand, I wanted to hear it from the horse's mouth. The man was now seriously late for his practice but when he heard this final request he smiled and relented. 'It all started when I was practising in Florida in the winter before the start of the European tour back in the 1980s,' he said animatedly, as if he had never told this story before.

'As I was a Swede who came from Stockholm in the winter I was very pale, so I decided to flip the rim of the cap up to get a little sun on my face and obtain a tan. This I achieved, but what I didn't expect was to discover that my putting would improve markedly once I'd removed the brim of the hat from my view. To this day I've worn the cap like this, even when it's cloudy and there's no sun in the sky. At first, people must have thought I looked stupid, but now I think everyone's accepted it. I think, maybe, they even like it.'

I think, maybe, they do. As I left Parnevik to his own devices and wandered up and down the driving range watching consummate professionals sometimes make the most minor of adjustments to achieve their intended one per cent improvement, my past view of golfers was proving to be somewhere wide of the mark.

Golfers were obsessed but in very different ways. As Bo had said, 'I'm no different to you when it comes to golf. It's like being an alcoholic. You really don't want to have a drink, but something makes you. It's the same with golf. It has a complete hold over me.

'One of the most fascinating aspects of the game, I find, is that someone's true personality reveals itself out on the course. I've often met the most charming, intelligent and caring people who can revert to being a complete asshole when out playing golf. It's as if the dark side of you emerges in golf. I find that very interesting from a psychological point of view. All the bad habits and all the flaws in your personality are revealed out on the golf course.'

'Don't you think all professionals are like that?' Tommy Armour III asked, when I told him that the public perception of professional golfers out on the course is often one of robotic, colourless individuals who took themselves and their work far too seriously. 'I mean, when you go to the doctor does he or she crack jokes in the surgery and not be particularly bothered by the performance and outcome? You've got to remember, we're doing our job, just like anyone else. Every mistake costs money. It can be a lot if you're challenging for a title, or it can make the difference between obtaining your tour card for the following season or not. I've never known so much pressure in golf as there is now.'

As my meetings with various golfers had already proved, off the course they are very different people. Some are charming and humorous; others reveal multifaceted characters that are impossible to be seen during play, but all have had their struggles, their share of disappointments, and their dreams. It is their dreams that keep them coming back.

David Toms, the 2001 US PGA champion, strode by, taking in the scenery of a course and a tournament that had adopted the Louisiana golfer as their adopted son. Indeed, Toms was the defending champion at the Compaq Classic, having beaten nearest challenger Phil Mickelson to the title in 2001, and every other person he passed appeared to want to shake his hand, or gain his autograph. Even though Jack Nicklaus had arrived by then to observe his son, Gary, play the first couple of rounds, Toms still seemed to be the main man at English Turn.

Chip and I started to follow Jordan for the first nine holes of the tournament. Despite Pete's negative mindset he began reasonably well, although a putt that slammed against the hole and then produced a circumnavigation round the lip before settling an inch outside was unfortunate. 'That ball's seen more lip that Bianca Jagger on her wedding night,' Chip observed. That was a new phrase to me, and one that I made sure I remembered for future use.

I would be departing for England that night. Part of me wanted to stay and see how the tournament would unfold. Another part of me fancied a night at Tommy Armour's party, too, for that matter. But the European Office Putting Championships beckoned the following day, that prestigious tournament that lured particularly strange people from all over the continent to a large office block in London. Having already laid claim to the fact that I was the 17th best ice golfer in the world, this was my chance to add another feather to my golfing cap.

Pete Jordan, meanwhile, made the cut and finished the Compaq Classic on one under par with a score of 287, leaving him in joint 62nd position together with Jesper Parnevik. Fulton Allem was on his way home after two rounds, while the eventual winner was K.J. Choi from

South Korea, with a final score of 271 after four days' play in the colourful city of New Orleans.

Although I had enjoyed New Orleans immensely, I had found it frustrating not having played any golf myself. This, I considered, as I leant back in my overnight seat some 30,000 feet above the North Atlantic, was something of a turn-up. I was beginning to suffer from the cold turkey effects of not having played any kind of golf for eight days – this, after having played three rounds of golf in the first 38 years of my life.

To pass time en route home I flicked through the pages of *Golf Digest*, the prestigious American bible of golf on that side of the pond. This, too, was another indication of my slow but undoubted transformation. I used to look at pin-striped suited businessmen sitting on the train, on the way home from a day's work, with their heads face down inside the pages of golf magazines, with a disdain bordering on contempt. How sad were these people, I wondered, in my remarkably arrogant superiority. To my mind, it was as bad as reading *Trains Today*, or *Computers Made Easy*. Now, eight months since I first picked up a golf club with intent, I was reading them all, from the UK's *Golf World*, *Golf Monthly* and *Today's Golfer*, to America's *Golf Digest*. I had started to look forward to the sound of these magazines dropping through my letterbox at home and to the floor amid the newspapers and children's comics, as if they were birthday cards or letters from a lover. Indeed, I was flaunting the fact that I was reading them in public now, because in doing so I was telling the world that not only did I know a thing or two about golf, but I could obviously play it.

A throwaway remark made by Lee Trevino in *Golf Digest*, however, made me stop, blink, and read it over and over again just to make sure he had actually said it. 'Only bad golfers are lucky,' he commented. 'They're the ones bouncing balls off trees, curbs, turtles and cars. Good golfers have bad luck. When you hit the ball straight, a funny bounce is bound to be unlucky.'

It made me relive some of my best shots so far, the chip via the bunker and the rough to a couple of feet from the pin at Sundridge Park and, even more so, the four iron off the tree to close to the pin at Cliftonville. That latter shot had initiated a particularly exciting purple patch of form, but now here was Trevino telling me all that it proves is that I played a bad shot. Deep down I knew he was absolutely correct in his assessment, but for some reason I took this to heart. Even my highlights were merely examples of my poor play!

Now it is arguable whether you can class office putting as a kind of golf at all, but considering that a lot of people get up to it, coupled with the fact that I had not picked up any kind of club in anger for what had appeared to be a lengthy period of time, I could not wait to throw myself into the fray.

My only other sortie into putting on a carpet had produced a successful conclusion, albeit at 3 o'clock in the morning of New Year's Day, 2001, when I had won a mini tournament following a closely contested play-off with a fellow drunkard, in front of a small and extremely intoxicated audience in a friend's front room.

Although the European Office Putting Championships were sponsored by Glenlivet, and there were therefore copious amounts of whisky available, this time I would remain stone-cold sober in my attempt to become a European champion in anything for the first, and most probably the last, time.

The event was held at The Ark, a state-of-the-art office block situated beside the Hammersmith flyover in west London. Although I was jetlagged after arriving back in England that morning, the sight of so many golfers, complete in full golfing clothing despite the venue being the fifth and sixth floors of this spacious office block, soon woke me up. I thought this was going to be a snip, but clearly there were plenty of participants here aiming to win.

There were players from France, Spain, Portugal, Sweden, even Russia. And although this was supposed to be the European Office Putting Championships, a few Americans, Australians and South

Africans, who happened to be working in London at the time, had entered too: 250 competitors split into 20 groups who had to wind themselves round a five-hole course spread out over the sixth floor of The Ark. Tables, chairs, filing cabinets, even the odd potted plant stood in the way of the 'hole', which turned out to be a bottle of Glenlivet. Touch any of the obstacles and you were back to the start of each hole. The winner of the group, the player who had won most points deriving from one point for an outright win of the hole, and half a point for sharing the hole, qualified for the grand final.

After two holes I had no points, and found myself in last place out of the six in my group. The others had played sensibly, two-putting if need be to ensure their target was found. I, true to character, went for broke, becoming the 'Seve Ballesteros' of office putting. Although this policy did not at first pay off, a half-point at the 3rd hole, then an outright win at the fourth (in which, rather craftily, I felt, I putted beyond the single-storey filing cabinet into a vast expanse of bare carpet well to the right of the bottle, before sinking the resulting putt past the potted plant) placed me as joint leader with one hole to play.

This hole required a near impossible putt to hit the bottle in one. All tried and failed repeatedly, except one from Israel who pushed a conservative effort close enough to the bottle to ensure a two had been scored. If I could hit the bottle with a first putt that was like threading cotton through an eye of a small needle, I would qualify for the final. I didn't. My ball crashed instead into a chair leg, but with my second shot, a putt that I knew had to find the bottle, I got lucky, and thus set up a play-off to determine which of the two of us would go through to the final.

I lost, thanks to a gold-plated pot that got in the way of my putt, and thus my bid to become European office putting champion ended. Afterwards, though, Natasha Duval from Glenlivet revealed that by having played in one of only a few play-offs that evening, I was officially placed at 23rd in the rankings, a fact that cheered me up no end.

So, not only had I become the 17th best ice golfer in the world, but could now lay claim to being the 23rd best office putter in Europe. Whether that could compare to Tiger Woods's seven majors to date was open to debate, but as I went home that night I came to what I thought was a magnanimous decision. Tiger was clearly better than me on grass, but until he had tried his luck out on frozen oceans and carpets I would continue to hold the upper hand.

11

The Young Pretender

It was now early summer in England, the best time of the year, when the temperature was pleasantly warm, the first smells of freshly cut grass pervaded the air and golfers, some content to dress like boy scouts, flocked on to the courses to make the most of the lengthening hours of sunshine.

May also meant the first major tournament of the year on the European PGA Tour to be played in this country, the Benson & Hedges International Open, hosted by the De Vere Belfry golf course, on the outskirts of Sutton Coldfield in the West Midlands.

For me this was a chance to meet one or two professional golfers on this side of the Atlantic, see a little action and attempt to gate-crash the pro-am competition that takes place the day before the first round proper of the tournament on the Thursday. After all, I had now become a golfer. Having acquitted myself competently on ice and carpet, it was time to raise the odds a little and test myself on grass.

On the Tuesday I arranged to walk the famous Brabazon championship course with Justin Rose, the young upstart who had taken everyone by surprise as a 17-year-old amateur at the Open at Birkdale, in 1998, by finishing fourth. Turning professional immediately afterwards, he proceeded to miss 21 consecutive cuts, a run that soon had the world's media spotlight cast over a young man who was, judging by his

Birkdale achievement, supposed to be evolving into one of the finest golfers in the game.

Just when his game was looking desperate, Rose's father, Ken, the driving force behind his son's rise to prominence, contracted leukaemia, a turn of events that clearly made a telling impression on his son. Despite, or maybe because of, the personal anguish that had invaded his life and made missing cuts suddenly appear largely irrelevant to a youngster who had previously lived and breathed golf, Rose began making it into day three of golf tournaments, then twice finished runner-up in 2001, before finally ending any lingering suspicions about his long-term future by winning three tournaments on three different tours before May in 2002, two in South Africa (the Dunhill Championships on the European Tour and the Nashua Masters on the South African Tour), and one in Japan the week before the B&H, the Chunichi Crowns on the Japanese Tour, from where he had just returned.

It was Justin who suggested we walked the course, enabling us to have at least a couple of hours to talk, and giving him the chance to play a practice round before the following day's pro-am. Ian Poulter, the English professional who found himself agonisingly in eleventh place in the PGA European Order of Merit, and therefore just one place out of the Ryder Cup team, joined us for the morning as we set off from the first tee.

'It's been a rollercoaster ride,' he smiled with a mixture of irony and satisfaction. 'I've had four years crammed with the most amazing experiences and I wouldn't have changed it for the world.

'Things happened quite easily for me,' he recalled, as we stomped down the middle of the first fairway following a firm drive off the first tee. 'I became the English under-16 and then under-18 champion when I was just 14. And then Birkdale.'

At the 1998 Open, Rose, in front of hundreds of millions of television viewers, chipped in from 45 yards at the 18th green to finish fourth and become, by some distance, the highest-placed amateur. Overnight he became a sporting sensation, not just in Britain, but around the world.

'Rosemania' hit the newspapers and the teenager found photographs of himself published having a haircut, while his friends were being interviewed by reporters.

'It was pretty crazy,' he recalled, with another wry smile, borne out of his later experiences. 'After the Open things went bananas. Don't get me wrong: it was fantastic how people took to me at Birkdale and supported the underdog, but afterwards I became a little embarrassed by all the fuss.'

The general misconception is that Rose immediately turned professional as a knee-jerk reaction to his surprise fourth at the Open. The plan was always to turn pro after Birkdale, he insisted, once a 15-foot putt had been rattled in on the first green and we made the short trip over to the second tee. It just so happened that he finished fourth and people assumed it made him leave his amateur status behind him. The truth was that he and his father had set out a three-year plan, which was how long it took for him to establish himself on the professional circuit.

He had lost sight of the three-year plan after Birkdale because by finishing fourth, it opened so many doors for him. He found himself having practice rounds with Nick Faldo and Ernie Els, playing alongside Nick Price, and getting to meet Tiger Woods. It became almost easy for him to play well and he felt very comfortable with the position he found himself in.

'What had happened at the Open came out of the blue. I had only lost a major at the age of 17 by two shots, so it gave me a glimpse of my potential.'

He paused just long enough to set up a £10 wager with Poulter for the next hole – even in a practice round there had to be an element of competition – before signing a few autographs for a gaggle of golf-mad kids who had sprinted up to us once Rose had been sighted. I had already taken note of how both he and Poulter seemed to do things with their ball that I could not, particularly off the fairways. Even when I managed to hit a good iron, my ball needed to land some distance away from the pin in order to allow the ball time to come to a halt close to its intended target. What Rose and Poulter seemed to manage with consummate ease was to loft their ball high into the heavens, no matter what club they used, before dumping it from a great height on top of the pin. This kind of shot was the norm, achieved by the pros with an expectant expression, and witnessed by me with incredulity.

We walked on, Rose, myself and Rose's caddie, bent over by the weight of the massive golf bag strapped across his back. After Birkdale came the rapid fall. Following his first three tournaments he'd missed the cut on each occasion, something that quickly brought him down to earth. He found the first few tournaments difficult, probably as a reaction to Birkdale, coupled with the fact that the world and its dog were now obsessed with his performance.

The longer it went on, and the more cuts he missed, the bigger an issue it became. Birkdale soon became a millstone around Rose's neck. Every time he was close to making a cut, a camera would appear from beneath the trees adding to the pressure. He started to panic and it got to the stage where he would start a tournament with the single aim of just making the cut. He couldn't understand how golf, something that had come so easily for him, had suddenly turned so difficult.

'There were times when I was telling myself my game was no good any more, and that whatever I had before was now lost. This wasn't just in my imagination, either. My game was horrendous. The Justin Rose at 14 would have beaten the same guy four years older than him. In hindsight I put too much emphasis on obtaining my tour card and earning money. Now I realise that at 17 and 18 it wasn't important at that stage, although at the time I believed it was the only thing that mattered in the world. I'd lost my flair, I wasn't playing the game for the right reasons any more, and I simply wasn't enjoying golf.'

Rose was sounding like a hard-bitten, weather-beaten, old pro as he cruised through the outward nine holes, looking every inch like a tournament winner from the week before. In reality he was still just 21 years of age, although the highs, lows and finally highs again of his career in golf had probably stuck another 10 years on to his psyche.

The comeback, when it finally began to rear its head, was the result of family support, advice from the best in the business, and self-belief that was tested to its limit, but never fully broken.

'I had my doubts, of course, and there were times during the past four years when I've been extremely down, but the deep-seated belief in my ability never quite deserted me. Somewhere, lurking at the back of my mind, I always knew the game would come back to me. It took hours and hours on the driving range and the putting green. I can't tell you how many times I've holed a putt to win the British Open at home on my putting green. Probably hundreds and hundreds of times, actually.'

David Leadbetter (recognised as one of the best and most high-profile coaches in the world) was extremely helpful throughout all this, too. He kept telling Rose to keep his self-belief, that he was incredibly talented, and that he'd never seen any other golfer as talented at his age. It was what Rose needed to hear.

His fellow professionals kept their distance, however, an interesting point that perhaps reveals the dog-eat-dog competitiveness of the circuit. 'I've got to be honest with you and state that no professional went out of his way to help me out,' Rose smiled wryly. 'Not one of them. It would have been nice if an icon in golf had lent me a little support, I suppose, but I almost take pride in the fact that I've pulled through the bad times on my own without relying on the help of any other golfer.'

Rose was at pains to make it clear that he had no complaints about the other professionals. 'They all had their own pressures to make cuts and grind out a living, just like me. In their defence, maybe it was hard for them to relate to a 17-year-old. Perhaps, also, there was a slightly cynical view taken towards me as well. "So, this game's not quite as easy as you thought, hey, youngster?" After all, many of them had been playing on the circuit for twenty years. They probably didn't take too kindly to this young upstart arriving on the scene with a bang, finishing fourth at the Open, and then turning professional with the expectation that I was going to continue to record top ten finishes from the word go. I can understand this. Funnily enough, I reckon I may have earned more respect from my fellow professionals because of the way I handled myself during the hard times rather than the fact that I've now started to win tournaments.'

At the turn of the year it seemed only a matter of time before he would be holding aloft his first professional trophy. Then cancer provided a harsh and unwanted dose of reality. 'My father contracted leukaemia,' Rose explained, with understandable heaviness in his tone for the first time all day. 'In the grand scheme of things it made me realise, probably for the first time in my life, that missing cuts really was not the end of the world. It taught me a lot about myself and about life. I have applied these lessons to the way I lead my life, and the way I approach my golf. I have also come to realise that you can apply what you've learnt in life to your golf, and that, conversely, you can apply what you've experienced in golf to life.'

Most father-son relationships are close, but in Rose's case his father had thrown all his energies into backing, supporting and guiding his son to the position he finds himself in today. Sometimes this kind of intense partnership can backfire – the disastrous mother- and father-relationships with professional women tennis players provide copious examples of this fact – but in Justin's case the opposite appears to be nearer the mark.

'I've only ever seen my working relationship with my father as positive. I can't tell you how important this was when I was missing all those cuts and descending into such gloom. My father, and my mother, Annie, too, were always there for me, always telling me it would come good in the end, and never deserted me. I didn't come through those 21 missed cuts on my own. My family saw me through. Really, I owe everything to them. That's when you realise how much blood ties you together. That's also when you realise who your friends truly are.'

While his father underwent the twin traumas of chemotherapy and radiation, Rose battled back on the circuit, taking positives from his father's unpleasant situation. 'I worked even harder on all the things he's taught me,' he said. 'I was very worried for him, and there was definitely a sense of wanting to win for my father. I knew, especially when he was on the edge and not good at all, that if I could achieve something in golf it would make him happy and could benefit his recovery.'

Fuelled by a kind of motivation which far exceeds sporting goals Rose delivered his pledge in Johannesburg, where he was born before he left for England as a small boy, by winning his first title on the European Tour. (The 'European' Tour also stages tournaments in countries as far-flung as Australia, Malaysia, South Africa and Dubai.) His timing could not have been better. 'Dad was right in the middle of a series of chemo- and radiotherapy sessions when I won my first title. I had to go on to Australia, but sent the trophy straight to the hospital where it stayed beside Dad's bed. Later, Dad told me my success had given him a real lift. He's not yet fully cured, but we're hopeful.'

The Benson & Hedges would be the first tournament in ages that Ken Rose would be attending. His son was understandably ecstatic about this, and desperate to play well over the next few days. The difference now was that Rose had set his sights on winning the whole tournament, not just making the cut. 'One of the many things I've learned over these past few years is that you've got to try your hardest to take your opportunities when they come your way in this game. It's something I've started to do. The difference now is that I believe I'm a winner at this level, but I also understand that it doesn't necessarily go for you every time. If I don't make the cut I'm not going to have sleepless nights over it. I'll know my chance will come again soon and when it does I'll give it my best shot. Looking back, I have to laugh at my ambition of just making the cut. If I came here to the B&H aiming to make the cut, there's no way I'm going to win the tournament. My aim now is to win, and that's the only way I can pull it off.'

Once Rose started to win, so the plaudits flooded in. He was particularly taken by John Daly, the winner of both the Open and US PGA titles who, despite his personal problems deriving from alcoholism, took time to congratulate him. 'John pulled me aside after my first win in South Africa and said: "You really gave it to them, didn't you!" I thought, that came from a good man.'

Yet the comments that are held dearest to Rose's heart come from one of the greatest of all time. 'Gary Player has sent me a letter after each of my three wins so far,' he explained. 'I don't know whether it was because I was born in South Africa, or whether he just feels it's good to see a young player come through after all the adversity. Whatever the case, he always ends his note in the same way: "And remember, the more you practise the luckier you get."'

Nobody had taken much notice of what score Rose had rattled up during his practice round, least of all him. From time to time he'd take two or three drives off the tee, a couple of irons off the fairway, or a number of putts on the green, sometimes across the shorn grass on the green far from the actual hole in order to test out the lie and the pace. By my reckoning, though, he had notched up a totally effortless 69, or three under par. Produce four rounds of those come the tournament and he would be close to claiming his most prestigious title yet.

As soon as the round was over I headed off to the administrative offices, while Rose looked for his parents. Later, I would glimpse the happy sight of Ken Rose standing dutifully behind his son at the driving range, as if nothing had happened to either of them in the past six months. It seemed like business as usual.

My short sortie to the tournament office, past the temporary stalls and shops springing up in time for the tournament selling clubs and clothes, prints and pots, sun cream and toiletries, was to discover whether I had been selected to play in the next day's celebrity pro-am tournament.

Having shot sub-100 scores in each of my last six rounds, I felt confident I could do myself justice in such a tournament, even if it was on the famous venue for the Ryder Cup, in the presence of a golf professional, and in front of what I assumed to be a small crowd. In my previous half-dozen rounds I had enjoyed a purple patch of six or seven holes where I notched up pars or bogeys and, on the basis that each four-man team in the pro-am would rely on the top two scores per hole on a Stableford points basis, I fancied a high handicapper like me would be scoring heavily for my team.

Fiona Foster, from the Karen Earl organisation in charge of the pro-am and the week's affairs at the De Vere Belfry, had some news for me. 'You're in the pro-am,' she said. 'Your professional will be Bernhard Langer.'

'Bernhard Langer?' I asked. 'You mean the twice US Masters champion, the nine times member of the European Ryder Cup, apart from Faldo and Ballesteros the best golfer to come out of Europe, the winner of 41 tournaments on the European PGA Tour, the most consistent and most resilient golfer in Europe over a period of 20 years? You mean that Bernhard Langer?'

I was quite pleased with my knowledge of the German, acquired since I had decided to throw myself into the game, although it was still a rather stupid question. 'That's the one,' Fiona answered politely.

I walked away from the office in a frenzied state of mixed emotions. A part of me was delighted and excited to be given the opportunity to be playing golf, my new-found love, with one of the true greats of world golf. Bloody hell! I was playing with Bernhard Langer. Another part of me was growing increasingly anxious by such a prospect. Bloody hell! I was playing with Bernhard Langer.

I telephoned home to relate the barnstorming news. 'You'll never guess what?' I said to my wife, with breathless excitement and panic.

'What, we've won the lottery' she asked.

'Well no, but I am playing golf with BERNHARD LANGER tomorrow.' I announced Langer's name like a master of ceremonies at an awards function.

'Is he a golfer, then?' my wife asked.

I told Justin Rose my news later in the day.

'I wish you luck,' he said. 'I've got a feeling you're going to need it.'

12

Don't worry, be happy

Loitering in the middle of the well-manicured practice green beside the clubhouse was a figure that, despite his size, stood out from the rest. Diminutive in stature, with a shock of unruly hair, wearing a bright, fluorescent yellow jacket, and puffing incessantly on a cigarette, a middle-aged man appeared to be the centre of attention.

Retief Goosen arrived and headed over immediately to consult with the little guy. Goosen, the South African who had transformed himself from journeyman to US Open champion and European Order of Merit title holder in the space of twelve months, was leading the money list again by May in Europe, and had emerged as one of the most serious challengers to Tiger Woods on the world scene. Yet he still stood transfixed by what the unlikely figure was saying to him.

The man was Jos Vanstiphout, a 51-year-old Belgian psychologist who had emerged in a little over seven years from being something of a joke figure on the circuit to being in heavy demand. Jos was the mental guru to the golfing stars. Although his methods were not widely known, some of the more interesting antics he got his pupils to follow, such as singing on the golf course, or putting with their eyes closed, had seeped out into the public domain.

Although psychology, especially in sport, has become an accepted practice these days, there still remains an image of men in white coats with electric hair. Vanstiphout, happily, does little to dispel this. 'I was always interested in the mental approach,' he explained, in his Euro-Pop accent. 'I used to work with managers and sales people. Then I took up golf and funny things happened inside my head. I found this really weird. There was I, a pretty assured kind of guy, experiencing all kinds of negative thoughts whenever I played golf. So I started to read sports psychology books, and the one that made a huge impact on me was Timothy Gallwey's *The Inner Game of Golf.*'

When Vanstiphout said 'huge impact' he meant it, as his subsequent actions would prove. 'I said to my company: "Bye bye, I'm off." It was my intention to travel to America and meet this man Gallwey. My company asked me what I was hoping to achieve. And I told them I was planning to become a golf coach.'

He paused to light a cigarette and observed me for so long that I felt mentally raped. Outwardly I showed no emotion, just interest, but inwardly I was thinking that this little Belgian must have been bonkers to have reached such a dramatic decision.

'I trekked across America looking for Gallwey. In the end he came to me. I was with a colleague of his who contacted Gallwey and said: "You've gotta come down straight away and meet this Belgian man because he's crazy." Gallwey and I spent a month together before I returned to Europe intending to start on the tour.'

Gallwey's disciple soon found work in the shape of a struggling Dutch golfer called Rolf Muntz. He'd heard about Vanstiphout's intentions and asked him to come up and see him at his club in Holland. He worked with Muntz for three hours and agreed to accompany him both to the Portuguese and Moroccan Opens. Muntz had been struggling to make the cut in tournaments, but after he finished 14th and then 7th people started to take notice. At first, when they saw Vanstiphout getting Muntz to sing at the driving range or on the tee, other golfers and caddies looked at him as if he were diseased.

'After they saw his improvement, though, the feeling towards me began to change. At first it was the lesser players who started to ask for my services. Then some of the better-known ones started to knock on my door. We're a small family on the golf tour, you see. We travel together, eat at the same restaurants, share the same courtesy cars, play the same courses, so whenever anyone finds any new way to become successful everyone else wants a piece of it.'

In the past few years his clientele has included the likes of Darren Clarke, Sergio Garcia, Ernie Els, Paul McGinley and Thomas Bjorn. 'It's becoming a lot easier now because golfers with greater natural talent are coming to me. You can make a mule run faster, for sure, but you can't make them win the Derby, can you? But the best players have the best computers inside their heads, and all I have to do is to help them find a way to reprogram some of their thought processes.'

It was two particularly notable successes, however, that really made the golfing world take this man seriously. Thomas Levet was a little-known golfer ranked way down the Order of Merit List until he worked with Vanstiphout. Shortly afterwards, the Frenchman won the 2001 British Masters at Woburn. It was a result that barely seemed possible just a few weeks earlier.

His most high-profile result, however, came with Goosen, who overcame his innate shyness to win the US Open in 2001. The manner of his victory at Southern Hills, from a mental standpoint, was especially impressive. Having gained a winning position on the 18th green, he went on to three-putt and force a Monday morning play-off with Mark Brooks. To have even reached the stage of being so close to becoming a winner of a major was, in itself, a remarkable improvement. To return in the morning, having thrown away the chance of winning the US Open the night before, and win the play-off emphatically proved how far the South African had mentally travelled.

'On the Sunday evening after he had three-putted I asked Retief how he was feeling and what he had learnt from the day's events,' Vanstiphout recalled. 'He said: "Now I know I can beat them all." That was his big breakthrough. Most golfers would have said: "I've blown my big chance." But not Retief. He'd crossed over the bridge of fear. He'd turned his misfortune into a positive. I told everyone that night: "Watch my boy from now on.""

One of Vanstiphout's favourite sayings was 'blah, blah, blah'. He often completed a sentence with 'man' and would liberally throw in every swearword in the book to enhance his argument. Although I had heard he had always been reluctant to discuss his methods, I was still fascinated to know why he felt golf provided such rich pickings when it came to psychology.

'Golf is the most mentally demanding sport in the world by a long, long way,' he stated. 'There's absolutely no doubt about that. If you play in a team game like soccer you have others around you, always. You can hide behind them so that nobody can see how big your dick is.'

I recalled Tommy Armour's analogy with nudity out in New Orleans as Vanstiphout's phallic example was uttered. 'In golf you're out there on your own. And you know what your biggest enemy is?'

'Yourself?' I answered, in a questioning tone.

'Time. I tell you. It is because of time, man. In soccer, even if you are going through the middle of a nasty divorce, you have no time to think about it because someone's just passed you the ball and you've got to find someone else to pass it on to. In golf a round takes between four and four and a half hours to complete, and in all that time you're only striking the ball for three minutes at most. So what do you do for the rest of the time?'

'What people should do – and I'm talking about all kinds of players, from professionals to amateurs – is look at the blue sky and the beautiful course, listen to the birds singing and enjoy a very nice walk. But they don't, of course. They're either thinking about how bad the last shot was, how bad the next shot's going to be, or looking at the bunkers, the lake that's in front of their next shot, the stream, the bunch of trees they must avoid, and so on. What I have to tell everyone all the time is that they must look at what they want to achieve, not what they're trying to avoid.'

'You know who's the strongest, mentally?' he asked. I thought about this question for a few moments. Was Tiger Woods too obvious an answer? I wracked my brains for a few seconds more but came to the realisation that when it comes to the best in every facet of the game, it has to be 'my' Tiger.

'Yes, of course, Tiger Woods,' replied Vanstiphout, wondering why it had taken me so long to come up with the answer. 'Just look at his face, especially in the last round of a tournament. Cameras are clicking and flashing around him, people are shouting things out, and none of it bothers him. He's in the zone and he doesn't even hear or see anything else but the ball and his next shot.

'He's the exception rather than the rule, though. It's perfectly understandable, too. How many people could withstand hitting the worst shot ever at, say, the Masters, with the knowledge that 250 million television viewers are watching, as well as all your friends and family?'

Vanstiphout's philosophy is simple. It is a firm belief that we underplay our potential. 'You've gotta understand that the average guy uses a maximum of only seven or eight per cent of his brain's ability. There's absolutely no doubt that we're capable of using more, a lot more. It's all about becoming the person that you think you are. Why is it that, from time to time, you hear stories of old women lifting up a car in order to free an injured child? It happens, doesn't it? You would think this is physically impossible, but on seeing a trapped child that old woman suddenly tells herself she has to free the child, instead of convincing herself it is a physical impossibility.'

If this is the case, then, why is it so difficult for golfers to adopt a permanently positive approach to the game? Vanstiphout leant forward at this point, as if already prepared for the question and his answer. 'Life is full of negatives, my friend. Children are brought up being told they can't do things, when they should be encouraged to give it a go. Even if it fails, we should be saying well done, and next time you'll do it. Watch out, be careful, stop that, you mustn't do that. Our world is full of negatives from the moment we're able to walk. It all becomes embedded in our subconscious. Golfers are no different to anyone else. They happen to have a physical talent when it comes to hitting a ball with a club, but in every other way they are as average as you or me.'

To solve this problem Vanstiphout makes personalised tapes. 'Golfers need to change their thinking in order to change their behaviour,' he explained. 'Our self-conscious is our computer, don't forget, so I make tapes recording their weaknesses and saying the right things to transform them into strengths. It lasts only eight minutes, but it is intended to provide a deep state of relaxation.'

Couldn't he just produce one general tape? Vanstiphout laughed at this question, a deep, wheezy laugh, until he coughed and spluttered. 'Do you think I'd be here if I could produce just the one tape and sell millions of them around the world? No, I'd be sitting on my boat in Monaco, that's where I'd be. Every player is different, so every tape has to cater to their individual needs. Of course it helps reminding them, too, because sixty per cent of what I say to them in each session is forgotten by the time we next get together.'

Vanstiphout suggested that he take a look at me on the driving range so I eagerly followed him out of the clubhouse. Every so often a golfer, coach, caddie or manufacturer would walk past, nodding their heads towards the Belgian in recognition. I would smile pleasantly at them, often adding a 'Hi.' Vanstiphout's standard reply to them was: 'Fuck you, too.'

I attempted to explain the standard of golf I had reached in nine months, relaying the string of sub-100 scores recorded in the past six rounds, and the triple and double bogeys that normally preceded and then followed a purple patch of six or seven holes where pars and bogeys were scored. During the purple patch I felt good and didn't think too much about my game, but as soon as I hit a poor drive, or scuffed an approach shot, the doubts would creep in. I should have known better.

'Listen to yourself. Already, by telling me this, you have ordered your subconscious to register it, to keep it all in mind, and to let it out just as you're standing on the first tee tomorrow morning with Bernhard Langer looking on. So, unless we change your mindset, your personal

120

computer has logged the fact that tomorrow you expect to shoot some good holes knowing that you'll lose the plot completely after a bad shot.

'What did I tell you back in the clubhouse? You're asking for it and you'll probably get it, too, because you've created your own future. It's all about trying to achieve, not looking to avoid.'

We arrived at the driving range. Vanstiphout collected some balls, handed me a five iron and said: 'Now, what I'm hoping to achieve here first is to discover what your character is, something that will reveal itself here on the range. I want to see whether you know who you really are.'

This appeared daunting in itself. My God, what was he going to discover about me that I didn't know, lurking beneath my skin, deeply embedded in my inner self?

'Before we start I always like to shake hands,' Vanstiphout said, interrupting my flow of thoughts. 'It's a nice way to begin a session.'

This, so I would discover, was a trick. I shook his hand like I shake anyone else's – firmly. 'Whoa, tough guy, macho man,' my psychologist exclaimed, shaking his hand in mock pain and grimacing. 'What are you, a rugby player or something? We're here to play golf, you know. Loosen your grip, relax, slow down, take life easy.'

I positioned myself in readiness to drive the first ball Vanstiphout had placed in front of me, making sure that my grip on the club was loose, but before I could begin my swing my new guru stopped me. 'You're tense,' he said, as a statement of fact.

'No I'm not,' I said, sensing that I had just snapped.

'You see,' Vanstiphout replied. 'Look at your lips. They're all tight and taut. Here's something I tell my golfers to do. Loosen your lips. Make a noise like a horse by blowing on your closed mouth.'

I looked at him and blinked.

'Go on, go on,' he insisted.

I made a noise of an equine animal, which was supposed to be a horse but sounded more like an ass.

Vanstiphout ordered me to hit the ball. As always I was a little inconsistent, but the more he cajoled me to relax and be horselike in my approach, so the fluidity of my strokes and the line and length of my drives improved.

'Bet you can't hit two great shots in a row,' Vanstiphout said.

I proceeded to hit two, great successive shots.

'Bet you can't hit three in a row,' Vanstiphout teased.

I went on to strike three consecutive beauties.

'There's no way you can hit four in a row,' Vanstiphout added.

I laughed at what I thought was an obvious example of trying to motivate me by proving him wrong, and then hit a drive so sweet I hardly knew my iron had struck the ball.

'Hah!' shouted my teacher, as if he were Archimedes in the bath. 'You were smiling, in fact even laughing a little.'

I told him that it was because his methods of motivation were rather obvious and that I was always going to recognise this fact. Wrong, again.

'No, no, my friend, you misunderstand me. I wasn't trying to motivate you at all. I had a feeling you would play better if you were outwardly happy because then you would be in your most relaxed state. Smiling is the opposite to fear, remember. The message your subconscious is saying is that the boss is happy and everything's OK. Judging by that shot, I'd say that was a correct assessment. So, already we have learnt something very important about you.'

'What's that?' I asked, having given up trying to keep up with Vanstiphout's assessments.

'The subconscious never lies, man. The body can cheat on you, but not your subconscious. You want to be a smiley, happy person. That's when you are at your best. Look at your last drive. You were smiling away and produced a beautiful golf shot. That's what you must do from now on. Be happy when you're hitting the ball. Try and think of something that makes you smile. Even laugh as you're playing. It may sound strange, but I think it works for you.'

Right! So I had to make the sound of a horse and laugh as I drove off the tee.

Vanstiphout did not stop there, however. 'This is something I learnt from Gallwey,' he began. 'Think of your mind like a glass of water. Make sure it is full to the brim. You can't add anything to a full glass of water, can you, because it's already full. It's the same with the brain. Fill it up with a simple thought process so that no negatives can get in. You go to the toilet and lock the door so that everyone keeps out. It's a case of no entry, man. That way you don't have to bother fighting negative thoughts, which just creates tension. Just ignore them. So, when it comes to striking the ball, say quietly to yourself "back" when the club's gone as far back as you intend it to do, and then "hit" at the precise moment the club hits the ball. If it helps, say these words out loud. If you say "back" at precisely the point where the club will not extend any further, and then "hit" at precisely the point the ball is struck, then you will hit a good shot every time.'

I took a long look around me to ensure that nobody was watching or listening, and then went through the three exercises my psychological tutor had instilled into me. Crouched over the ball, I first blew out my lips noisily like a horse, then started to laugh as I began to swing my club, before shouting out first 'back' and then 'hit' as I completed my drive. To my utter astonishment the ball soared high into the heavens and far out to the horizon. Vanstiphout stood there smiling and clapping. 'We have a result,' he declared, appearing genuinely pleased with the workout.

Like any sane man I had my doubts about whether imitating a laughing horse would improve my game, but after witnessing first hand my improvement I would be happy to canter down the fairway in the morning, clip-clop into the bunkers and gallop to the greens, stopping at the odd lake for a slurp of the water and a sugar lump from the watching gallery.

'Don't try and compete with Langer tomorrow,' was Vanstiphout's final piece of advice. 'Just remember that you are very lucky to be playing with him, and that you are playing on one of the best courses in Europe. So, the first thing is you'd better enjoy yourself. And, my friend, if you don't want to look like a fool, don't fight with yourself. Just relax, hey?'

On the subject of looking like a fool, I asked whether it was really acceptable to re-enact the laughing, talking horse technique during the pro-am.

'Of course, of course,' came back the emphatic answer. 'It works for you. Do the lips, have a laugh, remember "back" and "hit", and just see what happens.'

Well, I surmised, as I drove to a nearby hotel for the night: if it works for Retief Goosen then I suppose that's good enough for me. But I couldn't help thinking, one way or another, that things would not turn out quite how I expected them to in the morning.

13

Belfry blushes

From the moment I woke I felt nervous. By the time I had made it to the administrative offices at the Belfry to register my name for the pro-am, my stomach was churning. En route I happened to pass a certain Bernhard Langer, practising his bunker chips. Each shot landed within a few inches of the pin, as if the German had been using a remote control to steer the ball.

By rights I should have possessed a handicap to compete in the pro-am. A swift explanation that I had not actually gone through the mechanics of obtaining a handicap because I had played on so many different courses and thus had not joined any one golf club, together with a letter from David Young from the World of Golf confirming my standard, saw me through this potentially tricky hurdle. I was down for 18, the highest handicap allowed in such a tournament, but still two lower than my best score, unless you include my 90 in Greenland. This could hardly count on a day like this one because, the last time I had checked, there were no icebergs on the Belfry fairways.

A glance down the tee-off times made interesting reading. I would be away at 11.40 a.m., following on from Jean Van der Velde, the hapless Frenchman whose story Stewart the caddie recounted at Carnoustie, and preceding Ireland's Paul McGinley. Apart from Langer my colleagues for the day would be Geoff Irvine, the owner of Bedford

Rugby Club, and Clive Woodward, the England rugby union national team manager.

I cursed my luck on seeing Woodward's name. I had got to know Clive pretty well over the years and liked his company, but I knew full well that he would derive mischievous pleasure in seeing me squirm on the golf course, just as I would if the roles were reversed. Already I was losing the battle against negative thoughts that were invading my mind like a plague of locusts in a corn field.

Having played all my golf so far with a half-set of clubs, I thought it was time to come across a little more professionally in such exalted company. In the golf shop at the back of the clubhouse I treated myself to a one wood, a four iron and a pitching wedge, which meant that with these extra additions I was lacking just a driver, a six iron and an eight iron from a full set. Added to this, I also bought a couple of woolly club heads, which were inserted on to the heads of the one and three woods, a Ping cap, a waterproof top and a rather naff royal blue V-neck sweater, with the words 'Ryder Cup 2002' emblazoned on its left breast. I ended up not wearing it on the day, nor indeed ever since.

Down at the practice range I spent twenty minutes clubbing drives with my irons and woods. The one wood felt terrible, as did the four iron, which was a bit of a blow seeing that I had just bought them. Alongside me, the minute figure of Ronnie Corbett practised his swing with a driver that appeared almost the same length as him.

Over by the chipping areas, I then made a hash of my attempted lobs to the green with my new pitching wedge. Costantino Rocca, a five times winner on the European PGA Tour, had clearly been watching me for a while because I suddenly felt my wedge extracted from my grip by a roly-poly Italian, who proceeded to show me how it was done.

'Look,' he said, pointing to his feet. 'You see where they are?' he asked, demonstrating how close they needed to be together in order to control the direction and strength of his chips. 'You are like this.' Rocca went into an exaggerated stance, with his feet so wide apart he almost tumbled forward.

I muttered a grudging thank you for such a public lesson and headed back to the first tee to watch some of my predecessors in the pro-am. On the way, I was introduced to John Daly by a mutual friend, the big-hitting American, who had won both the British Open and the US PGA despite an on-off affair with alcohol and numerous wives.

'What's it playing like, John?' I asked, trying desperately to sound as if I knew what I was talking about.

'Oh, pretty good,' John replied. 'It's not playing too badly at all.'

I told him I would be partnering Langer very shortly. Daly gave me a mock-concerned look and blew out his cheeks. 'I'm gonna wish you luck because, man, you're gonna need it.'

Rose yesterday, Rocca a few minutes before, and now Daly. The professional world of golf was inadvertently trying its utmost to screw up my mind even before I begun the round. The sight that met my eyes on arriving at the first tee hardly helped, either. I had been expecting a small crowd of maybe twenty people. Instead, there must have been a good two hundred of them, all crowding round in the hope of not only seeing a famous golfer playing with a well-known celebrity, but a well-known celebrity completely cocking up his first drive.

Cliff Thorburn, the former world snooker champion, stepped up on to the first tee to drive off. He was playing with Denmark's Thomas Bjorn. After what seemed like an eternity he finally sent a sweet drive straight down the middle of the fairway, and received a round of applause for his efforts. 'Thank God,' the Canadian shouted out, with a relieved expression.

Soon it would be my turn. I walked over to meet my playing partners at the first. Clive Woodward had brought his son, Joe, to caddie for him, and Geoff Irvine was employing a local man. There was no sign of Langer yet, although he would be using his trusted, long-term caddie, Pete Colman. Which left me, out on my own, as the only player of the group not to have a man carrying my clubs for me.

Van der Velde arrived, looked at us and asked: 'Are you the unfortunate ones to have me today?' We explained that we were early, and he was close to being late. 'Ah well,' he laughed, his heavily accented English making him sound like Inspector Clouseau. 'Then you are the lucky ones.'

I just had time to double-check my bag. Apart from my clubs, old and new, I had ensured that twelve balls were buried in the pockets. To lose a dozen golf balls in one round would spell a complete disaster, but I was leaving nothing to chance. I checked that I had enough tees, a spare glove and a towel. Finally, I searched in another pocket for my camera.

The camera had accompanied me on each occasion I had ventured out on to a golf course, even at Royal Melbourne back in the previous July. The reason was simple, if a little embarrassing. It was there in case I scored a hole in one. After all, it would simply be terrible not to record such a moment on film. To hope for such a feat inside your first year as a golfer really is pushing new boundaries in optimism but, like the man who stuffs a condom in his wallet when he goes out for the evening in the hope he might get lucky, I always packed my camera.

Mike Tindall, the Bath and England rugby player, was standing on the other side of the ropes beside the first tee. When he caught sight of a rather anxious novice attempting to look calm and collected, he beckoned him over.

'You're not playing in this, are you?' he asked, slightly incredulously.

'As a matter of fact, I am,' I replied.

'Fantastic,' Tindall responded. 'I'm going to completely piss myself if you slice your first drive into the woods.'

I thanked him for that final, welcome dose of psychology just as Langer made his grand entrance. Like an actor given a minute's warning before his first speech on stage, Langer had waited until the very last moment and then arrived bang on cue. If it had been me I would have been in a terribly flustered state, but the German, dressed in a slightly hideous yellow jumper and black trousers, appeared totally at ease. Why waste a few precious minutes hanging around the first tee with a bunch of amateurs when you could be honing your game somewhere else? 'You might be a better golfer than me,' I thought to myself. 'But you wouldn't catch me wearing that!'

We lined up as if at a royal premier as he shook hands with us all, before stepping purposefully to the tee. After an introduction that seemed to go on for ever as the tannoy announcer listed the German's more notable achievements, Langer smacked the ball straight down the centre of the fairway. Follow that! Clive Woodward did precisely this, after a somewhat shorter introduction. I was hoping Geoff Irvine might be next, but the announcer called my name up, to a polite if small ripple of applause.

I had been telling myself in the seconds before this moment to be calm, to be relaxed, and to treat this shot like any other at the driving range. Then I remembered the routine Jos Vanstiphout had recommended the night before. Standing over the ball, my lips made the noise of a horse, I let out a small laugh that I hoped was not audible, and said quietly 'back, hit' as I hit the struck the ball good and hard with my three wood.

It could have been a lot worse. Steve Backley, my golf fitness coach who had played earlier that day in the same competition, told me how once, when teeing off at a pro-am, the seven handicapper performed a complete air shot. Yet it could have been better, too. There was no problem with the length, but on bouncing between the centre and the left edge of the fairway, the ball took a wicked deviation to the left and ended up in a bunker. Great! What made matters a great deal worse is that while I was impersonating Shergar, I could hear a couple of people giggling in the crowd. The animal noises, I decided, as well as the laughter, would have to go.

Everyone's first shot encapsulated the round. Langer's went exactly where he intended it to. Woodward's, too, was hugely impressive. Irvine's was a bit wayward and uppish, but did no major harm. And mine ended up in a bunker. I topped my second shot out of the bunker, managed to get close to the green on my third, chipped to around five feet of the pin and then two-putted for a double bogey six. That was the way I always seemed to begin rounds of golf, and so I was not duly concerned.

On the 2nd, my drive went to the right and into the trees. All I could do for the next shot was knock the ball back on to the fairway, but in attempting to find the green with my third, I deposited the ball into the stream that ran across the fairway a few yards from the front edge of the green. End result, a triple bogey seven. I managed to avoid the lake beside the 3rd green as another double bogey was notched up, but ended up in the wide river crossing in front of the green on the 4th.

And so this went on, Langer picking up birdies and Woodward scoring pars or bogeys, and me finding every obstacle placed in front of me. By the 7th I felt wretched by my performance. It was time for a pit stop. Van der Velde and his group were just about to tee off, so we took time out for a coffee and some food. Although Vanstiphout would have been tearing his wild hair out by now, I decided to change everything about my game in the hope that things might pick up. Off came the top, to reveal just a white polo shirt in rather cool conditions, while the ball was changed, as was the tee. 'You'll see a big difference now,' I declared, as Langer looked on wearily and smiled.

This desperate attempt to improve matters seemed to pay off at first. I scored a bogey at the par three 7th, and a bogey five at the par four 8th, scoring vital Stableford points for our team that was lagging well behind the top of the leaderboard. At the 9th, Trevor Payne, a member of the public who had been following our group around all day with his father, took pity on me and offered to be my caddie. Now I felt like a proper golfer, although I couldn't help but think that Trevor was deranged to be wanting to carry my bag at a tournament brimming over with golf stars and celebrities.

As I was starting to play reasonably well, I thought I had earned the right for a chat with Langer. Quietly mannered, and clearly at peace with himself, the German seemed pretty content with his lot. A devout Christian he helps organise the regular meetings of the Tour Bible Class. You would never have guessed that this was the same man who endured many years of back pain and the putting affliction known as the 'yips'; or that he missed a crucial six-foot putt at the 1991 Kiawah Island Ryder

Cup in America, which would have won the trophy for Europe instead of losing it – a putt that Seve Ballesteros later said that no one should have been asked to take. This was also the man who once treated golf as if it were more important than life or death, as he battled his way to the top despite having no tuition and no real system back in his native Germany.

'Golf was totally consuming my life from the age of 15 through to 25,' he said, as we walked along the Belfry fairway grass. 'It meant everything to me. It's also true that I have suffered a great deal through health problems and technique, and these were not good times. But you must persevere and not give up.

'In the beginning it was a real struggle for me. There weren't many German amateurs and absolutely no professionals at all when I started getting serious about the game in the 1970s. The problem was that the golf season in Germany was only seven months long and I'd spend a good couple of months during the season finding my best form after such a long lay-off. I didn't have a golf course to practise on, any money to travel, or any lessons. In fact, I didn't have a lesson for the first seven years of my golfing career. Instead I watched others and learned from them.

'Then, when I started to make ground in the game, people told me that I was obviously talented but I was doing a great deal wrong. I used to be a caddie, and then became an assistant professional teacher. I won a tournament in Germany when I was 17 and decided to give it a go for two or three years and see how it went. That's when golf took over my life, which was not so good, but I got married, had a family and became a Christian, and suddenly a missed 3-foot putt isn't the most important thing in life.'

Which was just as well because my improving round took a sudden turn for the worse again. My new clubs were still performing terribly, and my old clubs were, as a result, playing likewise. At the par three 12th, a Toyota car was on offer to any amateur who scored a hole in one. Of course, by winning the car you would have to relinquish your amateur status, something which would pose all sorts of problems to your communal garden golfer, but to worry about such a possibility was, in my case, an absurd waste of time. At 208 yards it was a long par three. I hauled out my new one wood and noticed Langer looking at me, and the club, with great interest. Eventually he asked: 'You're planning to go for the green with that club?'

'Just exploring all the options, Bernhard,' I answered, hurriedly sticking it back in the bag and taking out my three wood instead. My drive hooked the ball out of bounds to the left of the green, a shot I personally blamed Langer for. At the par three 14th, where Faldo recorded a hole in one during the 1993 Ryder Cup singles matches, I achieved my first burst of applause from the watching crowd after chipping the ball close to the pin. It had taken fourteen holes to achieve a few claps, something Pete Coleman, Langer's caddie, pointed out with a hearty belly laugh. I acknowledged the crowd with a rather self-conscious wave and a touch of the cap. The touching of the cap was something I had never performed before, but had noticed golfers doing this in tournaments. I then managed to miss an easy putt to score a bogey and shatter the illusion.

By the 17th my game had gone to pieces again. I was cursing my luck, and kept insisting to Woodward: 'I'm a lot better than this, really.' Clive had been playing unbelievably well throughout the round, but couldn't help the odd giggle when he saw my downtrodden expression stomping up the fairway behind him.

At the par five 17th, I hit my best drive of the day from the tee. On a dog-leg to the right I felt I couldn't have hit the ball better, landing it bang on the corner in full view of the turn to the right and the green in the distance. First Langer and then Woodward smacked their drives seemingly into and over the trees to the right. I didn't say anything, but secretly I felt pleased. 'About time those two hit duff shots and I led the way,' I thought, as we all walked down the fairway. On arriving at my ball, I watched as Langer and Woodward walked some 50 yards further on to where their balls had perched, perfectly around the corner and well clear of the trees, in a perfect position to chip on to the green. A shot later, Langer produced his ungainly-looking broom putter and swept home a birdie.

Meanwhile, after a bogey that did little to cheer me I came to the 18th tee. I had no idea what I had scored up to this point, but I knew that unless I produced my best hole of the day, I had run up three figures on precisely the worst day, at the worst place, and with the worst company imaginable.

In front of us stood a particularly testing final hole. Danger was everywhere, from the huge lake that dominated the whole fairway to the bunkers on each side of the green, and even the three-tiered green itself. Langer, Woodward and Irvine all smacked big drives over some trees and the corner of the lake and on to the fairway on the other side. I hit another good drive and assumed I had followed suit. Instead a marshal was waving his red flag. I had failed to make the opposite banks of the lake by a foot, which meant that while the other three walked on, I was called upon to place my ball in front of the lake and try again. My second effort went straight into the water as well, so that by the time my third drive landed on the other side of the fairway, albeit well over to the right and in a bunker, I had already scored 5.

It took me two flustered attempts to scoop the ball out of the bunker, just as Langer was landing his ball on the green, and when I then attempted to strike a colossal effort over the lake that had swung round in front of the green, the ball plopped once more into the water. From there I found the bunker to the right of the green.

The others had waited for me, which was a kindly gesture, even if it did unwittingly underline just how far behind them I had fallen. They watched as I played my bunker shot straight towards the pin. For a split-second I thought the ball was going to drop into the hole. Unhappily it did not, instead turning its inexorable way down the steep slope until it ground to a halt some 45 feet away.

At this point I was heckled. I was actually heckled! Some wag from the crowd shouted out: 'If you hole that putt from there I'll bare my arse!' Now I knew how Colin Montgomerie felt. Poor old Monty had endured so much abuse, especially in America, that he had recently announced that he had had enough and would not play there any more. Of course, he relented, but I could understand his actions. I felt like proclaiming that I would never play at the Belfry again after that, except that such a decision would only provide mass relief to the organisers of the pro-am. Still, there was worse to come.

As we all walked up to the pin a man held out an autograph book and shouted for us to come across. 'Bernhard,' he said. 'Can you sign this, please?' Langer smiled and scribbled out his name.

'Clive,' the man said, turning to Woodward. 'Would you mind?' The England rugby manager duly obliged.

'Ian,' the punter then said. 'Can I have yours too?'

Now every so often someone who has read one of my books asks me to sign my name. It doesn't happen often, but it does happen, usually at book signings or speeches. I ambled over to where the man was standing behind the ropes beside the edge of the green and stretched out my hand to grab his pen.

At the very last moment he snatched the pen away from my grasp, burst out laughing and shouted: 'Nah, I was only joking.' All I could do was walk away while he and his friends had a good laugh at my expense.

Two putts later, I completed my round with an 11 at the 18th. Even though Langer was terribly nice about it, and Woodward gave me a consoling pat and presented me with an England rugby cap, I felt like the village idiot. The wheels had totally come off at the Belfry, in the full glare of not only Bernhard Langer, but a good number of the golfing public too. During the drive down south to my home that night I had made up my mind. Golf was a bloody stupid game and I hated playing it, watching it, or having anything to do with it at all. And I really, really meant it.

14

Fanny

My God, this game is just so bloody brilliant, isn't it? What could be better than spending a late afternoon that rolls into a beautiful summer's evening, on a lush, green golf course, playing the game with a friend and enjoying a drink afterwards at the 19th hole?

OK, so there's been a pretty dramatic change of heart here, but for good reason. Things, against all expectation, turned for the better after the nightmare of the Belfry, although my transformation in fortune began in humiliating fashion.

Adopting the old adage of getting right back into the saddle, I sought an hour-long, double lesson at the World of Golf with my coach, David Young. Before we began I opened up my golf bag, hauled out my one wood and my four iron and asked David what was wrong with my new clubs. 'I can't seem to hit a thing with them,' I proclaimed, in disgust. 'See if you can do any better with them.'

David examined them for a split-second and asked a curious question. 'Have you had a major operation recently?'

'No, of course not,' I answered, wondering what he was getting at.

'Oh, so you haven't had a sex change, then?'

'No, what's the point in saying . . .' Whatever I was about to say trailed off as I observed my coach curled up in laughter.

'You've only gone and bought ladies' clubs,' he said, once his guffaws had died down. 'What the hell would Langer have thought of that?'

Oh shit! Double shit! No wonder Langer gave me a quizzical look on the 12th when I pulled out what now appeared to be a ladies' one wood. There's no doubt that playing with Langer, in front of all those people, and on such a demanding and prestigious course as the Belfry had got to me, but it hardly improved my chances when a good number of my shots had been played using ladies' clubs! Then I recalled my almost dismissive manner with Langer's enquiries. 'Really, it's all right, Bernhard. You think I don't know what I'm doing? Next, you're going to tell me that small, white round thing is called a ball. C'mon, give me a break!'

For most of that toe-curling round of golf I had done my best to impersonate Norman Wisdom in a B-rated golf movie. Yet only now had the full horror of the most embarrassing incident of the day dawned on me. At the time, I dismissed Langer's half-smile for nothing more than his usual friendliness. Now I faced the truth. Langer was smiling at me, but much more to himself. The former Masters champion had found me out. To make matters worse, I wasn't even aware of it. If there's one thing worse in life than knowing you're making an idiot of yourself in public, then it's not knowing this at the time and discovering the fact much later on.

I wonder if Langer had contemplated telling me there and then at the tee? I was once in the company of Will Carling, the former England rugby captain. Unbeknown to Carling, who was eating a plate of lasagne at the time, a large dollop of béchamel sauce had nestled firmly on his chin. I sat and stared at this food on his face for ages, deciding whether to tell him or not. The little angel inside my head told me to do the decent thing immediately. The little devil cohabiting urged me to let him find out for himself, preferably after a series of important business meetings half a day later. The angel won the day, but it was a marginal decision. Langer, in comparison, let it be – although in hindsight I was probably grateful to him for this. If it had all come out then and there, I doubt my shattered defences could have taken any more that day.

I tried to look at the positives. So it wasn't me at all, then. It was my clubs! Good workmen can blame their tools, too. By the end of the hour's lesson I was hitting the ball sweetly again, watching it disappear over the numerous flags which dotted the driving range.

Within a week, having exchanged my two ladies' clubs for the male versions, I played the east course at Sundridge Park on a glorious, early summer's day, with a retired banker friend of mine called Archie Herron. Although I began the round in time-honoured fashion with a triple and then a double bogey, something remarkable then took place. My purple patch, which came to me in every recent round save the Belfry debacle, arrived early. Not only that, but instead of staying with me for five or six holes before buggering off again to leave me to my own, self-destructive devices, it hung around. After nine holes, the last seven of which I scored four pars and three bogeys, I was out in 44. Drives off the tee on the par threes sent the ball straight on to the greens. Chips from off the greens landed within a few feet of the pin. Even 6-foot putts I missed on a consistent basis at the Belfry veered straight into the hole.

With a final score of 86 I had obliterated my previous lowest score by six strokes and gone well under the 90 barrier. '86,' I spluttered, as I arrived home. 'It was only 86 today.'

'Really,' came a voice from the kitchen. 'I knew it was hot today, but I didn't realise it was 86 degrees.'

Another mass of emails, messages and faxes were sent round to the usual suspects following my first sub-90 round. Understandably Clive Woodward refused to believe the same man who had played so disastrously with him could make such a score. In the end I posted a photocopy of my Sundridge Park scorecard to him as proof.

Within a few days, Tiger Woods, on one of his rare sojourns over to Europe, had won the Deutsche Bank SAP Open in Heidelberg, beating a rejuvenated Colin Montgomerie after three holes of a play-off. Justin Rose, incidentally, had demonstrated his new approach to golf in perfect fashion by missing the cut at the Belfry, before then finishing a highly impressive third in Heidelberg. Langer, meanwhile, was placed well down the field in both tournaments. It seemed to me that Woods and I had both hit good form with some interesting challenges ahead. For Woods it was the small matter of the US Open in New York. For me it was the opportunity to reveal my new-found game in the company of someone who had witnessed a few good rounds over the years. Incredibly, despite this rather obvious discrepancy in our golfing careers, I was managing to equate my goals with Tiger's.

Yep, 'we' were both doing well. Tiger and I had now become an item. The more this came into being the more I realised that I would have to meet the man, face to face, no matter how difficult it may prove to engineer. However, to my dismay, an official approach made to Tiger's management company for a brief audience with the man was turned down flatly and somewhat incredulously. The gist of IMG's message was that I clearly had failed to realise how busy Tiger was.

Clearly, I would have to rethink my Getting To Meet Tiger strategy. In any case, if it were ever to happen, I wanted to ensure that first I had explored all aspects of golf in the company of the very best. In the attempt to come across as more professional, the purchasing of new golf clubs to top up my collection had backfired on me, but at least I could console myself with the fact that I had obtained some very unique advice from one of the world's best-known golf psychologists.

It therefore seemed only natural next to turn my attention to the world of the caddie, the unsung hero in the partnership with a golfing professional. Along with Steve Williams, Tiger's New Zealand-born caddie, Fanny Sunesson is the best-known bag-carrier in the world, partly because of her hugely successful partnership with Nick Faldo, but also because of the stark fact that she is a woman in what is still very much a man's game.

Through the ever-helpful Faldo, Fanny agreed to be my caddie for nine holes at the west course at Wentworth, two days after the Volvo PGA Championships had been concluded at the famous Surrey course.

Wentworth was Fanny's suggestion because she had already marked out all the yardages for the course during the week before, when Faldo had been competing. David Rennie, Wentworth's club professional, agreed to accompany me as a playing partner for the morning, no doubt interested to see whether I had improved since our previous round together back in September on the east course, which had left a lot to be desired.

We decided to play the inward nine holes, prompting me to suggest to David: 'If I've scored, say, 40 after nine, I might just go on to see if I beat 80 over the full eighteen holes.'

Rennie threw back his head and laughed at this notion. 'I'll tell you right now, there's no way you'll manage 40,' he said. 'This is the west course, the greens are treacherous, and they've toughened it up just this year to make it more of a challenge to the pros at the Volvo PGA.'

It was always good to receive such an encouraging verdict. Taking a prior look at the west course during the Volvo PGA I saw my mental guru, Jos Vanstiphout, at work on the putting green. Beckoning him over, I explained that I'd shot my worst round in ages at the Belfry after an almost complete mental breakdown. Then, a week later, I shot my best round ever when I was full of self-belief.

Vanstiphout seemed pleased with this news. 'Well, it's simple,' he said. 'The boss [he meant my mind] was showing you what can happen if you let him take control, and then allowed you to take the helm. You see what a difference it can make if you can be in control of your mind? That's as good a reaction as I've had anywhere. I'll put you up there with Retief when I tell my story.'

Fanny and Nick had a good few days at Wentworth, too. Faldo finished tied fourth behind debut winner Anders Hansen, a credible display for a player, suggesting his halcyon days were not necessarily behind him. For Fanny, caddying for me as opposed to the six times majors' winner would prove to be an interesting exercise, and a graphic contrast between someone who is rather good, and someone who is rather not.

Not that this seemed to perturb the 34-year-old Swede as she produced a white towel, a bottle of water and an apple and shoved them into my golf bag. 'Do you always bring an apple for Nick or any golfer you caddie for?' I asked.

'Sometimes it's a banana,' she answered. 'It depends on whether I feel an apple or a banana is the right fruit to bring.'

I wondered whether she felt I was an apple or a banana golfer, and the reasons, which would obviously be technical, why she therefore brought an apple.

'Because I didn't have a banana in the house,' she explained.

Right! Fanny was in unmistakable guise: visor, sporting the US Masters logo where she had helped Faldo win two of his three Masters titles, thick bob of blonde hair bouncing up and down behind her as she walked purposefully along the fairways, checking her measurements already written down from the week before; Taylor Made waterproof jacket and trainers.

I was hoping to don, for the first time, a new, blue and white stripy Nike top favoured often by Tiger. In truth, it had concerned me when my wife announced that this was my worst top yet in an increasingly foul collection of golf clothes, and that it made me look, to quote her, 'about seventy'. As if that was not bad enough, I liked it. Genuinely. What was happening to me? And how come when Tiger wore it he looked so cool, but when I slipped it on I looked seventy? The rain, however, that alternated between drizzle and downpour, forced a waterproof jacket to cover up the monstrosity.

An occupational hazard of caddying, namely a bad back, meant that Fanny had to dash off mid-morning for an appointment with a podiatrist in central London. 'Quite a few caddies have back problems,' she explained, which is hardly surprising considering the weight of a packed golf bag and the amount of time it sits across a caddie's back.

I find it hard enough carrying what had now had become a three-quarter set of golf clubs, so what must it be like for a woman to carry the whole pile? 'Actually, I've always been pretty strong,' Fanny insisted. 'I find the bag feels heavy when Nick's not playing well, and nice and light when he is.'

Still, because of her current condition, and the fact that her London appointment beckoned, I carried the bag for most of the morning. 'Hmm, I could get used to this,' Fanny said, as she looked on approvingly at her golfer with his clubs over his own back. 'It's quite a novel idea, isn't it. The caddie gets the golfer to carry the bags, leaving me to concentrate on my work. Maybe I'll put the suggestion to Nick.'

The half-round between me and David Rennie proved to be a mixed collection of horrendous, acceptable and, just occasionally, brilliant. The horrendous was best highlighted by the tee shot at the 11th using a three wood. A couple of men had been working on the fairway close to the end of the tee, some thirty feet away. One stopped astride his lawn mower by the right-hand side and waited patiently for David and myself to tee off. David's ball soared high and far down the fairway. Mine was topped and sliced, forcing the ball to shoot past the mower like a bullet, at knee height, no more than a few feet away from the workman. To his credit he did not move an inch, but Fanny's jaw dropped a mile. 'You could have killed him,' she said.

At the long, par three 14th, an example of how a golfer should follow his gut feeling reared its head. Fanny suggested I should use my seven wood off the tee. I had never actually teed off using this club before, didn't say anything, and promptly scuffed the ball as it hooked over to the left and into a clump of bushes. 'I would have preferred to have used my four iron,' I mentioned, rather belatedly.

'Go on, then,' Fanny answered. 'Have another go.'

This time I struck a slightly short but clean drive that fell just a couple of feet from the green. 'Every golfer is different, and there are lots of ways of hitting the same ball the same distance,' was Fanny's conclusion from this. 'You've just proved how a golfer must go with his or her favoured club, even if others wouldn't necessarily use it.'

At the 17th I drove straight into the trees on the left of the fairway. I had noticed whenever a small hunt had been required to find my ball that Fanny always insisted on searching until it had been discovered. Because of the time limitations, my natural impatience, and the fact that this was only a half-round designed to see my caddie at work more than to record a score, my inclination had been to drop a ball and press on. Fanny, on the other hand, would always emerge triumphantly from a bush, a small thicket or a patch of particularly deep rough, pointing to where the ball lay.

On this occasion, though, the ball defeated her. 'When I was younger, I used to spend half my time looking for lost golf balls so that I could play with them,' she said.

I laid the blame for not finding this ball squarely on Fanny's shoulders. 'Not this time,' she replied. 'Not after a shot like that. That was really horrible, wasn't it?'

In between the horrendous came a few flashes of brilliance, all from my usually suspect short game. A bunker chip landed just a couple of feet from the pin. Another chip, this time from the lip of a bunker, ended with similar results. 'Nick would have been happy with those shots,' Fanny announced, which was ironic considering that it was Nick Faldo who had taught me how to chip in the first place.

The most spectacular shot of all came from Fanny's own advice, however. The ball had been plugged deep into another bunker by the side of the 15th green. Ordinarily, I would choose to hammer the ball out of the hole, which would have either sent the ball soaring into the next county, or merely left the ball unmoved and a large dent in the bunker. Fanny suggested I turn the face of my sand wedge round, and then to hack down on to the ball as if I was chopping wood. It seemed a ridiculous notion, and felt even more so as I went about her instructions, but the outcome was incredible. The ball ballooned out of the bunker, shot up in the air, and plopped to within six inches of the hole some twenty feet away.

'Awesome, awesome,' Fanny shouted, appearing genuinely pleased. 'That's the best shot I've seen here this week.' I would have liked to have taken the credit for the chip, but actually I had no idea how it had happened.

I noticed how, for just about the only time in the round, Fanny walked slowly to the next tee. Normally she'd been bustling along, leaving David and me in her wake, but this time her progress was measured. 'It's to calm you down. I do the same with Nick. When he's playing really well, especially when it's looking as if a title is on the cards, I become very calm and walk slower just to prevent him becoming over-excited. Over-excitement on a golf course is usually not good news. It's cost some players titles before.'

On the 17th green, Fanny then used the powers of positive thinking to see me home. Up until this point my putting had been inconsistent, although the fast, turning greens at Wentworth had hardly made putting an easy task. As she and I eyed up a tricky looking, ten-foot putt, Fanny looked straight into my eyes and declared: 'You'll hole this one, absolutely no problem.' The ball rammed subsequently into the hole as if it was never in any doubt. 'See,' she added, looking pleased with herself. 'I say the same kind of thing to Nick, too.'

At the 18th I scored my only tactical win over Fanny when, some 40 feet away from the pin off the green, she suggested I chipped using an eight iron and I plumped for my putter instead, sending the ball to within an easy putt of holing. This triumph was soon shattered when, as an exercise in discovering how difficult it can be for a caddie to read a lie correctly, I advised Fanny that a 12-foot putt she faced would swing from right to left, and that she had to aim a good foot away from the hole to stand any chance of sinking the ball. She duly followed my orders and watched as the ball swung from left to right to leave her effort way wide to the right of the hole.

'Sorry, Fanny,' was just about all I could muster, as she gave me a look and said: 'Right to left, hey?'

Back in the clubhouse, Fanny explained how a woman from the south of Sweden became the world's most recognisable caddie. 'Actually, I wanted to be a professional golfer and for much of my childhood I was obsessed with playing the game,' she admitted. 'I got my first club at the age of 6 and by 14 I had a single-figure handicap. I sold newspapers on

Sundays all year round and spent the rest of my time playing golf.'

Having played as an amateur in a Swedish tournament on the European Ladies Tour and reached a five handicap, Fanny was then asked to help carry a bag for a couple of European Tour events played in Sweden. 'It seemed to make sense. I was doing all kinds of jobs in a hotel – room service, chamber maid, waitressing – and at least by caddying I could travel a bit and stay close to golf. Initially I planned to do it for a month. I was 18 and it seemed like a fun thing to do, but then I was asked to caddie for a season on the men's European Tour. Even then I thought it would only be for a year, but having first carried the bag for Mark Wilshire, the one-eyed golfer, for a short while, I worked with Andrew Murray.'

He finished seventh in their first tournament together and people began to take notice. Fanny's apprenticeship was short. 'Picking up a bag did not seem to be a problem,' she said, referring to the high turnover of caddying jobs on the circuit. Spain's Jose Rivero, Sweden's Anders Forsbrand and Britain's Howard Clarke came and went, with the Spaniard sacked by his female caddie after he took someone else to the 1987 Ryder Cup.

Then, at the end of 1989, Fanny was offered the best job in her business. At the age of 21 she had already gained respect on the circuit, helped guide Rivero to a tournament win, caddied at the Ryder Cup, and then had the courage to sack her golfer, which was the flip side of how player-caddie relationships normally end.

Working at the Australian Open, the music-loving caddie organised a trip to a Eurythmics concert. Faldo came along and afterwards asked her to carry his bag. 'I couldn't believe it at first,' Fanny admitted. 'He was the biggest star in world golf, and I was a 21-year-old Swedish girl, but we soon hit it off and then spent ten wonderful years together.'

Within three months of being hired she had helped Faldo claim the Masters. Another three months on and he had won the Open at St Andrews. Not only had Fanny raised the profile of the caddie from simple bag-carrier to adviser and confidante, but she trailed the way for women caddies who have now become regular features on tour, and even helped to pioneer the double strapping on golf bags that has made lumping clubs around courses so much easier.

How, then, does such a close, working relationship gel? 'Well, you spend so much time together that you just have to click as people, not just as professionals. You have to both like the person and respect the player, otherwise it would make life very difficult. The chemistry's so important. You need to share the same ambition, you need to be as driven as your golfer, and it helps if you think the same. Often I'd go to bed thinking about something to do with Nick's game, like his swing, or something to do with his clubs. Anything, really, to perfect his game. Then, in the morning, I'd say to him: "Do you know what I was thinking about last night?" Nick treated me like a caddie, not a woman, which was fine by me.'

And the others? 'Oh, nobody minded their Ps and Qs because a woman was standing on the green. They swear a lot in front of me, believe me.'

When the times were good they were very good. Together they won four majors. In the process Fanny became a star in her own right, not only benefiting from a percentage of Faldo's earnings, but gaining various and lucrative sponsorships from, among others, a telephone company, a club manufacturer, and a Dubai-based jewellery company that paid her to wear a £12,500 pearl necklace. I put it to her that she had inadvertently become famous. She was clearly uncomfortable with the notion. 'I don't see myself as famous at all,' she argued. 'But I suppose I've become reasonably well known in the golfing world. As far as I'm concerned, though, I always see the player as the star. If I can help at all, then that's great.'

A combination of Faldo's loss of form and the sheer length of time they had been together inevitably forced a split in 1999, initiated by Fanny. 'I just needed time off,' she explained. 'It was good for me, and it was good for Nick. I felt bad about it at the time because I knew things weren't going well for him, but it was something I had to do.'

For the next 16 months she would carry the bag for the exciting if combustible Spaniard, Sergio Garcia, the American, Fred Funk, and his compatriot, Notah Begay, one of Tiger's best friends on the circuit. For a variety of reasons these relationships did not prove to be long term, and when Faldo asked Fanny to caddie for him in 2001, the old partnership was back together again.

'It's how it used to be. Nick's playing better, he's listening to me, and I'm feeling a lot happier about working with him than I did a couple of years ago. The break was difficult to force, but I'd like to think it's done us the world of good.'

She laughed at the notion of dumping Faldo for me. 'Actually, I found being your caddie a really interesting experience. I've only ever caddied for one other non-professional before, but I got a lot more out of it this time. I can definitely see that you can play and yet you're still a beginner, but on the evidence of today I see no reason why you can't get down to single figures before too long.'

It had been a fruitful day for me. If I could take one positive piece of advice to add to my steep learning curve in golf from every meeting or round with anyone connected to the game, then I would be happy. I was a sponge, eager to soak up everything and through spending half a day with Fanny I had not only picked up some useful tips concerning my game, but had seen a supreme professional at work. On top of that, I liked the woman. She was fun, she was level-headed and, by association with all her successes, I felt just a little more worthy on the golf course.

Fanny talked animatedly of how much of a kick she derives from being a dare-devil off the course. 'I shoot, I've been dog-sledging, scuba-diving, I have completed a sky-diver's course, been diving with great white sharks off the South African coast—'

'Sky diving? What does Faldo think of that?'

'Well, I don't do it any more because of my back, but I know he wasn't exactly keen about me doing it.'

And diving with sharks? 'That's when you go inside the metal cage and they swim up to you. It was very exciting at the time. The most dangerous part is getting into the cage. The organisers were shouting: "Don't fall in the sea." Nick thought I was completely mad.'

It came as no surprise that Fanny's latest dream is to climb to base camp at Everest, some 18,000 feet above sea level. 'I really want to do it. It would be a dream for me to do so.' She revealed an innate knowledge of the world's highest peak, its history, some of the climbers who have scaled or failed its challenge, even some of the many Everest stories created over the years, from Mallory to Hillary, and the disastrous series of deaths in 1996. Did she honestly believe that, one day, she would fulfil what she had admitted was a lifelong dream?

'Oh yes. For sure.' And with that she was away, leaving me convinced that she will be walking around base camp high in the Himalayas in the not too distant future, marking down yardages and discovering golf balls given up as lost many years before.

15

Out of the frying pan . . .

There had been another reason for spending the day with Fanny Sunesson. The following morning I would be playing in my second pro-am tournament, this time at the Victor Chandler British Masters at Woburn and, after the horrors of the Belfry, I was determined to be as well-rehearsed as I could be.

At home the night before the pro-am, Alan Shearer telephoned. The former England and current Newcastle United captain had been trying to find a date in his packed diary for a round of golf with me, but in the meantime, he thought he would make contact to reveal his own obsession with the game of golf.

He turned out to be quite a useful counsellor, too, for a guy who had made such a public imbecile of himself at the Belfry but was about to set up the possibility of a repeat performance at Woburn in the morning. 'It's a funny thing,' he said. 'You've probably seen me take a penalty for Newcastle or maybe England? [Er, just a few.] Well, even though I'm going to do it in front of, say, 50,000 at St James Park and a television audience of many millions, I'm not too nervous about it. I suppose it's because I know I'm a half-decent football player and I know what I'm doing.

'But golf? Golf's another proposition altogether. I played in the Duke of Roxburgh Challenge a year or two ago with Jesper Parnevik. There were probably 3,000 people watching, and as I stepped up to the first tee I was absolutely shitting myself. Honestly, I can't tell you how relieved I felt when I managed to smack the ball with my three wood down the middle of the fairway.

'There was another time at a pro-am at Turnberry when I pulled the trigger for the shotgun start, stepped up on to the first tee and, in front of another large group of people watching, managed to hit the ball all of five yards.'

Hardly missing an open goal, though, is it? 'Oh, but it felt like it,' Shearer insisted. 'I felt just as bad, and just as embarrassed, maybe even more so. And when I finished that round at the Duke of Roxburgh pro-am with a birdie in the company of Parnevik and another big crowd at the 18th, that, I can assure you, felt just as good as scoring at St James Park.'

We learn two immediate things here about Shearer, then. Outstanding footballer though he is, when it comes to golf he is exactly like you and me. The fact that he has been scoring goals at the highest level for ten years means absolutely nothing when he stands over a golf ball. If Shearer is, to quote the man, 'shitting himself', then you can be forgiven for thinking the same way, too. Keith Wood, the Irish rugby captain, had said more or less the same thing to me, too.

The other revealing aspect of all this is that Shearer is clearly obsessed with golf. Scoring a birdie is as good as scoring a goal for Newcastle in front of 50,000 home fans? I rest my case, m'lud.

It may seem difficult to accept that a man like Shearer has his sporting heroes but, again, off the football pitch he is as human as the rest of us. Nick Faldo, he confessed, had always been a bit of a role model. 'He's a winner,' said the voice down the telephone. 'He's always been determined, single-minded, a great golfer. And he possesses a touch of arrogance which any top sportsman needs.'

Yet the man he respects, appreciates, nay even looks up to the most, is the man everyone respects, appreciates, nay looks up to the most, whether you happen to be an Olympic athlete like Steve Backley, a psychologist like Jos Vanstiphout, one of the world's greatest footballers like Alan Shearer, or even me, someone who had no views on him at all ten months before, but now would do just about anything to meet him.

'No matter what aspect of golf you want to look at, you just can't escape from Tiger Woods,' Shearer said. 'You have to have the greatest admiration for him, and I'm speaking having played top-level sport for many years. The aura he exudes is massive, the pressure he's under huge. I can sometimes hide behind my teammates if I make a mistake. Tiger's out there on his own. If it goes wrong, it's his mistake and his mistake alone. Mentally, he is the most impressive sportsperson I've ever seen in action.'

Fortified by this unexpected conversation with Shearer, I drove to Woburn the following morning in readiness for the pro-am.

On the way I thought about Tiger. Having been rebuffed once already by Tiger's management company, I decided that it would do no harm to try again, this time with more delicacy and caution, saying that I appreciated just how busy Mr Woods must be but how even the very briefest of meetings would be considered a great honour . . .

I had arranged to meet Malcolm Mackenzie for lunch at Woburn, a long-serving professional on the European Tour I had not heard of until a few weeks previously, when his win at the French Open produced a beacon of light for every single, struggling, downcast golfer trying to pay their way around the golf courses of the European Tour.

Mackenzie, a professional for twenty years, who had twice lost his tour card in the process and spent most of the remainder of this time often failing to make the cut, had held the somewhat dubious record of the largest consecutive number of tournaments played on the tour without a win. Over twenty years Mackenzie had notched up a quite staggering 509 tournaments – that's 509 – without a win until, at the Novotel Perrier Open de France at Le Golf National, he saw off the likes of Ian Woosnam and Jose-Maria Olazabal to claim the title, and a first prize of £205,794.

This was, by some distance, the largest cheque he had ever received from the game, more than the Englishman had won for the previous two years combined and, in the process, moved him up from 146th place in the Order of Merit to a lofty seventh. As if all this were not enough, he needed to have produced the shot of his life to set up a birdie four on the final hole, when it had begun to look as if he had thrown away his best chance ever to finally win a tournament.

One shot ahead at the start of the final round, Mackenzie had opened up a three-stroke lead with four holes to play, but a run of three successive bogeys from the 15th left him tied with South African, Trevor Immelman, playing the 18th. When Immelman, in the group ahead, made par, Mackenzie realised he needed to make a birdie to win and avoid a play-off. He achieved this thanks to a miraculous two iron that left him with two putts from just 15 feet away. Talking to him about all this only served to underline not only the pressure in golf, but the enormity of Tiger's achievements.

'I'll tell you what pressure does to you on the golf course,' Mackenzie said, as we sat on the terrace of the Victor Chandler Pavilion and looked out over the 18th green at Woburn. 'After 14 holes during that final round I was feeling great. Then one bad shot at the 15th resulted in a bogey and strange things started to happen. I began to feel really tense, my throat felt so tight I found it difficult to swallow, and my strokes, which had been smooth and flowing, were punched suddenly from my ever-tightening grip.'

Worse still, that nasty, malicious, sadistic voice that has impregnated all of us at some point or other, paid Mackenzie a visit. 'The little man in the head had been absent all week but then, as I strode down the 15th fairway, he appeared, saying: "Oh well, you're not going to win this tournament. This is your last chance ever to win, but your next shot's going to end up in the water. This time you've really blown it."'

He must be a busy bee, this little man inside your head, because he manages to pay every single golfer in the world a visit, from a very fine golfer like Mackenzie to a football player like Alan Shearer and, of course, to me, where he seems to have permanent residency.

Somehow Mackenzie pulled himself together in time to make that spectacular two iron on the 18th. Afterwards, in this ruthless game, his fellow professionals were queuing up to congratulate the likeable 40-year-old from Leicestershire. 'I got the impression many of the other pros were rooting for me well before I actually won,' he said. 'They all knew about my tag of being the guy who had been playing longest on tour without ever having won. Much bigger names than I'll ever be made a point of congratulating me. Monty [Colin Montgomerie] was one. And when I got back home, Sam Torrance was on the telephone almost immediately to convey his good wishes.'

The surprise result has transformed his life. 'I've got money in the bank and I'm almost in the comfort zone,' Mackenzie added, enjoying his first taste of relative security for many a while. 'I have a two-year extension on the tour, too, as a result of winning, which means no more concerns about avoiding tour school for a couple of years, at least. Now I want to prove I'm not a one-tournament wonder, that it wasn't a freak result. I used to be scared of winning after so many years of failing. When I walked down that 18th fairway I had all the cameras focusing on me, something I had not been used to in my career, and I was scared of showing myself up and also of the reaction if I won. Afterwards, I wondered what the hell I'd been scared of for all those years. It was wonderful to be a winner. I only wish it could happen every day.'

If you have come to the conclusion that Mackenzie must be a remarkably persevering man then you would be right, but, understandably, he found this run of 509 tournaments tough going. 'In the early 1990s I was making a few top ten finishes, and even recorded a fifth place in the 1992 Open won by Nick Faldo at Muirfield. Then my shoulder grew troublesome. For a year my game ticked over, but from the mid-1990s onwards, surviving on the circuit has been a real grind. I can't tell you how many times I've somehow managed to dig myself out of a hole with a good performance at a tournament just when losing my card, or receiving a final demand from the bank manager, looked a certainty. A

#	Name										
104	Ramos Joaquim	POR	28	34	58	33	44	24	115		26
29	Bierfeld Christian	BEL	31	22	53	32	85	31	116		
62	Vallin Remy	FRA	37	23	60	27	87	30	117		
18	Marchiani Pierluigi	ITA	35	24	59	36	94	23	117	33	150
18	Beitans Kaspars	LAT	36	23	59	33	92	26	118	36	154
5	Antonis Danny	BEL	34	24	58	35	93	27	120	32	152
50	Pasquier Yannick	FRA	35	26	61	36	97	23	120		
96	Scarlatescu Ovidiu	ROM	24	34	63	35	98	23	121		32
103	Csórdás István	HUN	26	35	61	36	97	24	121		26
88	Toadere Dan	ROM	23	35	58	38	96	25	121		28
77	Pranti Michael	ITA	30	31	61	37	98	23	121		
4	Pavlič Danilo	SLO	27	36	63	35	98	25	123	26	
106	Ching Claudio	POR	21	38	65	33	98	25	123	28	
105	Balaszeki János	HUN	26	33	59	33	92	34	126	25	
46	Irmejs Didzis	LAT	36	31	67	33	100	26	126		
17	De Cremer Kevin	BEL	39	25	64	37	404	26	127	34	161
107	Csókás László	HUN	34	35	64	38	402	26	128		
99	Kulits Gábor	HUN	25	38	63	38	401	27	118	29	
102	Mesquita Carlos	POR	25	38	63	39	402	26	118	25	
38	Thibault Guy	FRA	36	27	63	37	400	28	128		
70	Kirkis Verners	LAT	40	28	68	32	400	29	129		
98	Helder Correia	POR	22	43	65	37	402	28	150	22	
84	Balek Boris	SLO	28	36	64	35	99	32	131	32	
14	Pirolles Jean-Yves	FRA	42	21	69	37	406	26	132	31	163
76	Piermann Christel	BEL	36	32	68	38	406	29	135		
2	Mangler Grégoire	FRA	38	30	68	39	407	29	136	40	176
83	Davies Tim	GBR	33	36	69	35	404	34	158	36	
86	Webb Michael	GBR	29	39	68	39	407	31	158	31	
109	Sőrés Miklós	HUN	28	35	63	44	407	33	140		
90	Parr Peter	GBR	35	37	72	34	406	37	143	27	
101	Pintér József	HUN	35	40	75	40	445	29	444	34	
87	Hladnik Ignac	SLO	40	39	79	30	409	40	449	28	
91	McIver John	GBR	46	38	84	41	495	37	462	30	
82	Stafford Ian	GBR	38	45	83	44	452	31	463	37	
19	Tervaskangas Anssi	FIN	32	24	53	33	86				

TOP Uummannaq, where the seals catch halibut and the men play golf!

ABOVE Thomas Zeininger, my unconventional coach.

RIGHT The scoreboard at the European Mini-Golf Championships makes painful reading.

PREVIOUS PAGE Playing golf on ice – as you do.

ABOVE The boys from Cliftonville.

LEFT On the Swilcan Bridge at the home of golf, St Andrews.

ABOVE Steve Backley reveals the fun you can have with a medicine ball.

RIGHT Lesson number one from David Leadbetter – 'this is a golf club!'

TOP LEFT Lesson number two from Nick Faldo - 'don't hit my car.'

TOP RIGHT Showing Fanny Sunesson how not to be a caddie.

ABOVE Laura Davies rubs it in after her epic penalty competition victory.

ABOVE The man synonymous with golf, plus Jack Nicklaus.

ABOVE RIGHT Ernie Els and "pards" on the way to losing a fortune.

RIGHT With Justin Rose the day before humiliation at the Belfry.

BELOW The Benson & Hedges pro-am line-up: Geoff Irvine (left), Bernhard Langer (centre), Joe and Clive Woodward (right), plus one utter clown.

ABOVE Addicted to golf: with Scott Gorham, Nicko McBrain and Glyn Johns.

LEFT Having 'fun with the guys': Chip Thomson (centre) and friend Clay in New Orleans.

LEFT BELOW Steaming at the Narita Golf Club, with Tai Kawata.

TOP LEFT Tiger Woods meets 'umbrella man'.

TOP RIGHT God's golf bag, complete with tiger and kiwi covers.

ABOVE Tiger tips to a cub.

ABOVE RIGHT I believe I can fly with Earl Woods.

RIGHT Tiger Watch – more than a few interested observers at the US Open.

scan on my neck revealed three joints were virtually worn out, but rest, far less practice, and a switch from a regular putter to a broom, which means I no longer loathe putting, has changed my game for the better.

'When I had to go to qualifying school for the second time in 2000, I decided that if I failed to win back my card I'd give up playing on tour and become a golf teacher instead. I had no idea how to go about finding such a job, but I had made a decision that I couldn't face much more disappointment, time away from my family, and grind.'

His wife, Natalie, had to put up with Mackenzie's promises, year after year, that some time, some place, somehow, he would come good. 'I think she'd given up hope on me, although she never told me,' he admitted. 'I kept telling her I had the ability to win the tournament and she'd say: "Yes, OK." The longer it went on the less she believed me. I never actually asked her because I probably didn't want to hear the answer, but after 509 tournaments without a win you couldn't blame her for doubting me, could you? If that little voice inside my head had beaten me, it would probably have been my last chance to win. I would have taken it really badly.'

With the type of money on offer these days in golf, the majority of professionals are more than happy to play for the rewards. After 509 previous attempts, however, Mackenzie's goal was simple: to win. 'To be referred to as a champion meant everything to me. Sure, the cheque's been gratefully received, but after twenty years I needed to win something very badly indeed. To have done so means so much more than just picking up a big cheque.'

His was a heart-warming tale, and I could have listened to him happily chatting away for the rest of the afternoon were it not for the fact that my time to teeing off was close. Wishing Mackenzie good luck I strolled over to the putting green, via the players' hut that sheltered a few of us from a sudden burst of rain.

At the first tee my three partners had already assembled. The professional for the round was the top French golfer, Raphael Jacquelin, a relative newcomer to the tour whose five years had witnessed a steady rise up the rankings and money list.

Playing with us were PY Gerbeau and Peter Gethin. 'PY', short for Pierre-Yves, was a well-known public figure in Britain, having been formerly in charge of the ill-fated Millennium Dome. In fact, the British media referred to him as 'PY Gerbil' during this time. Now the chief executive of a leisure facility in nearby Milton Keynes, the 37-year-old proved to be an interesting and highly entertaining character. He recalled how he used to be a professional ice hockey player in France. 'We made it to the quarter-finals of the Winter Olympics in Calgary in 1988, which was almost unheard of,' he explained. 'Then I got a bad ankle injury when I was 24 and ended up in a wheelchair for a year. Just about the only thing I could do was swing a golf club, which is how I got into the game.'

Now playing off scratch PY was clearly a more than competent golfer, and a competitive one as well. When he hit the occasional duff shot out came those French swearwords, or a furious swing of his club against his golf bag. It didn't help, either, that on this same day the Government had announced that it would be giving away PY's beloved dome to a business consortium for free. 'Bastards,' was a phrase PY would utter repeatedly throughout the round.

The only other occasion when PY lost his cool came about after he had left his cap beside his golf bag, which was dumped along the fairway to save hauling it up a hill to the tee. When the sun shone straight into his eyes he asked if he could borrow mine, the England rugby cap Clive Woodward had presented to me after my Belfry horror show. When PY saw the English rose on the front he almost had apoplexy. 'I cannot believe I'm going to wear this,' he muttered. 'It just shows how desperate a man I've become.'

Gethin was equally interesting. A former Formula One driver, Gethin won his only Grand Prix at Monza in 1972, driving a BRM car. Superstars of the sport, such as Jackie Stewart, Graham Hill and Emmerson Fittipaldi, were all jostling for pole position in this era, but for one day Gethin would steal the limelight. His golf, incidentally, was about as good, or as bad, as mine.

A round of 99 on my part was hardly something to be ecstatic about following my 86 a fortnight before, but it was still a vast improvement on the Belfry. The conditions – a heady mixture of sunshine, wind and heavy showers – were tricky, not least on the greens, and the course was testing, but the day was still more relaxed and enjoyable than on my previous pro-am experience. Jacquelin was supportive, friendly and in good spirits. From Lyon, he dreamt of becoming a footballer until a teenage injury put paid to this. As he lived beside a nine-hole course he took up golf and discovered he had a natural aptitude for the game. Now aged 28, he was beginning to become noticed on the tour. You could argue that a young French professional golf player, a high-profile figure in the British leisure industry, a former Grand Prix racing driver and an author may not necessarily have too much in common, but on this pleasant day we were all speaking the language of golf. Or trying to. And that immediately brought this unlikely quartet together.

Out of 50 pro-am teams competing we finished with a score of 65, or seven under par, obtained from taking the best net score from the four of us per hole. My round had been acceptable, but not a patch on Sundridge Park. In particular, my chipping game, so good only the day before at Wentworth with Fanny Sunesson, deteriorated so rapidly that on the 17th green I had deposited so much sand from the bunker in attempting four times to free my ball that Peter Gethin remarked on how I had just created a beach on the edge of the green.

A lesson at the World of Golf on bunker play and chipping followed, in readiness for my third pro-am of the summer at the Compass Group English Open, at the Forest of Arden, just one week later. This time I was determined to put on a good show and actually play a significant part in my team's ultimate standing.

That was the intention. The reality was somewhat different. My playing partners for the day were Mark McNulty, the experienced and consistent money winner from Zimbabwe, together with Barry Richards, the former South African opening batsman, plus a friend of the cricketer.

When I sent my first drive from the first tee 200 yards down the middle of the fairway, and then followed this up with an approach shot leaving me 30 yards from the pin, things were looking good. A reasonable chip, a putt that flirted with the lip of the hole (a Bianca Jagger) and then a simple tap-in handed me a bogey. I should have felt satisfied with this, but the little man made an early visit to my head and gave me a rollicking for not scoring what should have been a par. Moreover, my partners pointed out that the putt for par would have scored a net birdie for the team, and three valuable points.

That was it. Although my chipping and putting remained solid enough, I somehow lost the ability to drive, save for a few unexpected exceptions. Out of 14 fairways I managed to knock four drives down the centre. The rest either sliced into the trees on the right or, worse still, were topped 20, 30 and sometimes even just a few yards in front of the tee.

The interesting company sometimes made me forget my woes. McNulty, in particular, was a colourful character, and no slouch either when it came to his career. Playing in his 25th season on the European Tour, the Zimbabwean had won 16 tournaments and had earned consistently big money for much of this time, including a tied second with the late Payne Stewart behind Nick Faldo at the 1990 St Andrews Open.

Although McNulty revealed his interest in impressionism, the piano and koi carp, what really made me sit up and listen were his laments on the state of affairs back in his native home, with Zimbabwe seemingly ignored by the world while the re-elected president Robert Mugabe continued to betray all semblance of democracy. Like many others, McNulty's family had suffered.

'My parents were driven out of their farm,' he explained. 'In the past 12 months they've aged ten years. Do you know, at a polling booth near to them sixty people turned out to vote. You wanna know what the result from that booth was? Mugabe won with a 35,000 majority.

'What pisses me off is how the British Government have totally ignored the situation in Zimbabwe. South Africa have turned a blind eye in return for the help the ANC received from Zimbabwe in their fight to end apartheid. Zimbabwe were right to help the ANC, of course, but that doesn't mean that now anything goes back home. It's a fucking shambles.'

We played in silence after this for a while as my play deteriorated. My driving, in particular, had slumped to the standard of total beginner. On this display I would have struggled to have won the Uummannaq golf challenge open only to the Inuit locals. In fact, it had become so bad that when faced with a charity challenge of hitting the 18th green in return for a dozen golf balls, Richards was telling me he'd bet me odds of 100-1 that I would fail. I did, naturally.

Although McNulty was terribly understanding and kind about it all, I felt pretty wretched afterwards. My chipping and putting had somehow made a potentially disastrous round bearable, but the driving had become an embarrassment. Once again I was asking myself what McNulty was thinking to himself as I topped balls into lakes, bunkers and trees. Miraculously, our team finished seventh out of 50 in the competition, just one place out of the prizes. If I had scored just one par out of the nine bogeys I recorded, we would have moved up to sixth place and McNulty would have earned the princely sum of £60 for his troubles. In terms of my contribution it would have been no worse if I had not bothered to turn up. As the day wore on, so the urge to explain to McNulty that I really was a better golfer than this became so strong that, eventually, it became unbearable. It was one thing telling Clive Woodward at the Belfry. It was another telling Mark McNulty. 'I'm a lot better than this normally, you know,' I pleaded with my professional, and immediately felt even worse as a result. Now I had scraped the very depths of the golfing barrel.

As I trudged disconsolately off the 18th green, I tried and failed to work out why, once again, my game had let me down. How could I have shot an 86, hitting all 14 fairways in the process, just a fortnight before, and then play as badly as this? Once you've learnt how to ride a bike, that's it. You can ride a bike for ever. So why isn't this the same in golf?

How can you smack the ball straight down the middle of the fairway with absolutely no bother whatsoever, and then have a total malfunction of the brain and forget completely how to drive for much of the rest of the round, to the extent that those around you must be wondering whether you have ever actually played this game before?

Perhaps, I reasoned, it was golf's way of reminding me that just because I shot an 86 within nine months of starting up the game, it doesn't mean to say it's always going to come as simply as that. I hoped that this was the case, although on the basis of my performance with Mr McNulty and company, I wondered whether I would ever score anywhere near to 86 again.

Maybe it was my clubs. After all, I had stuck with the same, modest half-set, topped up with a couple of clubs, since Royal Melbourne. The man with the answer would be Eric Rogers, a tour representative for Taylor Made Golf on the European Tour. I managed to set up some time with him that same evening through his wife, a rather useful contact named Fanny Sunesson.

Eric could be found where he is always found at a European Tour golf tournament, in the huge Taylor Made van, parked close to the driving range at the Forest of Arden. The sight of so many company trucks parked alongside each other reminded me of a Formula One Grand Prix paddock, where the likes of Ferrari, MacLaren and BMW-Williams all sport their massive motor homes. Here, in the West Midlands, Taylor Made, Mizuno, Titleist and Wilson all jockeyed for the best position as close to their golfers as possible.

The term 'van' is pretty misleading. 'It's 50-feet long, and can cost anything from £100,000 to £250,000, depending on its size,' Eric explained, in his southern Californian drawl. Originating from San Diego, Eric had moved across the pond to tour rep in Europe and spend more time with his caddie wife.

His job specification was clear. 'To get as many of our drivers in play on the tour as possible,' he explained. 'It's partly a game of marketing. The public want to use what the pros use. We have fifty per cent of the market right now, and have been market leaders for the past two years, but we also have to make sure our professionals are happy with the product.'

As a result, the vans arrive usually on a Sunday before the start of a tournament the following Thursday. Inside the van a veritable workshop can be found, where engineers and technicians are hard at work meeting the specific demands of each individual professional. Inside the Taylor Made van, for example, the likes of Retief Goosen, Ernie Els, Sam Torrance and Justin Rose all had their personal preferences displayed in the form of drivers in all shapes and sizes.

'These guys are so fine-tuned that they're looking for a one per cent improvement in their game,' Eric continued. 'Sometimes we take some loft off their irons, which reduces spin on the ball. Sometimes we're looking to produce a different and better ball launch. It's not just about marketing. We've got to identify problems and give a correct analysis.'

Over the years Eric's come across a few tales from within the van. 'In my first year on tour a professional came into the van and told us how, while lying in fourth position in the tournament with just three holes to play, his shaft snapped on his eight iron in mid-swing. He was penalised a stroke for this which, he worked out, ultimately cost him $28,000. His question to me was: "Are you willing to pay me $28,000?"' Eric's answer, by the way, is unprintable.

Another time a professional insisted on performing all his own mechanical work on his clubs. 'He was in a bunker, on national television, and as he hit the ball the head of his sand wedge flew right off on to the grass. Afterwards, we suggested he should quit doing his own work. Luckily, he saw the funny side of it.'

The fact Eric revealed that really made me think, underlined how most of us are not using anything like the right equipment. 'It is very, very common for the amateur to buy some clubs and then add to them,' he said. I was one of them. 'What they fail to realise is that a golf club should be specific and very individual. Fifty per cent of drivers used are incorrect for the user. In fact, they are detrimental to the player's golf.

You'll find the lofts and lies on at least three of your irons are not right. For instance, you'll find that you're more or less hitting seven and eight irons the same distance.' Again, that's me.

'The loft or the lie of the club will dictate the ball's flight. If the club's too upright the ball will hook. If it's too flat then you will slice. There should be four degrees between each club, but I bet you'll find that's not the case with yours.'

I produced my clubs rather nervously from my bag and watched as Eric pored over them, his face furrowed with concern as he began to take measurements. He looked up and exclaimed: 'Aha, just as I thought.' It emerged that the difference in degrees between my three and four, my four and five and my five and six was not enough, whereas between six and seven, and especially seven and eight, it was too much. 'You're not doing yourself any favours,' Eric concluded, as he bent my eight iron into slightly better shape using a vice.

As I hauled my set of clubs over my shoulder, I mentioned my inexplicable breakdown in the driving department to Eric and his Taylor Made colleagues, in the hope that they might come up with a technical reason that could easily remedy the problem. Instead, their explanation was the same illogical one that I had heard so often during the past few months.

'That's golf,' Eric said, with a world-weary look on a face that suggested he had been there himself many times before. 'It's one of the few remaining mysteries of this world. But I can guarantee you one thing. Just when you're close to your wit's end, the game will hand you back a bit of slack. You may be hating it right now, but it won't be long before you're totally in love with it again. Golf's the boss, and it has you completely in the palm of its hand.'

Eric was right. Love, hate, fear, none of these emotions is as powerful or as uncontrollable as golf. Now every part of my being had been consumed by this infuriating, frustrating, fantastic game.

16

The most public piss in history

Like a yo-yo dangling on a string, golf had toyed with me these past few months, but my latest low was in no danger of causing any permanent damage. How could it, when I knew the chance to travel to New York and see not only the US Open but a first, really close-up glimpse of the Tiger was just around the corner? I viewed this like a child in the final countdown to Christmas.

The 2002 US Open was staged in Farmingdale, Long Island, on a public course for the first time in the history of the tournament. By the time, a week after my last pro-am, I reached the famous Bethpage Black course, Tiger mania was already in full flow.

The US Open was no stranger to the elongated stretch of land jutting out and away into the Atlantic from Queens and the Bronx. In 1995, Shinnecock Hills had played host to the event, but Shinnecock was further out towards the more salubrious Hamptons, where the wealthier New Yorkers retreat for the weekend.

The point about Bethpage is that it was less than an hour's drive from John F. Kennedy Airport, and this meant that the Open, for the first time, was extremely accessible to the baying mob from a city that provides the greatest hecklers and cat-callers in the world.

According to Chip Thomson, who had been instructing Pete Jordan in the last couple of days, the spectators had been true to form.

Take the hapless Colin Montgomerie, for example. Having declared earlier in the year that he would never play golf in America again, after enduring years of abuse from the crowd over his weight, his demeanour, or his perceived resemblance to Mrs Doubtfire, he changed his mind and should have capitalised on *Golf Digest's* crusade to welcome the Scot with open arms by issuing thousands and thousands of 'Be Nice to Monty' badges for the public to wear. All it would have taken was a few acknowledgements to the spectators, maybe donning an 'I Love NY' baseball cap, as Nick Faldo cleverly if somewhat cheesily had done, or even wearing one of the badges himself. Instead, he traipsed round the course with his face furrowed.

On the Tuesday before the start of the US Open, someone shouted out from the crowd: 'Hey Monty, I've been especially nice to you. Can I get an autograph?' Montgomerie kept on walking with head bowed. The man yelled back: 'I hope you miss the f***ing cut, I never liked your fat f***ing arse anyway.' Harsh.

Tim Herron, the US Tour player, was also on the receiving end of some local, caustic 'wit'. Known as 'Lumpy' on tour because of his sizeable bulk, he was asked by a spectator if he could provide him with a ball. Herron explained that he was in the middle of his practice round, he didn't know how many balls he might need, and that if the spectator were to meet him at the 18th he'd happily hand over a ball then. The guy in the crowd shouted back: 'Hey, you fat f***, keep your balls, I don't need them, and I've only got one stomach.'

Corey Pavin, the winner at Shinnecock Hills in 1995, was reminded of where he would be playing his golf that week. Someone enquired: 'Hey, Corey. Can I have your autograph?' Pavin replied: 'Afterwards.'

The hopeful recipient hit back: 'OK, Corey, but don't forget, this ain't Shinnecock.'

It most certainly was not. This was New York and here, at the Bethpage Black, they said it exactly how they saw it.

The Black reminded me of the Scottish links courses at their worst, save for the treacherous winds that blow in off the North Sea. Everybody expected any score under par for the tournament would be close to winning the whole shebang. Dudley Hart, the American professional who would enjoy a good tournament, was asked if he would take a score of four over by the end of the week. Hart replied: 'On which day?'

Pete Jordan did not start well. After five holes he was four over, including a double bogey at the fifth which provoked an angry hurl of his putter towards his golf bag. Scoring a 76 after the first day was not so bad after that start, but it meant he would be struggling to make the cut after finishing the first day six over par.

Tiger, meanwhile, had to endure more attention than even he was used to. On the Monday, some three days before the start of the US Open, some 10,000 fans followed him round as he completed 18 holes in practice with fellow American and close friend, Mark O'Meara.

He arrived two hours before his tee-off time on the first day, stretching his svelte frame out of a black Buick, before marching straight past me with purpose through security and into the clubhouse. Within ten minutes he was out again and heading for the practice green for a few putts, to be greeted by a huge cheer from a crowd as large as most galleries at other golf tournaments. As his ball veered towards the hole, people were yelling: 'Get in the hole.' By the side of the green stood Steve Williams, his trusted caddie, who has emerged through his cut of Tiger's winnings as New Zealand's highest-paid sportsman. The Woods' bag stood upright with the word 'Buick' printed in big white letters all the way down its side. I noticed that the driver sported a large, furry tiger as a cover, and that one of the woods was covered by a furry kiwi.

'Did you get that cover in New Zealand, Steve?' I asked, as I sidled up next to him and pointed to the kiwi. I didn't think it was a totally unreasonable thing to say to the man, but Williams replied: 'Well, what other country would sell a kiwi cover?' That rather abruptly ended the conversation.

I had already decided to follow every shot of Tiger's first round, making use of the media armband that allowed me inside the ropes along the fairways and greens. Having never been presented with the opportunity to do so before, I was fascinated to watch the best golfer in the world ply his trade under such intense public scrutiny.

Arriving a few minutes before his allotted tee-off time of 1.35 p.m., Tiger received the biggest cheer of the day as he underwent a few stretching exercises and gazed ahead at the challenge that awaited him. For the first time in US Open history there were two starts to the round, at the first and the tenth tee, and Woods together with fellow American Chris Di Marco and Northern Ireland's Darren Clarke were due to begin their day at the 10th. This meant facing three monstrous par four holes and a par five to begin with, and an extremely testing start to the round.

Wearing a Nike-emblazoned white shirt, black tank top and black cap, together with grey slacks and black, spiked golfing shoes, Woods possessed the kind of aura rarely seen in sport, a presence alone that would intimidate anyone playing alongside him. His air was one of confidence laced with a ruthless arrogance, not necessarily an unattractive arrogance but more one that let it be known he was very much the boss. It clearly turned on a crowd, measuring four to five thick all along the fairway. Some I had been talking to had been queuing for four hours just to see the man drive off. For them, and for many of the remaining 40,000 out in force that day in Farmingdale, Tiger Woods was the US Open. For me, too, for that matter.

The man in question drove down the middle of the fairway to shouts of 'Go, Tiger.' I suppose he must have heard these reactions, but acted as if he were completely in his own time zone. His second approach shot to the green left the ball some ten feet from the hole and, once more, achieved a huge roar, this time from the waiting gallery seated around the 10th green. He missed the putt by pushing the ball slightly to the left of the hole, after meticulous preparation with his putter, but safely made par. Tiger's challenge for the US Open title he last won in 2000 had begun.

As he moved from green to tee so I, and around 40 journalists and 40 photographers, followed him from inside the ropes. This, with some justification, annoyed some of the paying spectators who had waited all day for this moment, and I was at great pains to remain crouched in order not to spoil the view.

Someone from the crowd shouted out 'Jesus' as the ball fizzed over our heads from Tiger's drive at the 11th tee. I think this was a reaction to the way the ball shot forward like a bullet, although he might have been referring to the golfer. Whatever the case, as Woods marched purposefully down the fairway so we followed, accompanied by a small army of state troopers and NYPD officers. Clarke lit up the first of his trademark cigars and surveyed the mayhem for a moment. Both he and Di Marco had not started well, although how could they amid the circus around them? Tiger's approach shot left him with a seven-foot putt for birdie, which he missed by the narrowest of margins. An easy par left him level after two, and so far, there had not been a flicker of emotion on his handsome, focused face. This was his work, his business. This is what Tiger Woods did.

Before driving off at the 12th Woods chomped on a banana, the first of three he would consume during the round, A member of the crowd shouted out: 'It's a tiger sighting.' A kid beside him squeaked: 'Tiger for President.' The small boy would have to be careful not to put ideas into the player's head. Someone else turned the attention to caddie Steve Williams. 'Hey, Stevie,' he shouted. 'Can I carry your bag?'

After Tiger's drive, Williams uttered the first of many barked orders to a marshal some hundred yards away from where Woods would be playing his second shot. 'Would you stop moving there, please,' shouted Williams, in his unmistakable New Zealand twang that meant that the last word always ended on a higher pitch than the rest of the sentence. Meanwhile Tiger's mother, Kutilda, and his girlfriend, a blonde Swedish girl called Elin Nordegren, who had been previously employed by Jesper Parnevik as a nanny to his four children, watched from afar, perched on a golf cart. The approach shot presented Woods with another birdie chance. This time the ball dallied with the lip of the hole. Although he would probably not know this, Tiger had just suffered from a Bianca.

After three solid pars, Woods' first bad shot of the day came with his drive off the 13th tee. The ball pulled to the left and into the deep rough, striking a spectator in the left shoulder blade. The crowd gathered round the ball in a semi-circle and stared at it as if an alien had just deposited it from a spaceship. Woods failed to apologise to the spectator, one Bob Pietrobono, a software salesman from Pennsylvania, instead choosing to chide the writers and photographers who had gathered close to the ball oblivious to the fact that Clarke was in an identical position a few yards behind. While the big, burly Ulsterman shook his head and smiled wryly at the pandemonium, Tiger came to his aid: 'Darren is right behind you guys,' he said, before ushering them out of the way.

After both Woods and Clarke had escaped the rough, the local reporters set upon Pietrobono in a wild frenzy to claim the story. 'Nobody at home is going to believe me,' said the lucky man who had just been hit by Woods' ball. Pity he hadn't been knocked out by a blow to the head, or perhaps decapitated by Tiger's famed driver. That, he would have realised as he made his excited way home that evening, would have made him even more famous.

Meanwhile, back on the fairway, Woods slightly over-hit his third shot, leaving the ball nestling in the light rough on the edge of the green, 15 feet from the pin. No matter. Tiger sank the putt to a huge cheer and marched on to the 14th one under after four holes.

The par three 14th offered some light relief from the testing and eventful first few holes. Woods' drive with an iron left him ten feet from the hole. His putter was clearly on form because the subsequent putt found the hole without even touching the sides. It was as if he had steered it home using some kind of remote control device. Two birdies in two holes.

Then came the most celebrated bathroom stop in the history of sport.

En route to the 15th, Tiger stopped at a Portakabin to answer the call of nature. I suppose the reason why he can't have a leak beside a tree like the rest of us on a golf course is because the rest of us don't keep 4,000 watching spectators, plus an audience of many millions on NBC TV as close company. Anyway, it just so happened that as I was literally the nearest person to him when the marshals held their hands up high to allow him to make his impromptu stop, so I had the closest view, which I will now duly report to you as a world exclusive.

Tiger was in and out in under a minute, which was impressive. For the duration of his piss the crowd outside waited, silenced by the drama of the occasion. Quite what they were expecting is anyone's guess – white smoke from the top of the Portakabin to announce the next Pope? George Bush and Vladimir Putin emerging with Woods from the john, shaking hands? What I can tell you is that throughout his time inside the Portakabin, Woods kept his head incredibly still. This is a fact because although I couldn't see, nor wanted to see, anything going on from below his shoulders, I could see his head through the window which ran along the top of the makeshift loo. I have to say his bathroom style is similar to his golf swing: legs balanced well, straight head, eyes focused and looking down, and I guess a good grip. When he emerged Woods was met by another huge and rather merry cheer from the crowd. One shouted out: 'Wash your hands, Tiger.' Tiger smiled wryly and responded: 'Are you guys clapping because I'm potty-trained?'

Everyone laughed, like they do on Wimbledon's Centre Court when a top tennis player can say almost anything and still receive mass guffawing. The truth was that Tiger might as well have said: 'Look, why don't you all sod off and quit gawping at me taking a piss, you sad bastards.' You can bet everyone present would still have split their sides.

By now I had grown to understand something of the perennial spotlight cast over Woods. On the evidence of the first round at Bethpage this had reached ridiculous proportions. The game of golf is hard enough when it is just you battling against yourself to produce a decent score on a quiet, Tuesday morning. Just how many times must you multiply this, then, to get an idea of the kind of pressure Woods is under. Yet he is not only used to it, he appears to gorge off it. The more attention, the better he is. I was witnessing at first hand the man in his element. No other golfer came close to Woods when it came to personal impact on a golf course.

His drive off the 15th found the rough again, and from the resulting second shot out of the long grass, a large divot flew through the air and landed on a woman's shoulder. She was almost orgasmic with joy and promptly put the clump of mud in her handbag. It made me think that if there's money or stories to be made merely from a clump of mud driven by Tiger's iron, maybe I should turn back and stalk out the Portakabin.

As Tiger faced a 30-foot putt on the green, Williams turned his attention to the photographers. 'Can you guys get settled, please,' he shouted. Woods duly made the par safe with a third putt that stopped just short of the hole, as an airship hovered above filming the moment for posterity.

At the 16th he drilled another long drive left off the fairway and into rough. Not for the first time he got lucky. Either that or he employs the local grasshoppers. From the tee, Woods looked to be in deep rough, and therefore deep trouble. The ball, however, was sitting up in a favourable lie on closer examination. A pitch on to the fairway left a further pitch and a putt for a par. This looked on until a shout from a man perched up a nearby tree, a split-second before Tiger's putter made contact, seemed to unsettle the player. The end result was his first bogey of the day, and an angry stare towards the tree.

The par three 17th was negotiated safely, although Tiger needed a putt using a three wood out of the light rough at the back of the green to make the subsequent par simple enough. At the 18th, just for once, Clarke and Di Marco stole some momentary limelight. While they drove long and hard down the middle of the fairway, Woods struck another wayward drive that resulted in finding yet more rough. His playing partners strode down the centre of the fairway, laughing and joking with each other. I was too far away to hear what they were saying but, at a guess, they might have been enjoying a moment where they were in a comfortable position, and Tiger was up the proverbial creek. Woods produced a shot he had no right to play, landing the ball on the green close to the pin, and with the simple birdie achieved he made his way to the first tee which, on this strange day, would be his tenth, back at two under.

By this stage we were well into the afternoon and the crowd were growing noticeably more raucous as the beers were sunk. Woods received an appreciative roar as he pulled out of his bag his driver and removed his symbolic Tiger driver-cover. Eventually Williams was required, once more, to ask for quiet, this time in the stand. The ball was smacked over the trees and around the dog-leg to the right to land on the fairway. His second shot, a pitch, landed too long and into the rough at the edge of the fast green, and when his third left him with a seven-foot putt for par, a bogey looked a distinct possibility. Woods, whose putting had been exemplary all afternoon, made a difficult teaser look incredibly easy as another bogey was avoided. Later, he would admit that saving pars with long putts was more satisfying to him than making birdies.

En route to the second hole Tiger stopped for a second toilet stop. This time the crowd had been channelled away from him, which therefore avoided another high-profile stint in a Portakabin and, indeed, a first-hand account from me. His tee shot using a two iron set up a second approach shot with a low iron and a birdie putt, which he sunk without any bother at all. Three under now, after eleven holes.

The par three third and the par five fourth were both achieved, although Woods for once missed a birdie putt on the latter, which would ultimately prove not to be costly. Hole number five was also parred as Tiger marched on towards the par three sixth. Keeping up with Tiger was proving to be difficult, not least because while he was walking on the close-cut fairway, I was battling my way through long, thigh-length grass and bunkers. A machete would have been useful, although with all the NYPD officers surrounding me, it might not have been too wise to have produced one. Although his drive was good, his second shot landed over the green and in the light rough. The resulting chip set up a difficult putt for par which, just for once, he missed, As it became apparent that the ball would not find the hole, someone shouted 'Yes!' from the crowd, provoking a second, annoyed glance from the golfer.

There was more bother at the seventh. In the midst of Tiger's backswing at the tee a photographer's shutter could clearly be heard. Click, click, click. Woods stopped in his tracks, turned round to the offending snapper, and shouted: 'Oh, come on!' He regrouped and proceeded to smack the resulting drive 300 yards down the centre of the fairway. The approach shot was errant, leaving him a difficult putt to make par. The gallery was noisy, the climate hot and humid, and another dropped shot would leave him standing at one under. Woods seemed to have the eyes of the world watching his every move. No matter, the putt was sunk and we all moved on to the 8th or, in this case, 17th tee.

As if to underline the fact that the US Open had already become something of a Tiger-watch as soon as Woods had safely putted for a par three, half the gallery appeared to get up on their feet and follow the man over to the 9th. Di Marco and Clarke, meanwhile, still had to putt out themselves, but very few seemed interested in this, even though they lay 13th and 14th in the world rankings respectively, and were therefore very accomplished players in their own right.

At the final hole of the day, the 9th, Woods climaxed in perfect fashion by hitting his drive down the centre of the fairway, sending an approach shot with a high iron over the pin before backspin dragged the ball to 15 feet of the hole. In true, showmanship style, Tiger rammed the ball home and produced his biggest show of emotion all day by pumping his fist quite vigorously, as the gallery went wild with appreciation. Although we would not be sure at the time, a first day 67 would prove to be the vital round of the tournament, and for me, a stunned observer, I had witnessed from close up just exactly why Tiger Woods dominates golf. Nothing, it seemed, fazed the man. Realising that, in contrast everything appeared to faze me on a golf course, was a humbling experience. The leaderboard already had the expected name right at the top, and nothing would change over the course of the next three days.

On the Friday Woods followed up his first round excellence with a 68, leaving him some three shots clear of nearest challenger Padraig Harrington, and seven ahead of third-placed Sergio Garcia. Some big names had missed the cut, including Colin Montgomerie and the British

Open champion, David Duval. Pete Jordan was also heading for home after adding a 79 to his first round 76. Felix Casas, from the Philippines, carded a second round 92, which made me wonder idly whether if I, playing at my best, could beat him, playing at his worst.

On the Saturday morning, outside the clubhouse, I saw Jos Vanstiphout sitting on a bench. He was working his mind games on Ernie Els, among others, and was waiting for the South African to emerge. For some reason Jos had taken to me, slapping me on the back, laughing and referring to me as a 'Crazy English son of a bitch'. I told him that was a bit rich coming from a certifiable lunatic like himself. Fanny Sunesson joined us, peeled a banana, and told me that with my estimated 18-handicap there was no way I could break 100 on the Bethpage Black course. Before I had time to protest, Vanstiphout chipped in: 'Never mind 100, I say 120. In fact, if you break 120 I'll give you a crate of champagne. Moet & Chandon for 120. Dom Perignon for 100.'

A couple of caddies overheard this, Ricci Roberts, who carried the Els' bag, and Jimmy Johnson, who caddied for Nick Price. Incidentally, it is not a prerequisite to be a caddie with the sort of name that used to encourage people to approach you at a seaside resort claiming £5 for identifying you, but it helps. They threw in their thoughts to the debate as well, insisting that I stood no chance of scoring two figures, and not much of a chance of beating 120. Before we knew it US Open officials and more caddies became involved, so that by the time Nick Faldo arrived on the scene quite a small commotion was taking place.

'What's going on?' Faldo asked. Fanny and Jos explained the story and asked Faldo whether he thought I could break 100. His response was to let out a huge laugh. 'I'll give you some golf psychology,' he added. 'You don't stand a sodding chance.'

He went on to shoot 66 that day, the best round of the whole tournament, and his best-ever score in all the US Opens he has ever competed in. Woods shot a par 70, and although for a while the likes of Phil Mickelson and Garcia were closing in on him, two late birdies from

171

Tiger meant that by the end of the third day's play he had increased his lead to four strokes. It made the outcome a mere formality. Twenty-four hours later Tiger Woods was crowned US Open champion for a second time, after a two over par 72 handed him a final advantage of three strokes from his nearest challenger, Mickelson. In doing so he won his eighth major title, joining Tom Watson in the all-time list, leapfrogging the likes of Arnold Palmer, Gene Sarazen, Harry Vardon, Sam Snead and Bobby Jones. Part two of the Grand Slam attempt had been secured. Faldo's 73 finished him on a highly credible tied fifth, which suggested that his comeback was continuing to fare well.

The following morning, mindful of the crate of champagne riding on the bet, and hoping to prove Nick Faldo, Fanny Sunesson and half the US Open caddies wrong, I made my enquiries concerning a round on the Bethpage Black course. No go, I was told. The course would be closed for a further eight days due to the heavy rain and the huge crowds that had trampled all over it. This prevented me from proving everyone right, of course, and gave me the chance to cling to the argument that I might, just might, have proven them all wrong.

Whether studying the Tiger master-class on that first day would have helped me at all remained to be discovered, but I had never seen anyone make this infuriating game look so ridiculously easy as the new US Open champion. As a personal experience, watching the man perform was like, I imagined, watching Nureyev dance, or hearing Sinatra sing live in his heyday. It was effortless, it was awe-inspiring and it was beautiful. Really beautiful.

The tight security at Bethpage had made even a few seconds' conversation with the man impossible, but after the US Open I knew, more than ever before in my ascent of the golfing mountain, that the summit had to be, and could only be, Tiger Woods.

17

The Golden Bear

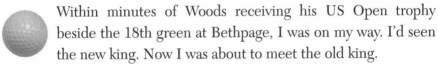 Within minutes of Woods receiving his US Open trophy beside the 18th green at Bethpage, I was on my way. I'd seen the new king. Now I was about to meet the old king.

If you go up into the north Georgia hills towards Dahlonega and the heavily wooded Chestatee River Valley, you'll find a town best known for the gold discovered in the surrounding mountains two centuries ago. On the outskirts, Birch River Golf Club can be found, the latest venture from the man they call 'the Golden Bear'.

It is always something of a culture shock to travel between the north and the south of the United States. The night before I had been in the noise and brashness of New York. Now I found myself in the south, where everything and everyone was a little slower. At the Atlanta Olympics I discovered just how big a rift there still seems to be between the north and south. A writer from a Chicago newspaper explained to me why so much of the organisation had gone awry: 'You're dealing with the Confederacy,' he said. He wasn't joking, either.

The record books provide irrefutable evidence that Jack Nicklaus is the greatest golfer of all time. His 18 wins in majors leave him far and away the most successful player in the big four tournaments in history, some seven championships ahead of second-placed Walter Hagen, with a first major win at the US Open in 1962, and a last at the Masters some

24 years later in 1986. In the process Nicklaus has most Masters' victories to his name with six, most US Open wins with four, and ties with Harry Vardon for most US PGA championship victories on five.

Few doubt that, in time, Woods will surpass this astonishing record, but for now, Jack William Nicklaus remains the man. The Golden Bear was officially to open his own golf course at Birch River GC mid-morning, hence my early start from Atlanta. Scott Tolley, who works for Jack from his North Palm Beach offices, had invited me along for the day, to see the great man at work, and to spend some time with him. If there were two people, and two people alone, anyone would wish to meet in the game of golf then they would be the best of them all: Woods from today's era, and Nicklaus from yesterday's.

For somebody who usually arrives at most events late, I surpassed myself by turning up a full hour early. This proved to be a big, though understandable mistake because, further to the south-east of the country, a minor drama had taken place. The Nicklaus private jet was forced to return to the east Florida coast after pressurisation problems were experienced in the cabin and cockpit. With the death of American golfer Payne Stewart, from similar circumstances, still fresh in the memories of everyone connected to the game, the mood in Dahlonega was one of both relief and disappointment. The rehashed schedule for the day meant that Nicklaus was unlikely to appear much before mid-afternoon.

It was beautiful here, if sticky and muggy with heat. Around the course were hardwood forests of oaks, maples and hickories interspersed with wild flowers, blackberries and migratory bird habitats. A sign close to the entrance made novel reading, especially to an English golfer who gets excited seeing a rabbit nibbling grass on the fairway: 'Please do not feed the bears', it read, referring to the large, furry and actually rather dangerous black ones who live up the slopes of the valley.

Scott and Jim Mandeville, the official Nicklaus photographer, sat in the clubhouse as the hot morning turned into an even hotter afternoon. 'Jack's a workaholic,' Tolley explained. 'I reckon he flies over 500 hours in a year. He can get real bored quickly. I can tell you, I've been to over sixty of these kind of events, and this is the first time ever that anything like this has happened to him.' Scott fixed me a stare for a while, before saying what his expression had already suggested. 'You must have jinxed him!'

Maybe it was all some kind of a prank. Apparently, the whole Nicklaus family are into practical jokes, often with Scott bearing the brunt of them. 'Oh, I've had his son Jackie put crabs down my back,' Tolley recalled, with the kind of weary expression an over-tired parent gives to a small child. 'Once, in the Dominican Republic, Jack asked me to fetch out a speech I'd left in my bag. When I placed my hand inside, a huge black beetle clasped its jaws round my wrist. I was in agony, but Jack and his son were almost crying with laughter.'

The club was beginning to lose some of the guests for the day, who needed to get back to whatever they had to do in the afternoon. The marquee, where we had all been wined, dined and shaded from the north Georgia sun that beat down on to the lush golf course, was beginning to empty. Of those who stayed some were entertained by an impromptu putting contest on one of the greens, and a longest drive competition. I got to talking to the head professional's family. Jeff Meier's wife explained how they had a bet riding on what shirt Jack Nicklaus would wear for his appearance once he finally arrived. His mother had ironed four shirts the night before in readiness, offering Nicklaus the choice between a yellow top, a blue one, and two blue and white stripy ones. A dollar was riding on the outcome.

At three o'clock an excited cheer was heard from outside the main entrance to the clubhouse. Local officials started to run about in all directions. Jack had finally arrived, after a 45-minute car journey from Gainesville Airport, once his repaired jet had flown to Georgia from North Palm Beach. Although Nicklaus appeared initially tired and hassled, by the time he re-emerged from the locker room in one of the blue and white stripy tops, he was smiling and waving. Amid the general cacophony of noise greeting the man's entrance, a smaller, personal cheer was heard from the Meier family. Mrs Meier had won the dollar.

The proceedings would begin with some warm-up swings in front of a crowd of around one hundred people seated on temporary stands constructed around the practice ground. Nicklaus, with a small microphone pinned to his shirt, began by explaining the problems with his plane, and then moved on to how, at 62 years of age, his back was causing him all sorts of trouble.

Starting with a couple of gentle swings that sent the ball no more than 60 yards, Nicklaus was quick to respond to a shout from the spectators suggesting that he played like Tiger. 'Well, he does what I'm trying to do,' he said, to immediate applause. 'He also does what I used to do. In fact he does it better than I've ever seen. I don't think he'll ever have a back problem like me. He's an amazing young man, as solid a golfer as I've ever seen. I wish him a lot of luck.'

It had taken less than five minutes for the 'T' word to have been brought up. Everyone, it seemed, wanted to know the former king's view of his successor, from the man who dominated golf in the late 1960s and 1970s about the man dominating the game today.

Eventually Nicklaus returned to his previous self-deprecation. 'Look at my back swing,' he said. 'My hands are nearly up to my waist. Wait until I reach for my driver. I'll be hitting 190 yards with that.' The comment received another round of applause and laughter, although as I clapped I reckoned 190 was perfectly acceptable.

The original plan was for Nicklaus to play the full 18 holes but, what with his late arrival and his bad back, this was revised. The ribbons were removed from the first tee and placed instead across the 18th, from where the Golden Bear opened the course officially, by cutting the ceremonial tape with a pair of scissors and making a short speech. Then, to the delight of all onlookers, he first drove a ball with a copy of the wooden driver he used to such effect in the early 1970s, before making an interesting comparison by emulating the shot using a state-of-the-art driver from today. The difference in distance in length measured something in the region of 80–100 yards.

With the formalities completed, some fifty-odd folks, as they say in these parts, followed Nicklaus while he played the back nine holes, although this number dropped considerably the further we strode away from the clubhouse. Like the pied piper Nicklaus led and the rest followed like a group of infatuated disciples.

For much of the opening holes he was inundated with autograph requests on hats, photos, posters, books and all kinds of paraphernalia. Either he failed to see or decided to turn a blind eye to the same people returning time after time with new caps or books to sign. Some of the autographed exhibits would sit proudly in people's homes. Others were clearly going to be sold. Even on a day such as this, money was being made. In fact, the only time Jack refused to sign was when golf balls were thrust towards him. 'If you knew the number of lawsuits Arnold [Palmer], myself and Tiger have gone through when it comes to signing golf balls, you'd understand why I don't any more,' he said, by way of an explanation that left most looking puzzled.

At the 12th, a par four with a sharp dog-leg to the right, Nicklaus smacked a beautiful drive straight and far but deep into a bunker. 'I've got a major driving problem,' he announced, as he set out for the bunker. 'I keep hitting it straight.' When his second shot from the bunker landed within five feet of the pin, he received the loudest applause of the day. 'You can still do it, Jack,' someone shouted out. 'You're still the greatest.'

In between the 12th green and the 13th tee I stopped for a drink. 'You've gotta try one of the cookies,' Scott Tolley suggested. On closer inspection I discovered that they were in the shape of a bear, a golden bear. I bit the head off one and munched away. 'You've just decapitated the Golden Bear,' Scott said, in mock horror.

Bill Clinton made a surprise return to the fray shortly after this. After being told various stories about the former President of the United States, both at New South Wales Golf Club in Australia and then at Ballybunion in Ireland, I had not heard a Clinton story since. At least, until now.

'I was playing golf with Bill Clinton and Gerald Ford,' Nicklaus recalled, which in name-dropping terms was fairly impressive. 'At the first tee Clinton hooks it way out to the left. I said: "Here, take another shot." Big mistake. He took about 60 mulligans during the round. It took six hours, 25 minutes, and at the end there wasn't another soul on that golf course.' He paused as people laughed and clapped, before adding: 'That's the absolute truth'.

'Anyway, the next day we played again. At the first tee he hit a good drive and parred the hole. At the second I said to him: 'Mr President, let's play golf today.' He only took three mulligans that day and as we walked towards the 18th tee he turned round to me and said: 'You know, Jack. If I make this par it's the first time I've ever broken 80.'

Once the laughter had finally died down Nicklaus continued with his round. Even though this was a leisurely late afternoon and early evening exhibition, it was interesting to note the competitiveness that remained within him. If a six-foot putt was missed due to a misreading of the lie, the attempt was reproduced over and over again until the man was content he had got it right. It transpired later that the following day he would be playing an exhibition round of golf in Kansas City with Arnold Palmer, Gary Player, Tom Watson and Lee Trevino. 'We're about 400 years old between us,' he declared. 'Watson will want to play, Palmer will try to play, Player will be grinding it and Trevino will be talking all the way round the course. There's gonna be some golf, and some goofin' around, too.'

At the 18th, before he holed his final putt of the round, Nicklaus made a couple of short speeches, thanking the organisers of the day and those instrumental in the creation and upkeep of the golf course, and wishing all the members present much fun over the years to come. It was a highly polished performance from a 62-year-old man who had endured a long and stressful day, and a memorable occasion for all those who had stuck it out during the unforeseen delay to spend a few hours with the greatest player of golf in the history of the game.

Scott Tolley had already introduced me to Jack much earlier in the day and, although we had exchanged a few words during the round, I was hoping I could spend some time alone with him later, away from the madding crowds who simply refused to leave the man alone. After we posed for photos together on the 18th, Jack invited me into the locker room for a private conversation as he changed and freshened up before heading off back to Gainesville Airport and on to Kansas. I felt slightly fraudulent standing alone in Jack's locker room, considering I'd only picked up a golf club in anger twelve months previously. It was as if Pavarotti had heard me singing in the shower and asked me to duet with him.

As I stood there, observing his holiness slump on to a bench and mop his perspiring brow, Nicklaus guessed my thoughts. Did he have to traipse around the country making these tiring appearances? 'Today's part of what I do,' he offered, before I had uttered a word. 'For much of my life I've gone out to play golf with the objective of being the best there's ever been. If that's your goal, and you go on to achieve it, then you also have to accept the responsibilities that go with it.'

He's not yearning for a little space in the late autumn of his life? Being touched and patted, slapped and followed for every step of his day is bearable? 'Absolutely,' he replied, slipping off his blue and white shirt that had made the Meier family one dollar richer. 'I don't consider it a burden. I consider it a responsibility. I also understand why golf fans do it. Heck, when I play a round with a sportsman I enjoy watching, I want to talk to them, too, ask them a whole lot of questions, and listen to what they have to say for themselves.'

So he's contented with his lot, then? 'Well, it's the lot I have, I suppose. If I'm honest I would have liked to have won more than I did.'

I let out a purposeful chuckle at this point and suggested that 18 majors and the tag of being the most successful golfer of all time was pretty good going.

'Oh, don't get me wrong,' he said, accepting my point with a wry smile. 'But when I look back I realise I had the opportunity to have won a whole lot more. If I'd focused on the game, like Tiger does today, I would have done, too. Tiger's more intent on being a golfer than anyone I've ever seen play golf. That's where his results come from. His and his father's focus.

179

'For me, golf was and remains a game. Just a game. Far more important to me is my family. (He is married to Barbara, has five children, 13 grandchildren, and another two on the way.) The reason why I worked so hard was for my family, but I never wanted my kids to grow up and leave for college without ever knowing they had a dad. My kids all knew me, and they all wanted to spend some time with me.'

What Jack said next really makes you ponder about what might have been. 'This approach and philosophy probably cost me 10 more majors as a golfer.' He waited for a few seconds while I digested this information. Ten majors? That would have put him on 28 majors, some 17 more than Hagen. Even Tiger Woods would be hard-pushed to get close to that figure. Nicklaus would have become untouchable.

Jack had not finished his point, however. 'If that's all it cost me in order to have enjoyed the relationships I have had with my wife and kids, then that's a very small price to pay. It really is.'

So, no regrets? The Golden Bear shook his head before splashing water from a sink on to his face and towelling himself down. 'After all, who really cares?' he continued, eventually. This comment drew another small gasp from his questioner. Who cares? Who cares? Well, how about the millions of golfers and golf fans over the past half-century? 'OK, so the golfing public may care, and the golfing historians and all that crap. It's all very nice but, to me, what really matters is what kind of a human being you are, what have you contributed to society, and what kind of a family have you raised? I'd like to think I've contributed to the record books, and to the enjoyment and fun of the golfing public, but what I've tried to do for my family is far more important to me.'

It was, of course, a very fair point and an ironic one, too. Here we had the very best the game of golf had ever witnessed – at least until now, that is – admitting that no matter what he had achieved in an area that has created so many millions of obsessive followers, on the greater scale of things it really did not come to much, not compared to what is really important in life.

When he looks at today's players, especially Woods, did he not regret he hadn't been born forty years later? 'Uh-uh,' he replied, as he leant forward over his thighs to tie up his shoelaces. 'I'm happy when I played. Truly. Who knows what I might have achieved if I'd been playing today? I might have dominated the game. I certainly would have won tournaments because I can't imagine any champion from any era not winning today. You look at the likes of Bobby Jones, Walter Hagen, Sam Snead, Byron Nelson. They all would have won because they were champions and they would have worked out what to do and how to win. Tiger is the same. He would have been winning fifty years ago, for sure.

'Making comparisons between any of the champions throughout the eras is like comparing apples and oranges, though. They're not playing the same game today as they did in my day, and I wasn't playing the same game that the likes of Jones and Hagen played. Time moves on and with it technology. Everything's changed, from the balls and clubs, to the courses and the spotlight. Sure, I lived in the goldfish bowl and still do to a degree, but not like Tiger does today. He seems to be able to handle it pretty well. I find him an extremely impressive young man. But he hasn't had a great deal of adversity yet in his career. It might be interesting to see how he reacts to it if things start to go wrong. At the moment he hasn't really got any challengers, has he?'

I recalled my time with Peter Thomson in Melbourne the summer before, an adversary of Nicklaus who won the British Open for a record five times but found his deterioration as a golfer hard to bear. With the Nicklaus back playing up so much, I asked if the man who once dominated the game in the way Woods does today was accepting it with a degree of resignation and an outlook that he had enjoyed an extremely good run.

'Actually, it's been a big blow to me to realise that my powers are waning,' he admitted, now fully dressed and ready to leave. 'I see no reason why I couldn't match the top guys today, if it wasn't for the fact that I don't possess the power any more. Even this week I've been working every day with physios on my back. I've gotten weak in the areas of support.

'The funny thing is that I can do anything and everything I want to with my body except play good golf. I can play tennis. No problem. I can scuba-dive, fish, hunt, walk. I can play all the things I want except for golf, and that really hurts me. As a result I can't really see me playing too much tournament golf from now on. I could still play competitively on the senior tour from time to time, but most of it is behind me now.'

So the playing days of a living legend are numbered, then? 'Let's put it this way,' the Golden Bear answered as he headed for a waiting car. 'I'll most probably stop completely if I can't play well enough to my liking.'

I'd been mulling over my head all day whether I should tell him of my golfing career, and whether he'd be remotely interested. As he shook my hand, it all gushed out.

'Er, Jack, actually I, um, only started playing golf a year ago and I'm down to a 15 handicap. What do you think?' This, if you go with my 86 in Kent, was strictly true, although if any of my pro-am playing partners had heard this remark they would have keeled over with mirth.

Nicklaus, true to professional form, did not bat an eyelid. 'Hey, that's great,' he said, putting on a well-used and crafted expression on his face and a tone in his voice that suggested he was genuinely interested. 'Maybe we'll have a game one day.'

I laughed. He laughed. I thought about adding: 'How's Tuesday week looking, in the morning, for you?' but thought better of it.

A small party had assembled to see the man off. As Jack was driven away in a people carrier, the first of a convoy of three, he gave a regal wave to the happy folk of Birch River Golf Club, who responded with a mass of waving arms and cheers. Only when the car had turned the corner and was out of sight did people finally turn round and make their way back to the clubhouse.

A couple to whom I had been talking earlier stopped and enquired: 'Have you just spent all that time alone with Jack?'

I confirmed this, trying to appear nonchalant about the whole event.

'Are you a golfer, then?' they asked.

'Yes,' I replied. 'I suppose I am.' Again, not strictly an untruth.

I felt happier than at any previous time since my decision to embrace the game of golf. Yesterday it had been Tiger, from close up too. Today it had been the man even Tiger idolises. Even a year ago I would have appreciated the significance of Jack Nicklaus and Tiger Woods. Twelve months on, though, as I turned the ignition key in my car, switched on the local blues radio station, and put on my sunglasses, I came to the contented conclusion that life could not get better than this.

18

Paralysis by analysis

That night I took the short flight from Atlanta to Orlando and checked in at the Animal Kingdom Lodge at Walt Disney World for the third leg of my latest American trip. Duncan Wardle, whom I knew when he worked in London, was now at the marketing office at WDW and had offered to put me up at what was still a relatively new hotel.

In the morning I was aroused by a bizarre wake-up call delivered by a certain M. Mouse. 'Hee hee hee,' he squeaked, leaving me to momentarily wonder in my state of semi-arousal if I had just become part of a Disney film. Taking tea on the balcony, I stared out towards an animal reserve directly below me. There, gazing nonchalantly at an Englishman naked save for a towel wrapped around his waist, were giraffes, zebras, ostriches, pelicans, impalas and kudus. I had already spotted a tiger and a golden bear over the course of the previous two days.

I had come to Orlando for a very good reason. David Leadbetter, the most renowned golf coach in the world had, in a moment of madness during the US Open up in New York, agreed to take a look at my swing and offer his advice. I use the word madness because the clientele of the man they call 'The Lead' is a veritable who's who of world golf. Not for the first time I was wading into water way too deep for the likes of a mortal such as me, but having just been in the company of Tiger Woods, tenuously, and now Jack Nicklaus, my hunger to learn and improve was greater than at any previous time.

The Leadbetter complex can be found in Champion's Gate, an impressive enclave just a 20-minute drive from the Disney theme parks. Jorge, a Hispanic, guitar-strumming cab driver, took me there and insisted on staying for what turned out to be many hours, before depositing me back at Orlando Airport. He seemed unperturbed by the prospect of a long wait. 'I have many tunes to learn,' he explained, lighting up a cigarette and resting his acoustic on his knee.

Although the main reception area is in a large building not dissimilar to the Beverly Hills hotel depicted on the cover sleeve of The Eagles' album, *Hotel California*, Leadbetter lived a short buggy's drive away beside the driving ranges, bunkers, chipping areas and putting greens, in a smaller complex of offices.

His office walls were inundated with signed photographs. Over the top of Greg Norman was scrawled: 'David, never have I known anyone have the knowledge as you did. Thanks for all your help and advice on my game, but most of all thanks for your friendship.' It was signed simply 'Greg Norman'. Nick Price had added his contribution to his own picture. 'David, one more time? Thanks for all your help and support – Nick.' And Ernie Els had contributed as well. 'David, thanks for all your time. It's been a lot of fun so far. Ernie.'

The photos were vying for wall space with framed magazine covers of Leadbetter, the most notable being *Golf Digest*, while shelves sported an array of books written by the coach, videos and various gadgets aimed at improving your putting, chipping and swing.

Two American professionals, aiming to play in the Canon Greater Hartford Open in Connecticut that week, had turned up unannounced at Champion's Gate, which meant that I had to bide my time. Leadbetter was happy to see me, but not at the cost of two visiting professionals.

I picked up one of his books, entitled *100% Golf – Unlocking Your True Golf Potential*, and started to read. Within moments I was staring at an uncanny description of myself:

The average player is someone who shoots around the mid-90s, who, on a good day, might hit two or three greens in regulation, has an acute sand phobia, who struggles to take fewer than 36 putts a round. Apart from the sand phobia, which wasn't acute with me but did, on occasions, rear its head, this was me Leadbetter was talking about. I read on:

Take a look around your club this weekend and you'll see golfers turn up to play in such a hurry that they won't ever find a few minutes to loosen up their golfing muscles or stroke a few putts before they tee off. They make a hash of the first few holes, throw away shots faster than you can count them, and then wonder why their game only begins to click on the back nine.

Yes, this was me again, more often than not. I continued to read, half expecting Leadbetter to write: 'Yes, Ian, I'm referring to you!' He did not, but he might as well have done.

Those who do make it to the range aren't always better off. Too many players think a balanced warm-up session is flirting briefly with the mid and short irons before wrapping their hands around a driver and hammering balls towards the boundary fence. By the time they've finished their tempo's shot for the day.

I was beginning to grow disappointed with my predictability as an average golfer. So far there was nothing in Leadbetter's description I could deny, and there was still more to come.

Are you tired of making the same sort of mistakes every time you go out to play? [he asked]. Do you step on to the tee confused by too much technical information? Is the general lack of consistency through the bag the hallmark of your game? When invited to play corporate or business golf is the overriding goal not to be too embarrassed? Are you one of those players who has all the latest gear but has a hard time breaking 90? Is that short walk from the practice ground to the first tee nothing short of a journey into the unknown?

I couldn't face any more of this. I drew all the strength I could muster to stop myself from sinking to my knees, breaking into tears and shouting out: 'Yes, yes, yes, I admit everything. It's all true. Every single question. Please, please help me.'

Fortunately, I recovered my composure enough in time for Leadbetter to appear. In his fifties now, he has maintained a fit, lean body. Wearing his trademark straw boater with the words 'Callaway Golf' emblazoned across his head, a red top and shorts, Leadbetter took me to a practice area where he could inspect my swing.

I was growing used to having my dubious game studied by golfing notables, but felt no more comfortable this time around than I did when Nick Faldo first asked me to swing a nine iron in his back garden all those months before.

Having handed me a five iron and a pitching wedge, Leadbetter disappeared for a couple of minutes to receive a phone call, leaving me to carry out a few swings by myself. This was a stroke of luck because my first two efforts dug huge divots out of the hitherto pristine grass. I was also concerned whether there was any room left in my confused head for yet more advice on my game. It had already been crammed full of tips from a whole array of professionals, and I had already wondered whether I was in danger of succumbing to the syndrome excellently described by Ernest Jones, a golf pioneer and guru of the 1920s. 'Paralysis by analysis,' he referred to it as. I knew exactly what he was talking about.

Happily, on Leadbetter's return, I managed to hit a couple of sweet drives with the five iron to send the ball soaring high and relatively far out into the driving area. I thought this might receive a favourable reaction and, at first, it did. 'Hmm,' responded Leadbetter, stroking his jaw and nodding his head. 'You clearly have good, athletic ability and eye to hand contact.' Then came the caveat. 'They help make up for the flaws in your swing.'

He suggested placing more emphasis on my back foot, shifting more body weight to the right of my body in the process. 'It makes the tail wag,' he said, by way of an explanation. I took a couple of swings and immediately felt more comfortable with this slightly altered stance. Not only that, but the resulting drives appeared to send the ball straight and further with the same amount of effort as before. I proceeded to send a dozen balls in the same direction, much to Leadbetter's approval. 'Well,' he proclaimed, after twenty minutes of this. 'I see no reason why you can't become a single-figure handicapper at least.'

I was exceedingly grateful that, just for once, I had not played like an idiot in front of a respected figure in the game. It had made a very pleasant and welcome change. Retiring to his offices, Leadbetter explained how the small matter of one inch had decided his fate.

'I hoped to become a tour player but missed out on getting my card by one stroke at tour school,' he recalled. 'I still remember it clearly to this day. It was 1977 and I had a ten-foot putt which would have given me a score low enough to have qualified. The ball looked like it was going in but, at the final moment, it turned just slightly, caught the lip of the hole, almost circumnavigated it before coming to a standstill an inch from dropping in. If it had gone in I would have definitely joined the tour, but it didn't and for a time I was really upset about it. It helped me direct my energies into teaching. I'd already come round to thinking this may be where my future lay.'

Before this defining moment in his life, Leadbetter, born in England but having spent most of his formative years in what was then Rhodesia, had a business course to his name, a two handicap and a part-time job as a club professional. 'Ever since I was a teenager I had my head in instructional magazines about golf,' he recalled. 'Arnold Palmer produced an instruction record in the 1960s and I used to spend my evenings listening to it. When I became a club professional I discovered I got a kick out of teaching others. I used to experiment with some players in the early days. Who knows how many games I've messed up? Anyway, I decided to explore golf teaching after I missed out on the tour card.'

Obtaining a job as a club professional at Staverton Park in Northamptonshire, he also started to help out with a couple of golfers he knew from back in what had since become Zimbabwe: Nick Price and Dennis Watson. When he realised that coaching was indeed his vocation, Leadbetter moved to a similar role at Oak Park, near Chicago. 'I threw myself into coaching to the point where I knew if I really wanted to make it I had to move to America,' he explained. 'I put my forthcoming marriage on hold and lived in not the most salubrious accommodation, but after I had gained a small reputation I moved down to Orlando and started to work with Nick and Dennis again.'

Price and Watson went on to win the World Series of Golf in 1983 and 1984 respectively and, in doing so, they made their fellow golfers aware of Leadbetter. One such golfer turned out to be Nick Faldo, who had told me his version of their story when he taught me how to chip the ball in his back garden.

'I would never repeat what I did with Nick Faldo again,' is how Leadbetter looks back on those scary days when he dismantled the swing of Europe's top golfer and reduced him, at least for a while, to an also-ran on the golf circuit. 'I got lucky because I found the only player who was able to put up with the one step forward, two steps back process. Nowadays players want instant success, so I adopt an intravenous method in which, drip by drip, they improve. There's no way they'd be prepared like Faldo to work on it for two years without any guarantee of success.

'Nick was the ideal student. I could have ended his career. It's as simple as that. A lot of players wouldn't have stuck with it and for that all credit to him. Yet, strange as it may seem, especially when he fell down the rankings list, neither of us ever had any doubt that it would come good in the end. When it did, when he won the British Open at Muirfield in 1987, it was the most rewarding thing I'd ever done.'

Now Leadbetter became recognised globally as the man who had turned Faldo into the best golfer in the business. The irony of the positive reaction was not lost on the coach. 'A few years earlier I used to turn up at putting greens and driving ranges at tournaments armed with a hulking great video camera and people used to look at me and wonder what the hell I was playing at. You just didn't get coaches, at least not full-time coaches who worked on a very regular basis with individual players. After Nick won the Open, we teamed up to write books, make videos, and I became inexorably linked with him.'

Soon everyone was knocking on his door, expecting Leadbetter, like Christ in the temple, to cure all golfing ills. 'It became a bit of a problem at times because some golfers expected to be improved without putting in the necessary mental effort themselves. I could often turn things around technically, but being able to transfer such changes into success could take time. That's what happened with Sandy Lyle, for example. He'd won Masters and Opens but came to me when his game had started to decline. We made progress but, at the slightest setback, he would revert to his old, negative ways.'

Sometimes change for change, sake can backfire, too. Take Ian Baker-Finch, the Australian who won the 1991 Open at Birkdale. 'I used to coach Ian, and even though he'd just won the Open, he decided he needed to be able to hit the ball longer. As soon as he achieved this, though, other aspects of his game crumbled. He got out of his pattern and the result was that he was barely heard of again, which was so sad.'

Leadbetter also worked with Seve Ballesteros for a short while. 'We'd worked well on improving the flaws, which were beginning to affect his game, to great success in 1992, but a couple of days before the 1993 Masters, his brother, Manuel, turned up and told him to revert back to his natural game. Seve's rarely challenged for anything since. The thing about Seve is, even now, he's still one of the best golfers in the world from 100 yards from the pin. His perennial problem is that he can't find a golf course.'

With Justin Rose he has enjoyed more success. Indeed, since I had spent that pleasant morning at the Belfry with the young Englishman, Rose had continued his fine form and was fast becoming talked of on both sides of the Atlantic. 'I was all for him turning pro at 17, I'm just not sure whether the way he was handled was the best for him at the time. You don't take a two-year-old racehorse and race him every week, do you? But now he's a very old 21, he's hardened a great deal mentally and I'm sure he's going to become one of Europe's greatest golf players.'

Even the slightest of glances around his Champion's Gate complex confirms that Leadbetter has been well-rewarded for his efforts, an unlikely development that arose following that missed putt all those years before. He recognises this, too. 'Only the other day I was with Tim Price, Nick's brother, whom I knew from my Zimbabwe days, and he said who'd have thought I'd end up signing autographs for people when I came from a little town in the heart of Africa. I never planned it this way, and I most definitely wasn't wrapped up in the whole American dream. All I wanted to do was teach and stay close to a game I loved but was not quite good enough to play, but you take what life gives you, don't you?'

He comes across as a contented man and this is probably due to the fact that he is forever presented with new challenges, many of which culminate in triumph. 'You never, ever stop learning this game,' he explained. 'There was a time when a coach was seen merely as a failed golfer, and that the only player who really needed to use a coach was a beginner. Well, life has changed markedly since those days, and coaches are recognised and respected in their own right, just as psychologists are now also becoming universally accepted.

'The point about the job is that you have to be all things to all men. Having the technical expertise is not enough because you are dealing constantly with different temperaments. This means that sometimes your approach is technical, other times non-technical. You must be a cheerleader one moment, a harsh critic the next. It takes time to get inside someone's head, to know their quirks and idiosyncrasies.

'And then there is the desire to remain always on the cutting edge. Right now I'm looking at a new development where, using electrodes placed on a player's forehead, you can measure how pressure develops when facing a particular hurdle, like a ten-foot putt to save par. This tells us how the mind responds to the situation. In effect, it shows us how the brain works. I'm sure we'll be using this device a great deal in the future.'

Over an hour had passed with the world's most in-demand coach, and I was aware that other, more notable golfers were waiting for his services. There was time just for one more crucial question.

'So, David, what advice can you give to turn me into that single-figure golfer?' Leadbetter seemed prepared for the inevitable, if belated request.

'Treat each hole as its own entity,' he began. 'It's your inconsistency that lets you down and prevents you recording low scores. That's a shame because you're clearly capable of it, but two or three bad holes spoil the day for you. It's all to do with how you practise before you begin your round. Treat it like a round of golf, playing every shot, and go through the same routine. Ivan Lendl once told me how he used to bounce the tennis ball seven times before he served. It got to the point where he did it without thinking, such was it a routine. Most amateur golfers' routines are dreadful. If you grow to rely on your routine, then there will be fewer highs and lows in your game.'

So that was it. The man who has guided so many of the world's leading golfers had just presented me with the keys to the kingdom of single-figure handicap golf. I couldn't wait to get started. It was now just a matter of time before I shot nine over in a round. A year before I would not have cared a jot. Now such a prospect meant almost the earth to me.

A family holiday and a trip to the Open meant that for the first time since I had begun this odyssey, circumstances beyond my control deprived me of playing golf for a few weeks, just when I was at my most eager.

At Muirfield, the scene of my own humiliation a few months previously, a Scottish storm blew Tiger Woods off course in his bid to claim a third major of the year, in what had become a much-hyped bid for the golfing calendar grand slam. An unbelievable 81 – yes, 81 – in his third round ended any hopes of reclaiming an Open title he first won in 2000, although a fourth round 65 proved not only his pride, but also his competitiveness. Tiger was not the only player to suffer. Colin Montgomerie shot an 84, a score that is plunging into the nether regions of amateur golfers, if it were not for the fact that it was at a stormy Muirfield. But the temporary demise of Woods proved to be the biggest shock.

Amid the mayhem Ernie Else managed to keep his act together to come through and claim his first Open title, albeit after losing a lead and scraping home in a subsequent four man play-off. Snapping at his heels whenever the big South African was off the course was his confidant and mind guru, Jos Vanstiphout.

The little Belgian was at his craziest best at Muirfield, revealing that deep down Els had been suffering from what was described as 'Tigeritis', a condition contracted after so many runner-up spots behind Woods over the years. This victory, Vanstiphout hoped, would provide the cure. Els also confessed that when he walked off the 18th, having just lost his lead to enforce a play-off, he expected a verbal onslaught from his (and my) advisor. Instead, Vanstiphout adopted the same approach used so successfully with Retief Goosen the year before at the US Open. 'I thought I'd be in trouble,' Els said. 'But Jos told me he was proud of me and that I'd already proved myself to be a champion over the past four days. I felt a lot happier after that.' The image of the huge, athletic Els receiving a dressing-down from the chain-smoking, fidgety Belgian was almost impossible to conceive.

Els had also worked with Leadbetter during a week that started poorly but ended wonderfully. 'There were a number of things wrong with his driving early in the week, but because his putting was good I felt we had a chance of turning things round,' the coach explained to me later. 'I think his win was destiny. The defining moment – his chip out of the bunker to three feet from the hole under such pressure – told how strong Ernie had become as the week wore on. If he'd ended up losing in the play-off, having led the way for so long, I'd hate to think what would have happened. It's very possible that the setback would have been too tough for Ernie to have come back from. Instead he's the Open champion, and to watch him achieve this was an incredibly satisfying moment.'

I managed to squeeze in three rounds in the following three weeks, all on testing courses that punished mistakes, and found a few elements wanting. For a start, I began to rely on my irons when teeing off, plumping for accuracy rather than distance. This ploy worked only to a degree. I still endured my patches of disaster that would last two or three holes and destroy what would otherwise have been promising scores. On all three occasions a score in the low 90s looked on until a lake, a ditch or an implosion in a bunker stuck an unwanted nine or ten on to my otherwise satisfactory card. Circumstances also dictated that, much as I wanted to, I failed to undergo Leadbetter's warm-up procedure. Traffic jams resulted in arriving at two courses just minutes before my official tee-off time, for example, which meant a rusty start and high scores in the opening few holes.

This was frustrating because on my return from the Open I had set myself a target which, a few months back, would have been unimaginable. I was convinced, buoyed by my one score of 86, that a score of 81 or less, or in other words a single-figure handicap score of nine over, was within my powers. I set myself a target of 18 months from my first round at Royal Melbourne to achieve this score. If I could just succeed, then I would have made huge advances towards becoming an accomplished player. These were faintly ridiculous goals to set, but after three days in the company of first Woods, then Nicklaus, and finally Leadbetter, my aspirations had risen to a dangerously high level. I decided that if I ever did get the chance to meet and talk to Tiger, I would tell him of my success.

Would he be impressed by this? Probably not. Perhaps my 17th in the Drambuie World Ice Golf championships or my 23rd in the European

Office Putting Tournament would mean more, if only for the fact that he could not make such claims.

You see, by now, Tiger had become an almost constant companion to my thoughts. What would Tiger think of this? Would Tiger approve of that? Could Tiger do it better? He was the equivalent of the invisible friend small children sometimes believe they have and talk to. I had, mercifully, not quite taken to asking an invisible Tiger questions aloud, even if they were rushing around my head. But it would only be a matter of time, surely, before I did.

Now it wasn't a question any more of whether I might, just, be able to meet the man, despite all the barriers that suggested I stood no chance. Now it was a matter of absolute necessity. Not meeting the very heartbeat of golf after all this commitment to his cause would be like Warren Beatty wandering through a harem without removing his clothes.

And how, I wondered, would Mr Woods fare in the European Mini-Golf Championships in Prague? It's a question he will never be able to answer, but this would be my next challenge, and the week that followed in the Czech Republic would prove to be one that was full of surprises.

19

A sting in the tale

I had always hoped that one day I would compete for Great Britain. I would have preferred to have scored a goal at the old Wembley stadium, a try at Twickenham or a century at Lord's. Given my newly acquired obsession with golf, however, a birdie at St Andrews in the Open would have done very nicely instead. Never in my wildest dreams could I have foreseen that I would achieve my dream, albeit in the European Mini-Golf Championships in Prague.

So concerned was I to leave no stone unturned in my devotion to the cause of golf, and so eager to impress a Tiger Woods I had no guarantee of meeting with my endeavours, that I felt participation and even possible success in the European Mini-Golf Championships would only add another notch on a belt that already included world ice golf and European office putting.

The president of the British Mini-Golf Association is Peter Parr. He, like Chip Thomson, had an apt name for a golfer. No doubt a day's research through the golfing annals would throw up a good many more: there's bound to be a number of Greens and Balls who play the game. Come to think of it, isn't there someone called Tiger Woods? I wonder just how silly a name you could come up with. Was there ever a Tony Divot, for example, a Chuck Albatross or a Billy Bunker? Wouldn't it be just grand if the Hollywood actress, Minnie Driver, turned out to be a golfer?

Shortly after my 23rd placing in the European Office Putting Championships I called Tim Davies, the man I met over a mini-golf hole on Channel 4 television's *The Big Breakfast* a few months back, to enquire if there were any other such events taking place.

You can imagine my surprise when Peter Parr made contact, promising me a place on the British team for the forthcoming European Championships. The selection process wasn't easy, you must understand. It went something like this.

'Would you like to join the British team and compete in the European Championships in Prague?' Peter asked.

'Yes,' I answered.

'Right,' replied Peter. 'You're in.'

The BMGA's president arranged everything for me, including purchase of a 'Fun Sports' mini-golf putter, complete with pink padding on the club head which made it different to, and somewhat camper than, your communal garden regular golf putter. All I had to do was turn up two days before the official start of the tournament in time for the opening ceremony.

The turning up bit had the potential of going disastrously wrong, however, on account of Prague unexpectedly being hit by the worst floods in over a century. During the week before the championships, the 800-year-old Czech capital and former seat of the kings of Bohemia was hit by devastating scenes as the waters of the Vltava River spilled over its embankments and on to the surrounding streets.

The Vltava was flowing at thirty times its normal speed, causing all but two of the city's many bridges to be closed. Some 50,000 people were forced to flee their homes, including Martin Tomanek, president of the Czech Mini-Golf Association and chief organiser of the championships, while dams of sandbags were constructed furiously by the police, army and volunteers.

It would be enough to deter most people, of course, from travelling to the place, but if you were to think this then you would be seriously underestimating the determination, nay bravery, of a mini-golfer. Life-threatening floods, earthquakes, attacks by aliens from space, nothing will stop us mini-golfers flocking to one of the most prestigious tournament of the year in the world.

And so I turned up early on a Monday morning at Stansted Airport in time to read various warning notices about travelling to Prague. 'Beware of pickpockets, petty theft and bogus policemen,' read one. 'Decline to show your money, ask to look at his credentials, and if necessary accompany him to the nearest police station.' Another one advised strongly not to visit the Czech capital at all. 'Only if your journey is absolutely necessary,' it insisted.

Well, of course, in my case it was. The taxi journey to my hotel went on interminably due to the devastation to the road system in the city centre caused by the floods. Thankfully, the mini-golf course, a further ten-minute taxi journey from my hotel, was on higher ground, unaffected by the burst river banks. I noticed as my journey neared its end a signpost directing drivers to a suburb called Slapy, something which caught my imagination somewhat. You'd pay good money, wouldn't you, to say that you lived in a place called Slapy.

The remaining members of the British mini-golf team met me at the Tempo Praha mini-golf venue of the European Championships. Apart from President Peter Parr, the other members were Tim Davies, a house-husband who used to work in computers, Ted McIver, employed by the Inland Revenue and Michael Webb, who worked for a firm of legal publishers. They had all been out in Prague for a number of days, honing their questionable skills on the two courses laid out in front of me, the 'Eternite' and the cement-based 'Betong'.

My initial assumption that they must be pretty good to have taken so much time in preparation was soon put right. The European Championships, apparently, were as good as the World Championships because the best nations in the world of mini-golf all came from Europe. The favourites, both from a team point of view and individually, were Germany, Austria and Sweden. The Czech Republic, Holland and Italy were also expected to fare well. Britain, in contrast, was a rank outsider.

In Germany, some 30,000 people are official, paid up mini-golfers. The players competing here were professional mini-golfers, believe it or not, with a government grant to train one day every week. The Brits were disappointed with the news that the Moldovans, the one nation in Europe worse than us, could not make the championships. We command the grand total of 30 official mini-golfers – or 31, if you include me. I knew from the moment I caught sight of the German team's official Formula One-style motor home that the week would not pan out as I expected. I made do with a plastic carrier bag.

The opening ceremony had been planned for that night in the city centre. In a variation of the Olympic Games opening extravaganza, we should have been paraded through the streets of Prague's city centre proudly hoisting our flag.

Unfortunately, or thankfully, depending on how you look at it, the floods meant that instead we were all transported out to a small town called Ricany, some 15 kilometres to the south of the city, where a barbecue was held in the grounds of a restaurant.

The mayor of Prague should have been in attendance, but was instead fulfilling his role as head of rescue operations in the city centre. The president of the World Mini-Golf Federation, a Herr Klaus Engels, was present, however, to deliver a speech and declare the championships officially open while all 109 male competitors and 30 female players, from countries as diverse as Latvia and Slovakia, Finland and Slovenia, looked on.

It was here that I was introduced to our coach for the week. That's right, the British team, who were fully expecting to finish bottom in the championships, with all five golfers battling it out between themselves to avoid finishing last individually, would be employing a coach. His name was Thomas Zeininger, a roly-poly Austrian player who had failed to make the Austrian team. As far as he was concerned we would all be taking the forthcoming few days extremely seriously indeed, which is why he announced that the following day, the day before the championships began, we would be practising between 8.00 a.m. and 1.00 p.m., and again between 6.00 p.m. and 9.00 p.m. Eight bloody hours of training at mini-golf! This was not exactly what I had in mind, especially when I discovered that the price of a large glass of excellent Czech Pilsner was the equivalent of ten English pence.

The practice day did not begin well. For a start, my hotel had mislaid my passport. I then spent ages searching for my putter only to remember that I had left it lying on the back seat of a Prague minicab. And then, on arriving at the course, Martin Tomanek announced that he had no record of my attendance and that I was not on the official start list. So, to recap: I had lost my passport and would be forced, therefore, to remain in the Czech Republic for ever, I had no putter to play in the European Mini-Golf Championships (which is kind of crucial in mini-golf), but the good news was that I wasn't entered in the championships in any case. Apart from that everything was just dandy.

Thomas Zeininger reluctantly agreed to lend me his putter for the day's practice plus the three days of competition. Actually, the European Championships would officially last for four, but seeing as the cut would be made on the penultimate evening, I figured my challenge for European honour would end after three days. I'm not saying I was lacking confidence, but I had booked my return flight for the night of the third day of competition. Martin Tomanek then decided I should be included anyway, especially when I informed him I was the 17th best ice golfer in the world and the 23rd best European office putter. He seemed quite impressed by this, and I wasn't going to dilute these achievements by painting the complete picture in front of the man who had the power to rule me in or out of the tournament. He decided to place me on top of the whole starting list, which meant I would begin the whole championships the following morning in a threesome with Tim Davies and a Slovenian named Boris Balek. This also meant that after my first stroke I would officially be leading the European Championships, and after my first round of three that day I would be the leader in the clubhouse, albeit for a minute or two. How exciting was that! Even my passport turned up later that night after an Austrian had mistakenly taken it before handing it back.

The British team members seemed to be practising for longer than any other of the 20-odd nations competing in the championships. This showed the level of commitment that only the best reveal. The reality was that the British needed to practise more than anyone else. In the clubhouse bar that night Heinz Weber, one of the top Austrians, and a friend of Zeininger's, explained how desperate he and his fellow countrymen were to defeat the Germans.

'When they've lost in the past they've ended up smashing up courses and tables,' Heinz said, with a weary shake of his head. 'And when they finished third in the 2001 World Championships, they took their medals off from around their necks in disgust during the medal ceremony. A lot of money's put into the sport in Germany and, as far as they're concerned, coming second simply means first loser.'

As the rest of my time that week would be playing non-stop mini-golf – three rounds on day one, a further three on day two, and then two more on the third day – I took my one spare afternoon off in between the practice times to take a look at Prague.

Paul Valéry wrote of Prague: 'There is no other place in the world where the magnificence of the whole is subordinated to so many precious details and cameos.' His point is easily appreciated in an afternoon's wanderings around a city centre full of treats, from the Gothic masterpiece that is the Charles Bridge, to Prague Castle, with its commanding position overlooking the river.

I took a cab back to the hotel from Prague 8 ('dead city', said Pavel the cab driver). I was soon brought back to stark reality when I made the mistake of answering a question Pavel threw at me. 'You like girls?' he asked, apropos of nothing.

'Er, well, yes,' I replied, thinking he meant as opposed to boys. This was a major error because a split-second later both his hands left the steering wheel and produced a handful of leaflets and cards.

'Theez very good girls,' he said, a proud smile on his face. 'I take you to them, yes?'

I looked down at the leaflets and observed a stack of naked Czech women smiling back.

'Well,' I said, choosing my words very carefully. 'Thanks, but I'm married. Besides, I'm in training.'

'What for?' he asked, with a quizzical stare.

'The European Mini-Golf Championships,' I replied. 'They begin tomorrow morning and I'm here to win.'

Pavel, taxi driver-cum-pimp, dropped me off at the hotel, laughed and shook his head. 'So, mini-golf is better than sex, yes?'

'Apparently,' I said, rather weakly, and waved goodbye.

In the morning the atmosphere at the mini-golf venue had changed noticeably. The day before, players practised in various types of T-shirts and shorts in a relatively relaxed manner. Now there was an air of serious intensity. Everyone was wearing national team tracksuits and tops, all sporting their country's name and flag upon their breasts. The British team had to make do with a cartoon figure of a lion. 'It's Lippy,' Tim Davies explained, rather drolly. 'Lippy the Lion.'

We sat by the clubhouse and observed as the other teams made last-minute preparations. The Germans assembled by their motor home and when Martin Tomanek announced that the first day's play would begin shortly, they hugged each other as if about to embark on a space voyage. The Czechs gave each other high fives, the Swedes seemed huddled in a group as a last-minute motivational session took place, while the Austrians jogged up and down, blowing out their cheeks like Olympic sprinters lining up for a 100 metres final.

Thomas Zeininger had insisted that we showed some passion as we played. I'm serious! Tim Davies and I therefore decided to roar like Lippy the Lion if we produced a great shot, growl if the shot was acceptable and mew if either of us fluffed it. There would be a great deal of kitten noises uttered over the next three days.

'Concentrate, Iron,' Zeininger kept repeating to me. Like all German-speaking people, Thomas could not get his head round my Christian name. I've never been able to understand why people from central Europe find it virtually impossible to say 'Ian'. No matter how many times I attempted to correct him, Thomas would still say 'Iron'. Even

Martin Tomanek got into the act over the tannoy when he asked the first group to make their way over to the first hole, 'Pyramids', on the Eternite course, to get the championships under way. 'And to begin with we have Iron Stafford,' Tomanek's voice boomed over the course to a polite ripple of applause.

Now, to the likes of you and me, each hole on the course seemed straightforward enough, albeit difficult. My approach would have been the same as whenever I played on a mini-golf course: hit the ball towards the hole and hope for the best. But this, quite palpably, was not the course of action to take at the European Championships. Not when there were two hundred mini-golf balls to choose from, depending on their bounce and softness. And not when there were both freezers and heaters provided to warm or cool your balls, in order to obtain the desired speed or slowness of the ball, depending on the type of hole that confronted you.

There was another worrying factor to all this. On the rare occasions I had played the game before, I would average between two and three strokes per hole, although there would always be at least one hole when I would persevere for ever in attempting to find it. This would not be good enough at this level. On the 18-hole Eternite course, for example, the top players would be looking for scores of around 20, which would translate into 16 holes in one, and just a couple of twos taken.

Although everyone seemed to gather round the clubhouse to watch the first play in the championships, I managed to begin my challenge for the title with an ace, finding the correct angle on the wall for the ball to crawl its way inexorably towards the hole via the side of one of three pyramids laid out on the course. One hole, one shot and I was winning the European Championships. The occasion demanded a growl, which was greeted with concerned stares from all those watching.

Boris Balek began just as well, and continued in similar style racking up five consecutive aces in the first five holes. Tim Davies and I exchanged nervous glances. Boris was not supposed to be particularly good, yet he was eating up the course with relish. I seemed to be faring well until I came to the sixth, the 'Cheese', which required an uphill putt via a narrow gap to a hole which, if missed, would result in the ball rolling back down to where it had begun its journey. Mine proceeded to do this on six occasions.

The ninth hole, 'Tube', needed the ball to pass through a pipe marginally wider than the ball before running on to the hole. The putt needed to be exact. I took a five. The 12th, 'Labyrinth', the 13th, 'Snail' and the 17th, 'Volcano', all posed problems too. My first-round score of 38 seemed pretty acceptable to me, but on later inspection I discovered that it was one of the worst. Indeed, on the official leaderboard, they posted up scores in various colours denoting their worth. Yellow, therefore, was considered awesome, green pretty good, red acceptable. My score, however, as indeed it would be for the remainder of the week, was in black.

'What does black mean?' I asked one of the Czech judges.

'Black means it was shit,' he replied.

Some of the competitors had to undergo drug tests after completing their round, although goodness knows how any form of chemical could enhance a performance out on a mini-golf course. I asked the same official if there was any chance of my undergoing such a test. He shook his head and a faint smile appeared on his face.

'Not with your score,' he replied. I never found out what this man's official role was at the tournament, although I'd like to think he wasn't the Championship's pyscologist.

A 41 on the harder and longer Betong course followed after an hour and a half's break in between rounds. The 'Betong', a type of cement, threw up holes such as the seventh, the 'Hammer Cage', which required you to chip a ball from 50 metres away, over grass and on to a shiny green which was faster than an ice rink. Chipping with a putter, of course, is not the same as chipping with a nice wedge, hence my score of six the first time I attempted this. On my third and final round of the day, however, back on the shorter Eternite, I posted a 31, including four initial aces in a row. I surprised myself at one hole by shouting at the ball, as it seemed to take an eternity to roll into the hole. This provoked a quiet reprimand from one of the numerous judges dotted around the course. Elsewhere, players were making all sorts of noises, from the gurgling red-haired German man, to the Swede who punched the air and sounded like a hot valve releasing air. The queen of the noise-makers was a German woman named Bianca Zodrow, who screamed so loudly each time she holed the ball it sounded as if she had reached orgasm. On reflection, maybe she had.

At the end of day one I found myself in 107th position, ahead of another Slovenian and Britain's Ted McIver. Although relieved not to be bottom, I found it disconcerting that I should have played reasonably well, at least in my book, and yet be so lowly placed. This, however, would be as high as I would get, for the following morning I made a fundamental error.

I blame Thomas Zeininger. Before play began he told me I putted like a golfer, when I should be putting like a mini-golfer. He persuaded me to alter my style so dramatically that by the time I was hunched over the ball at the first hole of the Betong course I resembled a contortionist. The immediate results were disastrous. After nine holes I had already scored 30. Reverting back to my former 'golfing' fashion, I made something of a comeback and took 19 strokes for the remaining nine holes. While I was shooting 49, Ted scored 41 and the Slovenian an impressive 30. My decision to change my style in the middle of the European Championships resulted in my plummeting to the bottom of the leaderboard.

My coach was beginning to show the first signs of cracking up. He had an interesting habit of standing in front of you as you made your putt, before throwing his head right back and shouting out 'No' to the heavens when you missed. It did wonders for the confidence, as you can imagine.

Frustrated by my performance and position I flung my putter – well, actually, Thomas's – down in disgust during my 37 on the Eternite. This, by all accounts, is the mini-golf equivalent of elbowing someone purposefully in the face in a football match. As my strop was in full show of a judge, it should have resulted in an official warning. Two such warnings would result in a dropped stroke. Instead, I appeared to get away with it.

Tim Davies, who was still partnering me during the round with Boris Balek, could not believe my luck. By the evening he could not believe his either. Tim had received an official warning, without apparently being aware that he was committing a misdemeanour, in asking coach Thomas Zeininger to show the precise mark where he should be aiming his ball off a wall. In fact, he had asked Thomas to place his umbrella over the hole to prevent other shadows from moving people affecting his focus. Michael Webb had also received a warning, this time for slow play. The Brits had two bad boys on the team already, something the rest of us made a great play about, and they were posted up on the naughty boys corner of the leaderboard. Quite a few others had joined them, too, ranging from a Portuguese man penalised for unfair behaviour – actually he was caught drinking a beer on the course – to Bianca Zodrow, whose very public orgasms had tested everyone's patience too much. She received two warnings for this, and lost a shot as a result.

On the morning of day three, the bottom three in the tournament would start proceedings as a group. This meant that Ted McIver, myself and another Slovenian, Ignac Hladnik, would begin play at the Betong course. My putter, incidentally, had been returned by a Czech taxi driver who clearly took one look at my pink-padded contraption and decided he had no use for it whatsoever. I decided, having already tried to make one change in my putting style with disastrous results the day before, that it would be best if I stuck with Thomas's putter.

Our group were made to feel a little like the classroom dunces. Indeed, as we approached one particular hole I declared to Ignac that I had performed exceptionally badly all week. 'We're all shit, my friend,' Ignac replied, in a rather doleful voice. 'That's why we've started first today.' Shit, it seemed, was an overused word in central Europe.

Thomas had undergone a transformation as the week had worn on. At the beginning full of hope and intensity, by Friday he had been reduced to a wreck, a state encouraged by the strength of the apple vodka and slivovic served up in the bar. While the Germans and Swedes collected their balls from their portable heaters, Thomas decided to warm our balls in a more animalistic way, sticking his hands down his trousers and producing them from the nether regions of his underpants. None of us was exactly eager to catch the balls when Thomas threw them towards us to play.

Discretion had long departed, too, from the mind of Thomas Zeininger. When Ted McIver underhit a putt our coach shouted out: 'Are you a boy or a girl?' And just as I was about to make a putt, he ran over to me as if about to deliver an important instruction.

'You see that girl over there?' he asked, pointing towards a rather sweet-looking Czech woman who was marking the scores at the hole. 'She has nice lips. Nice lips for blowing, *ja*?'

Somehow I couldn't see similar comments made to Tiger Woods from his some-time coach, Butch Harmon, just before he drove off from the tee. I thanked Thomas for his valuable contribution and proceeded to sink what should have been a difficult putt. Hmm. Maybe Thomas's unique methods worked, after all.

My 42 and 39 in my final two rounds failed to trouble the scorers. I finished on a score of 326 after eight rounds, some 17 behind Ted, 43 behind President Peter Parr and Tim Davies, and 54 behind the top Britain, Michael Webb. Needless to say, we all finished in the one hundreds, with my good self propping up the leaderboard. The three Slovenians insisted on taking a photograph of me standing by the 'Pipe' hole where, during my final round, I had scored a soul-destroying seven. 'You are a funny guy,' Boris told me, which would have been a nice thing to hear, if it wasn't for the disheartening fact that I'd tried to be serious about my mini-golf all week. Thomas Zeininger, meanwhile, went off in indecent haste to console himself at the bar.

And so, after my minor triumphs in the world ice golf and European office putting championships, the European Mini-Golf Championships had brought me down to earth with a vicious bump. I had finished 109th out of 109 male competitors, and had tried my hardest, too, for such an achievement. Normally, a numbered placing sounds better than the word 'last', but in this instance I was not so sure.

Half the field would complete the individual competition the next day, but I, the last-placed player in the European Mini-Golf Championships, would be on his way home. Then, moments before my taxi arrived to whisk me away to Prague Airport, a stroke of luck befell me from the most unlikely of sources.

News was delivered that a Finnish competitor, a Mr Anssi Tervaskangas, had been stung on the leg that morning by a wasp. The leg became rapidly inflamed to the extent that he was taken to hospital for treatment and, subsequently, had to withdraw from the tournament without completing his rounds. The leaderboard was revised as a result. Mr Tervaskangas was placed 109th and last. Mr Stafford was promoted to 108th.

Now that was much better. As I was driven across the Vltava River and to my waiting plane, a sense of satisfaction filled me. The ignominy of finishing last in the European Mini-Golf Championships had been spared, even if in questionable circumstances. If I were ever to enter such a competition again I would ensure that I would not change my putting style midway through the competition, that I would not leave my putter in a taxi, and would not listen to a coach who kept my balls up his arse and liked to talk dirty to me during my round.

Oh, and I'd pack some wasp repellent in my bag, too.

20

Steam baths with strangers

A Swiss mini-golfer named Michel Rhyn won the men's individual title at the European Championships, with Germans taking the next three places. I know this because the organising committee kindly sent me an official list of all final positions, a list confirming Ian Stafford in 108th place.

I didn't care. I was off to Tokyo in search of golf fanatics like the businessman who kept weeping at St Andrews. Here, in Japan, probably more than anywhere else in the world, my quest would be appreciated and understood, my hopeful climax in the court of King Tiger considered the ultimate honour. Now the day had arrived when I would travel to a fascinating country I had only visited fleetingly some 14 years before.

The Japanese Golf Association had ensured that my time in Japan would be packed. In fact, they had arranged a round of golf at the Narita Golf Club within an hour of my touching down at Narita Airport. Andy Yamanaka, the JGA's director of competition and international affairs, had been instrumental in the organisation of my time in Japan, and he was there at the arrivals hall to meet me, armed with an itinerary that would keep me busy right up until my departure four days later.

Taizo Kawata was waiting to play a round with me at the Narita GC. Mr Kawata, so Andy explained, as he drove me the 20 minute journey from the airport to the exclusive golf club, is a director of the JGA, a member of the R&A, a former top player and a well-known figure in Japanese golf. He also spoke excellent English which, surprisingly for a country that leads the world in electronics, is rare.

Within moments of our meeting he asked me to refer to him as 'Tai', a shortened version of his Christian name. I liked him immediately. It turned out that he had been educated at Ohio State University, hence his excellent English. 'Same place as Jack Nicklaus,' he announced.

The ever-busy Andy had to leave us to our round, but not before lending me his clubs, which were of a far better quality than the set I had left behind in my car boot. After a dozen or so practice swings I was as ready as one could be under the rather extreme circumstances.

Remember, I had just left a rather cramped seat in the cattle class of a British Airways 747 after 13 hours of no sleep and arrived in a country whose time was eight hours ahead. As my tee time at the Narita was 10.30 in the morning, I was about to begin a round of golf at 2.30 a.m. UK time, with a finish time of approximately 6.30 a.m. back home in London.

As if this were not enough, the temperature that morning had hit 95° Fahrenheit, which made life difficult, while the humidity was verging on the unbearable. Within a couple of holes I appeared to be leaking sweat from all parts of my body on a permanent basis. I recalled the Monty Python sketch where, in impersonating a host of David Attenboroughs in the Borneo jungle, Messrs Cleese, Palin and company were producing hoses of water pumping from their armpits and foreheads. Well, that was me at the Narita GC. Every time I stooped over a golf ball in readiness to play a shot, sweat would pour down on to the grass at my feet, forcing me to stop, stand straight, and wipe away furiously at my face with a towel.

After three holes, Sayuri, our female caddie, poured out a couple of iced teas into a cup and handed them to Tai and myself. While Tai took a couple of polite sips, I downed the liquid in one swift gulp, resembling an abandoned man in a desert who had just staggered to an oasis. 'You're thirsty, yes?' Tai asked, with a chortle. 'It's not quite St Andrews, is it?'

Indeed it was not. Sayuri, incidentally, was one of the 95 per cent of all caddies in Japan who are women. Unlike elsewhere, where caddies such as my new-found friend Fanny Sunesson are paid by the golfers who employ them, in Japan the caddie is employed by the golf club. Sayuri, bespectacled and seemingly fragile, happily pushed both golf bags along in a part-motorised trolley, while estimating to the inch the yardages to the hole without ever appearing to consult any notes.

Within a couple of strokes the effects of the iced tea had gone and I had returned to my former sweating self. By the 6th hole, I almost barged Tai out of the way in the rush to enter the halfway house shack for a second spot of refreshment.

Halfway houses in Japan – or at least at the Narita Golf Club – are something to behold. They are a haven of air-conditioning, of sweet fruit, and of ice-cold drinks, all served by a smiling girl behind a bar. We helped ourselves to a large tomato and a cold energy drink and lingered for ten minutes.

Back out on the course I was beginning to surprise myself. Despite the heat and my obvious tiredness (it was now nearly 4.00 a.m. UK time), I was beginning to play quite well amid the exotic birds, the strange animal noises coming from the trees, and the largest dragonflies I had ever seen in my life that swooped down in front of you and hovered for a while before zigzagging off to their next destination. A par at the par four ninth increased my confidence even more, but at this point Tai called a temporary halt to the proceedings. 'Lunch,' he announced. And that was that.

Lunch is an important part of playing a round of golf in Japan, I discovered. It is the recognised way of doing things in these parts, and although I was disappointed initially to stop, since my game was beginning to go rather well, I appreciated the fix of cool air-conditioning back in the clubhouse.

Over a lunch with cold Japanese beers we talked more. Tai's own story proved to be an interesting one. A talented batter and catcher in baseball, he turned down an offer from the Los Angeles Dodgers to become the first Japanese professional baseball player in American history.

'I'll never know whether I would have made it or not, but I have no regrets,' he insisted. 'I wanted to go back and live in Japan. It wasn't as if I could keep hopping back home in between playing for LA. In 1962, travelling across the Pacific was very difficult.'

He was clearly a talented sportsman: within two and a half years of taking up golf he competed in the Japanese Open as an amateur and has played ever since. 'I played off scratch for a long time but now I'm down to a handicap of three,' he informed me, shaking his head as if playing off three were some kind of failure. His life connected to golf has remained active. As vice-chairman of the JGA, Tai represents Japan on the World Amateur Golf Council and has refereed at every British Open since 1990.

'It was at the 1990 Open that Nick Faldo chipped in for a two on his way to winning the tournament,' Tai recalled. 'The ball stopped on the lip of the hole and stayed there for ages before dropping in. The TV cameras actually assumed the ball would not drop and left for another player driving off the next tee. Later, viewers phoned up and complained about Faldo's score. I remember being so nervous when I was summoned before Michael Bonallack, who was then the Secretary of the R&A, to confirm Faldo's score.'

The cold beers back out in the heat of the day had an initial adverse effect. For two holes I could barely hit the ball until, weighing up the temperature, the time and my performance, I decided to go for broke and use Andy's driver. Now, no driver and I had ever formed any kind of meaningful relationship throughout the past year, but at this stage of the afternoon, morning or whatever bloody time it was, I was past caring.

And then one of those minor miracles that have occasionally taken place in my fledgling golfing career happened. I struck the ball with Andy's driver and watched as it flew straight and long before landing some 240 yards down the middle of the fairway. The same thing

212

happened at the 13th, 14th and 15th. I started to par holes at will. It got to the point where I considered a bogey to be a poor score at any hole.

At the 16th, a major miracle almost happened. Taking Andy's three wood out of his bag I surveyed the 208 par three before me, smacked the ball and watched in growing amazement as it first pitched on the edge of the green and proceeded to roll straight for the hole. 'It's going in, it's going in,' I told myself, as Tai and I observed the drama in silence. Of course the ball did not go in – just as Elvis wasn't my playing partner that day – but it came to a halt less than one foot from the hole for what proved to be an easy birdie.

Tai slapped me on my back, shook my hand and clapped like a small child. 'That, Ian, was a beautiful shot, a beautiful shot. And let me tell you how happy I am that you did not score a hole in one.'

I laughed along with him before suddenly realising what he had just said. Unless I had misheard, he had just informed me how pleased he was that I had failed to score an ace. 'Why's that, Tai?' I asked, curious for the answer.

'I have been playing golf for 39 years,' he began. 'I have played in major tournaments, I have played on virtually every famous golf course in the world, and for much of this time I have played off scratch. In all this time I have never, ever scored a hole in one. And so, my friend, how would I have felt if you, a very tired Englishman straight from a plane, uncomfortable in this heat, who has never played on this golf course before, who is using someone else's clubs, and who clearly will become a very good golfer but is not quite there yet, had scored a hole in one in front of me?'

I could see his point. A score of 93 at the end of the round may not be a reason to celebrate, but under the circumstances I was just relieved not to have shown myself up.

After spending four hours in temperatures just below 100°, what would any sane man do? The answer, of course, is to take a piping hot steam bath. Obvious, really. So this is precisely what Tai and I proceeded to do, thus fulfilling the other important obligation during or after a round of golf in

Japan. If my body temperature had not already reached boiling point out on the course, it most certainly did once I had stepped gingerly into the steam bath beside the men's locker room in the clubhouse.

The conversation continued as it would between two men who had first met that morning, now sharing a bath. Tai explained that golf only really came to Japan 101 years before with the opening of a golf club in Kobe. 'For the first half of the past century only ten per cent of people played golf, and they were dukes and barons,' he said. 'Then, against all the odds, a Japanese team, fielding players nobody had really heard of, won the World Cup of golf in 1952, beating an American team with Sam Snead in it, an English team with Peter Allis, and an Australian team with Peter Thomson. That started the golf boom in Japan. Now, the only problem preventing Japanese golf from becoming more international is our own national inferiority complex compounded by the language barrier that has prevented our players from travelling.'

Tai had a pressing engagement in the late afternoon in Tokyo, an hour's drive away, so we changed back into our clothes before he drove me to the nearby Hilton for a much-needed break from the heat of the sun and the bath, and an early night.

As he bade farewell he told me that, apart from his own feelings, there was another good reason why I should be happy that three wood drive had just failed by inches to record my first-ever hole in one. 'In England it would cost you a round of drinks in the clubhouse bar, right?' he said.

I nodded my head. 'The prices here are a bit more expensive, don't you think?' He was right. A beer at the Narita clubhouse came to 2,000 yen, which was the equivalent of £10. There seemed to be plenty of people milling around, too, so the cost of that one shot might have been more than the price of my air ticket to Japan.

There was more. 'We don't just stop with buying drinks in the clubhouse in Japan, you know,' Tai continued. He went on to list a number of items, including planting a cherry blossom tree for the club, engraved clocks with all the facts surrounding the shot for relatives, cigarette lighters for friends, massive tips for the caddie, awarding the ball to the club, and so on. Praise be to the good golfing gods, then, that I failed by inches to score that elusive hole in one.

After a typically jet-lagged sleep and room-service breakfast that came complete with white bread and a toaster (what happens if you want eggs? are you served with an egg cup and a hen?) I checked out of the hotel, caught the airport shuttle bus and met my interpreter, Yusude Karata, at the Air Nippon check-in counter. We would be flying down to Fukuoka, the largest city on the beautiful southern island of Kyushu. Although, with its breathtaking scenery and smoking volcanoes Kyushu is considered to be the birthplace of Japanese history, Yu and I were travelling down south to pay a visit to the KBC Augusta tournament.

A typhoon was blowing up to the south of Japan, but was expected to hit the coastline and possibly venture as far north as Fukuoka later that day. I met this news with a mixture of excitement and alarm. Yu continued to read his newspaper without seemingly a care in the world.

'Typhoons are very common in these parts,' he remarked. 'And earthquakes. I wouldn't be surprised if a tremor or two happened while you are with us in Japan. They are that frequent.' The plane's pilot began to speak over the tannoy. Yu very unkindly translated. 'He said that we will get a lot of turbulence caused by the typhoon, even though the typhoon is further south than we're going. It might get really bumpy.'

After one, really bumpy 90-minute flight we arrived at Fukuoka Airport where I revealed yet more of my lack of local knowledge. The taxis in Japan, so I discovered the hard way, automatically open the rear passenger door on the left-hand side of the car closest to the kerb, without anyone touching it. One such automatic door smashed against my right kneecap, causing me to hop around like a demented frog and for Yu to giggle like a baby.

I then virtually fell out of the same taxi when it delivered us to the golf course on the outskirts of the city thirty minutes later. Having forgotten that the door automatically opened, I had to grab on to my seat belt to prevent the second half of my body joining the first half sticking out of the now opened door.

Andy Yamanaka was already in the clubhouse. We were ushered into a splendid boardroom overlooking the putting green where Toshimitsu Izawa was waiting to speak to me. Toshi was last year's money winner on the Japanese Tour and the second-highest ranked Japanese player in the world rankings at 34th, behind the perennially smiling Shigeki Maruyama, who partners Toshi whenever Japan enters a team tournament.

Toshi was all smiles on this day, too, partly because he had just become a father for the fourth time and partly because he had escaped the noise and commotion back in his Fukuoka home in order to meet me.

Unlike most of his compatriots, Toshi at least made the odd excursion across the Pacific to play in the US. In the 2001 Masters, he claimed a highly impressive fourth place and has become well known on the US Tour. Yet he had some revealing views about why golfers from a country as obsessed as Japan had not yet come close to dominating the sport.

'It's a mental thing,' he explained, through Yu. 'The Japanese feel the pressure more than others. The Americans, Europeans, Australians and Southern Africans can handle pressure better than us. It's down to our culture. If a Japanese player is leading a tournament he begins to feel terrible pressure. In Japan, if you make a mistake everyone points it out, so a Japanese golfer tells himself he can't afford to make an error. In America, people just say better luck next time. You made a mistake but it's not the end of the world.'

Toshi believed that although there were obviously technical areas of his game that needed to be improved, it was more his mental side that was lacking. 'I've never used a mental trainer,' he added, which got me thinking of contacting Jos Vanstiphout. 'Fuck you, you son of a bitch,' Jos would probably say to a bewildered Toshi on their first meeting. Maybe it wasn't such a good idea.

Even the ever-happy Maruyama is affected by this, according to Toshi. 'Shigeki told me that when he was leading the 2002 British Open, he couldn't remember anything that happened between the 10th and the 14th holes at Muirfield. Shigeki had completely lost himself.'

While the mental side may remain a problem for Toshi, he is determined to keep on improving the technical elements of his game, to the detriment of one of his great loves. The best player in Japan used to be hooked on 'Pachinko' parlours, huge entertainment rooms with row upon row of stand-up pinball games. 'I was crazy about it,' he informed me, with a large, toothy smile. 'I'd spend all my time at Pachinko rather than practise. Then I met Tiger Woods (there's just no escaping the man anywhere in the world) and realised that all my free time should be taken up practising golf, and that my hobby should be the same as my job – golf. So that's what I do.'

The subject of Japanese culture and golf was taken up again by Massy Kuramoto, who was produced for my interest by Andy an hour later in the clubhouse. Massy was and still is one of Japan's leading golfers, and certainly the most vocal. He's ruffled a few feathers in his time with his willingness to speak his mind, although the small, middle-aged man I found myself sitting opposite seemed jocular and content with life.

Curtis Strange had advised him to become a golf professional when they were at college together in America, after he had entered a tournament as an amateur and promptly won. 'I used to watch *The Wonderful World of Golf* on television back home in Japan and marvel at the likes of Nicklaus, Palmer and Player.' It was this early love, and Strange's advice that persuaded him not to turn to skiing, instead, as a profession.'Golf in Japan is like life,' he said, sounding like he was at the beginning of a long soliloquy. 'The Japanese look at the sun and the weather, plant their seeds and wonder if they will have the chance again. But the Westerner is like a lion. If he's not hungry, even if a rabbit hops by, the lion will not catch it and eat it. If he is hungry, however, the lion will try and catch anything, even an elephant. The Japanese lion, though, even if his stomach is full, will try and catch that rabbit because it happens to be there at the time and it may not come along later.'

Massy sat back, blinked a couple of times and crossed his arms in a way that suggested he felt he had explained his point perfectly. There was a silence in the room as I first looked at him, then at a bewildered

Yu, who was clearly wondering whether he had made a mistake in his interpretation, and finally at Andy. Eventually I said the obvious.

'Er, right, so where does the golf come into this little analogy, then?'

Yu put this point to Massy, who suddenly leapt back into life again as if he had merely been taking a short break before completing his story. 'In America or Europe, players will say to themselves: "This is my day, I'm playing perfect. I'm gonna take it all the way." But the Japanese player will say: "I'm playing too well. I must try and preserve some of this good form for tomorrow's round." If a Japanese golfer found himself at eight under par with two holes to play, he'd be happy to make sure his score stays at eight under, and not go for improving this in case it went wrong and he ended up at seven or six under. Tiger Woods (him, again) would try everything he could to transform eight under to ten under, though, wouldn't he?'

Massy had to go. I asked him if he felt he might win the tournament in Fukuoka. 'I don't think so,' he replied, with a broad smile on his face.

'That's not a very positive outlook,' I told him. 'And besides, why are you looking so happy about predicting you're not going to win.'

'Japanese culture, my friend,' Massy replied. 'Even if we think we're going to win, we never say so.'

'So,' I retorted. 'In reality you think you might win, after all.'

'Uh-uh,' Massy replied, shaking his head but still smiling. 'I can't even say what I'm thinking if I'm thinking I'm going to win because it's not in our culture to let people know this. So not only can I tell you that I might win, but I can't tell you that I'm thinking I'm going to win.'

I told him I understood, in the hope that by halting the conversation at this juncture, Massy's lions and rabbits would not enter the already confused scenario again. Japanese culture and golf were proving to be very strange bedfellows indeed.

21

Isao Aoki

Tokyo is spectacular, with no real centre but a myriad of neigh-
bourhoods merging seamlessly to produce a vast metropolis.
Much of it resembled an overgrown Piccadilly Circus, with
neon lights and large screens portraying music videos clinging to clusters
of buildings. Space in this city of 12 million inhabitants really is at a
premium, with the population scuttling around like ants and consistently
tall buildings stacked upon each other. Not a spare inch is wasted in this
mayhem, although further out one can take in the splendour of the Angel
Bridge, the gateway into the city over the Tokyo Bay.

The city was hungover from the football World Cup that had been
played out in Japan a couple of months earlier, with posters still evident
everywhere of either the Japanese national team or Manchester United.
David Beckham, in particular, seemed to stare out from most posters. If
you knew the right people to talk to, however, the game of golf was never
too far away.

I had met Iain Muir, from the golf equipment company Callaway, the
day before in Fukuoka. He had invited us to his office in downtown
Tokyo. As the only other British person I had come across now in three
days of visiting Japan, I took up his offer. Iain, a Scot from Paisley,
turned out to be the first non-Japanese golfer ever to obtain a tour card
on the Japanese Tour.

'I was crap,' he offered, with brutal honesty. 'I hardly won a yen. My parents were ex-pats so I spent most of my time doing what members of ex-pat families do, namely drinking and dancing. After flitting from job to job, I received an offer from the late Eli Callaway to help set up a Callaway office in Tokyo. This was six years ago, and I'm still here.'

His take on Japanese golfers was a similar one to that of Tai Kawata at the Narita GC. 'Big on numbers and statistics,' Iain explained. 'Ask any golfer what the degrees in loft are on his set of clubs and he wouldn't have a clue. Ask a Japanese golfer and he or she will reel off every single figure without even looking it up.'

Our next port of call would be the three-tiered driving range at Kasai, the largest range in the Tokyo district. I'd read about the monster driving ranges they have in Japan and wanted to sample one for myself. According to Iain there used to be a large range right in the heart of Tokyo city centre, beside the imposing red and white painted Tokyo Tower. 'It was open until three o'clock in the morning at weekends and became very much part of the Tokyo social scene,' he explained. 'Guys used to go out for a meal, have a few drinks and then go and hit balls until the small hours. It was also a popular place to meet girls, would you believe.'

The range was closed down a couple of years ago, but golf still existed in all sorts of nooks and crannies in the city. Some buildings had miniature ranges on their roofs, The well-known Seibu store housed a golf school on its sixth floor. And, according to a couple of guys I met at the Kasai range, there was even a brothel in Tokyo called the 'Hole in One', with a putting green in the waiting room.

The Kasai range was filled with the *kichigai* ('golf nuts') of Tokyo. It is estimated that fewer than one in six of the country's 15 million golfers has ever actually played on a golf course. The rest make do with the ranges. At Kasai, the range can house as many as 300 golfers at one time, on three tiers each providing 100 berths. It really is an imposing sight, especially with its 50-metre nets that can be automatically lowered to 25 metres if the winds from the nearby ocean pick up. At the weekends the range is open until midnight, with the most expensive floor being the ground, and the cheapest the top.

I drove balls there for half an hour, using another driver provided for me to surprisingly great effect. This was just as well because the impression was given that I was some kind of visiting British golf dignitary who could clearly play the game. Consequently, the general manager, the head of the Japanese Women's Golf Association whose offices were at Kasai, and a number of others crowded round to watch me drive. An embarrassment was thus avoided due to my sudden liking for a driver.

In the morning Andy Yamanaka arrived at my hotel, his flight back to Tokyo having skirted the edge of a full-force typhoon. We had been invited to Isao Aoki's house to meet the most famous golfer Japan has ever produced. Aoki is the only Japanese golfer to have become a household name throughout the golfing world and at 59 he was still going strong and winning tournaments on the US Seniors Tour, where he is often matching up against old adversaries such as Jack Nicklaus.

Yu was as keen to meet Aoki as I was, and came along just so that he could tell his friends that he had spent the morning with Isao Aoki. As Andy drove us to Aoki's house he filled us in with some stories about the man he referred to as 'Dad'.

'I was working with Dunlop when Aoki San was signed up by the company,' Andy explained. 'I ended up looking after him whenever he played overseas. I became his manager, his driver, his caddie, his wife.'

'His wife?' I asked, incredulously.

'Not after eleven at night,' Andy replied. 'Anyway, I caddied for him at the 1987 US Open at the Olympic Club, San Francisco, and then for all four majors in 1988 and ten or so tournaments a year after that. In 1990, when I got married, he was my best man and he gave me as a wedding present a brand new car he won at a Mitsubishi golf tournament.'

Aoki joined the seniors tour in 1992 and plays twenty or so tournaments a year, juggling his playing with commentating for Japanese television and organising his junior golf programmes back home in Japan.

'He's very different from most Japanese men,' Andy continued. 'He barely speaks a word of English but he has so many friends around the golfing world because of his attitude. Most Japanese feel inferior if they are unable to speak English, but Aoki San struts straight into a locker room and manages to communicate with everyone simply by laughing, nodding and slapping people's backs. He can't make an airline reservation or book a table at a restaurant in America or Europe, but he can speak the language of golf out on the course.'

Why did he bother playing golf elsewhere in the first case, though? 'Imagine how difficult it must have been for him,' Andy responded, clearly an unashamed admirer of Aoki. 'He was a typical Japanese man to begin with. He didn't like bread, didn't like meat, just Japanese food. Now, twenty years on, he eats toast and cornflakes and drinks coffee. He's tried very hard to adjust to a Western way of life when abroad because he wanted to improve himself as a golfer. He could have quite easily stayed in Japan, where he won the tour money list five times, and where he would have made more money than going to play all over the world. Everyone advised him to stay put in Japan, but he wasn't interested. He wanted to improve himself.'

We arrived in a quiet, plush suburb called Setagaya, close to the city centre, and waited initially in Aoki's offices connected to his house until a personal assistant took us to a hall at the bottom of a flight of steps. There we were required to take off our shoes and replace them with provided slippers, before being ushered upstairs to a waiting Mrs Chie Aoki, who greeted us and led us into a living room.

Standing by a trophy cabinet lining one long wall of the room, was the man they call the 'Tower', after the Tokyo Tower, because of his height. In fact Mr Aoki was six feet tall, which is hardly of 'towering' proportions, but in Japan it is. He looked lean, fit, healthy and indeed good for a 59-year-old.

On the way to sitting down, Andy and I both bumped our knees against a low glass table, which Aoki thought was extremely funny. His wife produced some iced coffee for everyone to drink before my audience with Japan's greatest golfer began.

'I had been playing on the Asian Tour and was on my way back home when I looked out of my aeroplane window down at Japan and realised how small a country Japan really was compared to the wider world,' he explained, through Andy acting as interpreter. 'That's when I realised I needed to play on a world circuit.

'In 1973 I was invited to play at the US Masters and Open, but when I got to the courses I was just excited to be there and didn't play at all well. I decided then to work really hard at my game to improve my chances overseas. Greg Norman became a great friend of mine because he, like me, found himself to be a strange foreigner in a new land on a new tour, and we ended up supporting each other even though we couldn't speak each other's languages. Then, at the 1977 US PGA Championships, I played alongside Johnny Miller and Tom Watson. I suddenly realised that these guys were nine years younger than me. Why should I have been intimidated by them?'

This is when Aoki's luck began to turn. In 1978 he won the World Matchplay at Wentworth, beating England's Simon Owen in the final. In 1979 he lost in the same final to America's Bill Rogers. Then, in 1980, came his famous battle with Jack Nicklaus at the US Open at Baltusrol.

'Jack hadn't won any majors for three years,' Aoki recalled. 'For Jack this was a major loss of form. At the 1980 US Open I found myself partnering him for all four rounds. On all four days Jack didn't make a single mistake. I played the best golf of my life, shot a six under which broke the existing record for the lowest score ever at the US Open, and still lost by two strokes to Jack.

'This still did me a favour, though. By breaking the existing record I received a special award from *Golf Digest* magazine. And by finishing as runner-up I felt accepted by the American people and felt at long last at home in America. It also motivated me to work even harder so that next time I could beat Jack.'

He never managed to beat Nicklaus when it really mattered, but maintained a hugely successful career that has kept him popular both in Japan and America. The fact that he remains such a star back in his homeland underlines what he perceives to be one of Japan's problems.

'In Japan, myself and Jumbo Ozaki have remained the best-known players for the past twenty years. I'm hoping this will change with players such as Izawa and Maruyama around now, but the point I'm making is that in America new stars have come along constantly, from Palmer to Nicklaus to Watson, to Miller, and now on to Woods. Some of the Japanese players tried to make it in America after me [namely Ozaki, Tommy Nakajima, even Massy Kuramoto, whom I met two days earlier in Fukuoka] but after two or three years they'd be forced to return to Japan in order to make some money.

'Japanese players are less likely to travel like I did because they have thirty or more tournaments to play in now on the Japanese Tour and there's too much money to be made in Japan, and lost elsewhere. But while they stay in Japan, Tiger Woods has raised the bar again in golf, just like Nicklaus did before. As far as I'm concerned, if I hadn't travelled and discovered the game on a global scale, there's no way I'd still be playing now.

'I've been playing golf at a competitive level for 45 years now and I consider myself to be a very lucky man to have earned a good living out of something I love doing so much. I'm nearly 60 years old and still have hopes and ambitions in my profession. How many at 60 can say the same thing in this world?'

Indeed, how many can? Aoki was, in fact, going to reach 60 the very next day. He was not entirely happy with the prospect. 'I think I will start going backwards from now on,' he declared, as he rose to his feet and we followed. 'Tomorrow I shall be 58 instead.'

He also informed us that the Aoki family would be holding a big party to celebrate the event. Whether or not I could have come along with Andy Yamanaka was irrelevant because that evening I would be catching a flight from Tokyo to New York, but it did occur to me, after Tommy Armour III's party invitation in New Orleans, that this was the second golfer's party I would be missing through my travel commitments. Somehow, as I looked around the serene environment of the Aoki household, I could not quite see the old man's gathering being similar to Armour's rock and roll bash back at his Dallas home.

Aoki San walked us to his front door and shook hands with all of us. 'Good luck,' he said, as we waved goodbye. 'And keep working on your golf.'

It had been a humbling experience to have been invited into the Aoki family home and made so welcome. To most followers of golf Isao Aoki is an obviously familiar figure, but few will have realised the personal battle he came through in order to establish himself on the global scene.

After a brief stop at a golf store where I bought a model of Tiger Woods complete with nodding head, it was nearly time to leave the country. The trip to Japan had only lasted four days, but it had felt much, much longer. Andy Yamanaka insisted on buying Yu and myself a final lunch in downtown Tokyo, refusing point-blank my vain attempts to buy him lunch instead.

I had arrived four days earlier complaining about my lack of sleep, the heat and the unbearable humidity, but I was now leaving touched by the hospitality and friendliness shown towards me from the professional golfers down at Fukuoka to Tai Kawata at the Narita Golf Club, to Yu, Isao Aoki and, especially, Andy Yamanaka, who had braved even typhoons to ensure that my time in Japan would be memorable.

'Now I think you have a better understanding of golf in Japan,' Andy said as he shook my hand.

And a better understanding of life in Japan, too. As the taxi pulled up beside me I took a backward step and watched as the rear passenger door automatically swung open and this time missed my kneecaps by a good couple of feet.

I gave Andy the thumbs up to acknowledge this successful manoeuvre. He let out a high-pitched giggle and clapped his hands. 'You are a quick learner, Stafford San.'

It's amazing how a couple of jarred kneecaps can improve your memory.

22

Mark the Shark

I was travelling on to New York for two reasons. It was on my way home from Tokyo (as true a statement as the one that argues that we're all related) and I fancied a stopover in one of the most ebullient cities in the world, but also I had arranged an appointment with the best-known, most successful sports agent in the game. It was this man, it can be argued, who transformed golf and every professional golfer's life into the big business the sport has become today.

Mark McCormack, founder and creator of the International Management Company (IMG), had agreed to see me at his New York offices on a late summer's Sunday morning in uptown Manhattan. The full picture had not really been explained to him which, I hoped, would be to my advantage. I was interested to hear his story, especially as this was the man whose company looked after Tiger Woods' affairs as well as managing a who's who of other top sportsmen and women from golf and a variety of different sports. McCormack was the man who first spotted the commercial potential of Messrs Arnold Palmer, Jack Nicklaus and Gary Player. Maybe he would feel the same vibes about me!

The impact McCormack had made on sports business had been very clear in Japan, where the marketing of Woods had reached a near frenzied state. Apart from the silly statue I had bought (there are rows and rows of smiling, nodding Tigers on display in that Tokyo store alone), you could buy virtually anything with either the Woods' signature or face endorsing the product. It was down largely to the efforts of McCormack that Woods had earned far more off the course than his considerable winnings on it. It was also down largely to IMG that Tiger's private life had become virtually non-existent.

The previous night's sleep over the Pacific Ocean and across the total width of America from west coast to east had been something of a disaster. I had arrived that evening at 7.05 which, according to both the hands on my watch and the date it showed, was precisely five minutes after I had left Tokyo. Either they've really speeded up passenger aeroplanes these days, or I had crossed over the International Date Line and gone back in time. My body clock, however, was not party to all this. It was just – and only just – beginning to come to grips with being eight hours ahead of London when suddenly, without any prior warning, it was asked to be five hours behind London or, worse still, 13 hours behind Tokyo. Clearly it had had enough of all this and went on strike. The anticipated night's sleep was instead replaced by channel-flicking in my hotel room.

Still, a typically Sunday morning feel to the day, as I walked up Madison towards the IMG New York offices in East 71st Street, perked me up considerably. The aroma of coffee was abundant as people either strolled past with newspapers in hand, or sat in the coffee houses drinking a long, lingering expresso.

Penny Thompson, McCormack's personal assistant, opened the imposing door and led me upstairs into a grand office full of leather armchairs, portraits and sketches on the walls, table lamps and an oak desk. Mr IMG would be along shortly, allowing me time to take a quick look around the office. After all, a man's office tells you quite a lot about the man.

The influence of golf on this particular subject's life was evident. A bronze statue of a golfer stood on a small table, putter in one hand as the other punches the air, with the words 'Get in There' inscribed below. An

All-American Collegiate golf award to Arnold Palmer was nearby, and on the wall a painting of golfers playing on the St Andrews links over one hundred years ago sat above a fireplace. Near the door, the world's top one hundred golf courses for 2002, according to a golf magazine, was hung up and framed. A quick inspection revealed a number of courses I had played (or tried to play) during the past year.

St Andrews, for example, was placed 5th. Muirfield was 9th, Royal Melbourne 10th, Ballybunion 11th, Carnoustie 22nd, Portmarnock 34th, New South Wales GC 47th and Wentworth 73rd.

I was still inspecting this list when a small cough broke the silence. McCormack had entered the room and was beckoning me to sit down next to him. At 71 years of age he remained as sharp as ever.

I assumed his career in golf began when, as a lawyer, he discovered Palmer. McCormack explained that I was wide of the mark by thirty years. 'Actually, it all started when I was six years old,' he said. 'I was hit by a car on my way home in Chicago from school and fractured my skull. The doc told me I wouldn't be able to play American football again. This was a big blow because, like all American kids in the 1930s, that's all I ever wanted to do. My dad knew I loved all sports, however, and started me up playing golf.'

The results were impressive. 'I went on to win the Chicago Prep School championships and then played as the number one member of the college team at William and Mary in Virginia. This, eventually, led to me appearing in four US amateurs, three British amateurs, as well as playing in South Africa and Australia.'

The 1958 US Open at Southern Hills, Tulsa, proved to be the end of McCormack's playing career. 'I shot a 78 and a 81,' he recalled. 'The point about this is that I had played as well as I possibly could have done in Tulsa and yet was still so far behind the best. Very early on I was one under and was actually leading the US Open. That's my one claim to golfing greatness. The truth, though, was that I realised I wasn't quite good enough to become a golf champion.'

This is very Mark McCormack. No emotions here, just a pragmatic approach and an immediate search to solve the problem. Working as a lawyer in Cleveland his wish was to stay connected to golf, and so he came up with what was at the time a novel idea.

'I figured that clubs would like a well-known golf professional to come and play at their club in an exhibition round and deliver a talk. I set up an exhibition company and soon those golfers who appeared were earning between $750 to $1,000 an appearance.' Which was a large sum of money in the late 1950s.

'Then, in 1960, Arnold Palmer told me he hated all his off-course organisation and asked if I would like to oversee his business affairs. He'd just won the Masters and finished runner-up to Kel Nagle at the British Open. Shortly afterwards, Gary Player came on board. My dad, who was in advertising, had a work friend whose wife was South African. As a result Player came to stay with them every year when he played golf in or around the Chicago area. I'd actually met Player when we both played in the '58 US Open. I approached him through my dad's friend and signed him up. A year later, a young Jack Nicklaus saw me at the tenth tee at a golf tournament to say that he was thinking about turning pro and would I be interested in working with him? Before anything had been arranged, Jack became a professional, but I went up to Columbus to meet him and his father anyway and an agreement eventually was made.'

At this point he produced a letter, dated 9 October 1961, which he wrote to Nicklaus expressing his delight in meeting him and his father, and how he hoped they would soon be working together.

All this was either astonishingly good luck, or equally astonishingly remarkable foresight on the part of McCormack. To his credit he is honest about these early days. 'I'd love to say I had the whole thing planned, but it was very much step by step. You've gotta remember that when they came on board, Palmer had won one major, Player had just started playing in the States, and Nicklaus had just turned pro. If they'd all shot 80 in their first couple of tournaments, I'd still be practising law now. Instead the three of them started to win everything, including the next six Masters in a row. I created "Big Three Challenge Golf", in which Palmer, Nicklaus and Player went on exhibitions all over the world, and this coincided with the advent of television into most people's living rooms.'

McCormack would venture into other sports. The cartoonist behind the Dennis the Menace cartoon lived in Geneva and put him in touch with a French skier named Jean-Claude Killy. A few months later, Killy became a sporting superstar at the 1968 Grenoble Winter Olympics. In the same year the most dominant tennis player in the world, Australia's Rod Laver, wrote asking for help. To prove this McCormack produced two further letters, to add to his own written to Jack Nicklaus, one from the cartoonist and the other from Laver. Then the Formula One motor racing star, Jackie Stewart, joined the ranks, too.

The next stage in the rise of both Mark McCormack and golf was down to television. 'I was offered a job as head of leisure time at a Los Angeles TV company,' he explained. 'I informed my law firm who came up with a unique solution. I should stay at the company and keep all the money I made from my outside work as long as I gave them all the legal work that stemmed from it. This was a pretty novel deal from a high-powered legal firm in the mid-1960s, but it was one I immediately accepted. I started up my company, called it first National Sports Management, then International Management Inc, and finally IMG. The beauty of the deal was that if it all failed, I was still a partner at the law firm.'

The conversation was interrupted by a telephone call from his wife, Betsy Nagelsen, the former American women's tennis star. McCormack was apologetic on his return, before moving on to how golf became big business.

'You're an exception, of course. Other than people like you, the vast majority don't get the chance to talk to, let alone play with their sporting heroes. But television brings these heroes into people's living rooms, from anywhere in the world. Golf also was conducive to commercialism because of all the equipment and clothing required. I soon realised that

Arnold Palmer, as my first golfer, would be better served known as a brand, rather than a golfer. You think that doesn't happen? Think of Lacoste and you think of a shirt with a crocodile on it, not a French tennis player of the 1930s. I see Palmer as Thomas Edison and Tiger Woods as Bill Gates. Tiger's been crucial to the growth of the sport in the inner cities and throughout the ethnic minorities. Golf now is truly a global sport, and it is developing fast in countries such as China, India and Indonesia.'

Ah, Tiger ... 'I find it a bit difficult with Tiger these days. I see him in Isleworth, where we both live, but I try not to bother him too much. It's a fine balance between wanting to let him know I care and at the same time not harassing him. If I say, come on over to dinner, he may think: "Oh no, then I've got to come." But if I don't, he might get the impression I don't care. Which, incidentally, I do. He's handled himself impeccably and in doing so has most probably become the biggest sporting icon on the planet.'

He has similar high praise for Tiger's father, Earl. 'Back in 1997 Earl started talking about his son being someone who is well beyond golf. He didn't quite say he'd be like Gandhi, but he got close to it. Well, at the time everyone was rolling their eyes and thinking: "Who's he kidding?" It's like Richard Williams announcing that his two daughters, Venus and Serena, would come to dominate women's tennis. They've both been proved right, though, haven't they?'

McCormack's own golf career has come grinding to a virtual halt. 'I stopped playing the game in the early 1970s for three reasons,' he admitted. 'I was once good enough to qualify for the US Open, when I could fade a ball around trees eight times out of ten and be able to hit a seven iron 155 yards, but then I found the fade wasn't working and the seven iron was only making 135. It also took too long for someone with my schedule, and it wasn't enough exercise. I took up tennis instead, where I expect nothing of myself and it can be done in an hour of good exercise. My wife tells me my only talent as a tennis player is picking my doubles partners.

'My golf these days is confined to playing with three good friends of mine: Michael Bonallack, the former Secretary of the R&A; Sandy Tate, the President of the US Golf Association; and Colin McLean, a former captain of the R&A. For the last four years we've been trying out different courses to play. Next time it's going to be in Ireland.

'The thing about golf is that you can learn a lot about the person you're playing with. If you've got a soft putt say from here [he gets up and stands in a corner] to here [he walks a few feet across the room] you can line it up both ways and hole it; you can pick it up as if it's conceded; or you can knock it in with one hand, a style that would guarantee you, say, two successes out of three, adding if you miss that you would have putted it if you'd tried properly. That tells me a lot about how people react to situations. I've learnt a great deal about people out on the golf course.'

In which case, he would have picked up that at times I can act like a child when it's not going my way on a golf course, and can be unbearable when it is. I declined to inform him of this, instead telling McCormack of my 17th place in the World Ice Golf Championships, my 23rd in the European Office Putting Championships, and my rise from 122 at Royal Melbourne to 86 in Kent in just one year. Strangely, I forgot to mention my 108th in the European Mini-Golf Championships.

There's nothing like impressing such a powerful man in sport, and this was nothing like impressing such a man. McCormack laughed, slapped my back as he led me out of his smart offices, shook my hand and made absolutely certain that I had left the premises.

I was still trying to work out Mark the Shark's response to my impressive achievements as I walked the 18 blocks through midtown Manhattan to Mark Hoffman's apartment. Hoffman, you may recall, was the excitable American real estate dealer I met on a windy day at Ballybunion Golf Club, on the west coast of Ireland. He was the one who informed me that he loved me after a particularly fine, if unexpected, five iron that deposited the ball inches from the pin.

We had spoken since, when I telephoned him briefly to ensure he was well following the September 11th atrocity in New York, but this was our first meeting. Over coffee in his top-floor apartment, overlooking much of the Manhattan skyline, Mark peppered me with questions concerning my golfing year before turning his mind back to 9/11, just a few days after we had played in Ireland.

Now, a year on (we were just a week away from the emotional first anniversary) Hoffman had recovered and was keen to see himself and his city move on. He had started up golf lessons again with the man who first taught him 25 years before, which meant a Sunday morning drive each week from Manhattan to Long Island for tuition. 'I love the game more than ever now because the lessons are definitely making an impact,' he said. 'I'll never master it, of course, but I feel that there are days now when the game allows me to gain the upper hand for a short while. Then I'm happy.'

As a parting gift he gave me a golf book on golf courses in the New York area and insisted that the next time I was in the area we would fix up to play at Bethpage or Baltusrol, or maybe even Shinnecock Hills, just a little further away. 'It's going to be some game,' he promised, as he waved goodbye.

That's another, crucial aspect to golf that I hadn't given much thought to until now. I had just spent an hour or so in a Manhattan apartment having coffee with an American I had met some 3,000 miles away in Ireland, on a golf course a year before. Despite our obvious geographical differences, a game had brought us together and, for one morning in Ireland, and another in New York, we had something only we could share.

All this from a stick and a ball.

Mark McCormack suffered a serious heart attack in January, 2003, and died after remaining in a coma on May 16th.

23

My part in America's Ryder Cup downfall

After so much travelling, my hunger for playing golf was now voracious, as was my now desperate desire to meet the greatest golfer in the world. Tiger had just lost out on the US PGA Championships, settling for second place after the American outsider, Rich Beem, clung on to his lead, and I was still searching in vain for not only that one exceptional round, but an audience with Mr Woods.

I had asked Mark McCormack to look into setting a meeting between myself and Tiger although, in the meantime, I had also received another firm rebuff from IMG. McCormack was the man who owned the company that represented Woods although, by all accounts, what Tiger chose to do or not was entirely down to Tiger.

In the meantime, buoyed by my sudden liking for a driver, I returned to Sundridge Park Golf Club, the venue of my orgasmic 86, and this time shot an 89. Not bad, not bad at all, but still three shots worse than my best caused mainly by a sudden malfunction in the putting department.

This concerned me enough a few days later to turn up at Harleyford Golf Club, in the foothills of the Chilterns, an hour ahead of my tee time in order to practise on the putting green. My partner for the day would be Sir Steve Redgrave, the five times Olympic rowing champion, and a man who gave me one of the most testing weeks of my life when I joined him and the rest of the British coxless fours boat for a week's training and racing a couple of years back.

Right from the off, Redgrave peppered me with a series of questions concerning my golf. What's my handicap? Where have you played? What's your lowest round? I thought we would be playing a friendly, leisurely round of golf, but Steve wanted to add a competitive element with a matchplay competition.

In his white golfing shoes with Union Jack flags printed on both and the name 'Steve' above, Redgrave certainly looked the part, but he was far from happy with his condition and his golf. 'I've grown fat and old,' he said, although he looked pretty fit to me. 'And I haven't played anywhere near enough golf to reach my goal.'

His goal was to become a single-figure handicapper in just over a year, now that he thought he would have the time to work on his game, but his enormous celebrity status, as befits a man who has made Olympic history, has meant rounds of golf have fallen way to speeches, appearances and charity work. It emerged that this round with me would be the last chance he would get to score nine under or less in a round before his time was up, and even if he did it would not be enough to reduce his handicap from 13.8 to 9.

Still, he did not appear unduly concerned by all this. In fact, Redgrave revealed the contentment of a man who had achieved everything he had set out to do as a sportsman and was now reaping the fruits of all his hard labours.

He was on good form too. When he saw a tee placed in my mouth he rebuked me. 'An old codger told me off for doing exactly the same thing,' he explained. 'Apparently, if you do that for any length of time there's quite a health risk from the fertiliser. This old boy knew of someone who was so severely poisoned by this that he ended up losing his leg.' The tee flew out of my mouth.

'I remember the first golf club I ever played at,' Redgrave continued. 'Farnham Park, near Slough. There was a sign there saying: "Golfers, please don't lick your balls on the course." Well, of course, we'd all shout

out: "Chance would be a fine thing."'

For the first nine holes it was nip and tuck. Steve would win a hole, then I would bounce back. I would surge ahead, then Steve would win the next hole, and so on until, at the turn, Steve held a slender one-hole lead. The highlights up to now included Steve nearly been clocked by someone's ball as we stood in the middle of the second fairway (we were in mid-conversation as the ball bounced past at head height a couple of feet behind him) and two 20-foot putts that he sank. My driving was going well but my putting was very ordinary.

'The way your golf has come on has followed the exact route I took,' Steve said, as we sat at the halfway house for a few moments taking in some refreshment. 'I bet you were scoring a birdie every other round, and a few pars, but also scored some horrendous nines and tens, didn't you, to begin with. But now you've become far more consistent and hardly ever score a birdie.' He was, of course, correct.

I knew the round would turn for the worse at the tenth where Steve mishit his bunker shot, blasting the ball so hard that it would still be travelling now if it was not for the fact that it cannoned off the lip of the bunker, ballooned high into the air, and plopped on to the green a couple of feet from the pin. From that point on my putting, which used to be so solid, disintegrated, and Redgrave romped to a 3&2 victory.

Over a quick drink back in the clubhouse, he revealed that his lowest score ever was 79, how he cannot abide practice, never visits a driving range and, indeed, only plays golf on a course, and is hell bent on reaching a single-figure handicap one day. 'I'm hoping I'll have more time soon to do this,' he said wistfully.

He also talked of his commitment to the charity, Sparks, which raises money for medical research. 'With money raised through numerous celebrity golf days, polio vaccines have been financed, as has research into ultrasound machines,' he explained. 'That's yet another thing about golf. You'd be amazed how much money the game raises through giving the chance to punters to play with either celebrities or professional golfers.' This made me feel rather ashamed of myself. I didn't mention this to Steve, but I had always been rather dismissive of the C-list celebrities who tend to converge at these golfing 'charidee' days, a gaggle of where-are-they-nows with their tired old patter and hangers-on. This was clearly rather harsh on my part and I vowed not to form such a view again.

Redgrave left with a final tale concerning the time he met his golfing hero, Sandy Lyle. 'It was a couple of years ago at Wentworth and Lyle was watching at a certain green when I played a bunker shot to six feet from the hole. I then managed to three-putt from there. I was rather embarrassed to have played so badly [hey, we've all been there], especially in front of someone I admired and looked up to so much.

'Anyway, a couple of holes later I holed a 50-foot putt, looked up and saw Lyle applauding the shot. No class to world class in ten minutes. That's what golf can do for you, isn't it?'

It certainly can, although my final score of 100, on an admittedly tricky, unseen course with horrendous greens, suggested I was still languishing in the no-class category. A putting lesson back at the World of Golf with David Young made me realise that in my quest to drive a ball I had neglected the most important part of the game. My hitherto solid putting style had been transformed into a nasty jab. Thirty minutes later, a smoother, pendulum style had returned.

Would this be enough to see me through the potential disaster that awaited me at Royal St George's, Sandwich, the following day? Well, yes, and no. Playing with the former Walker Cup player, Mark Brooks, I shot 101. When you consider that on previous Open venues I had been humiliated – St Andrews, Carnoustie and especially Muirfield come to mind – 101 was almost acceptable.

Add to this the fact that the course was long, the rough treacherously high, and the greens fast, and so undulating that often I faced 20-foot putts that required a right to left lie quickly followed by a left to right, incorporating a slope that if overhit would force the ball to run to the edge of the green, but if underhit would roll the ball back to where it had begun its journey, it could have been worse. And the putting, although hardly exceptional, was good enough to see a few ten-footers roll in. Indeed, on the par four 10th, I even parred a hole, the same one that probably cost Tom Kite the chance of becoming Open champion in 1993. 'Kite would have paid you a lot of money for that score,' Mark said, which immediately made me feel a better golfer.

There were, however, moments of excruciating humiliation, the pick being when we had to wave on a threesome behind us incorporating a 78-year-old, an 84-year-old and Mr Brian Pope, former England international rugby union scrum half, who just happened to be 94. 'Sorry to have held you up,' Mark shouted at Mr Pope, as he waved them through. We, in the meantime, were still searching for my ball in rough that was clinging to our kneecaps.

Life could have been worse, though. I had heard only that morning that Ken Rose, Justin's father, had died from the leukaemia he had been fighting so hard against over the past year. It was a cruel blow to a young man already forced to grow up so prematurely in his life.

The sun shone crisply on this early autumn day, with the French coast, some 23 miles away, clearly visible, and the ferries chugging in and out of Folkestone harbour just around the bay. A famous, old and traditional golf club, the tranquillity of Royal St George's would be transformed into pandemonium ten months later when the 2003 British Open would be staged there. 'The rough will be this high by then,' Mark informed me, as his hand went to almost waist height. Which was a daunting prospect, not only for rookie golfers like me, but for any spectator under four and a half feet tall.

A return to the much friendlier Purley Downs GC in Surrey resulted in a 91, far better but still a long, long way off that elusive 81 I required to score my first-ever nine over or less in a round of golf. I was beginning to worry that I had reached something of a plateau in my game. That maybe this would just about be it. My scores would fluctuate between the mid-80s at best and the three-figure mark at worst, depending on the severity of the course.

A typical round these days would shape up like this. I would start with a double bogey (slightly stiff and cold, not warmed up enough) and probably follow up with another two over score or maybe a bogey. Then I would play a number of bogey and par holes, driving well, and both approaching and putting reasonably solidly. This would continue until somewhere around the 11th or 12th when, inexplicably, my hitherto straight and accurate driving would fall to pieces and I would start splaying the ball into the trees to my right. Always to my right. I might get away with double bogeys here, but more often triples for two or three holes. Then I would improve for the remainder of the round without quite finding the form of holes four to ten, and often losing the ability to chip. Every time. Without fail.

I explained all this to David Williams, a former professional player on the European Tour, when we met at the De Vere Belfry for a rather important evening's work. Williams sympathised with my plight, and added that in his opinion Royal St George's was the toughest Open venue of all. '101's really quite acceptable,' he argued. I took to Williams immediately after this, even if he is a good liar.

It was now the eve of the Ryder Cup and I had sought and been granted permission by the European PGA's David Garland, the tournament director, to aid and abet Williams in the crucial role of deciding where to place the pins on the greens for the first day's play.

While Colin Montgomerie and Padraig Harrington, Darren Clarke and Sergio Garcia, Phil Mickelson and Davis Love were tucking into their eve of Ryder Cup dinner, Williams and I were about to play a significant part in how the following day would pan out for them. Jesper Parnevik was there, of course, in bad form seemingly on the course, but his usual good form off it. 'Where's your upturned cap?' I asked, when he ambled over for a quick chat. 'Where's yours?' he responded, rather surreally.

I'd spotted Bernhard Langer earlier in the day. He smiled and nodded at me from afar, a response that left me guessing at what was going through his mind. It was at the very same venue that I had made a total arse of myself in the company of the German in the Benson & Hedges pro-am.

Being the good Christian that he is, I hoped Langer's thought process went something like this: 'Oh good, there's that nice chap Ian, who tried his best and persevered, showing great character even when it went wrong, as he played a round with me. It really is lovely to see him again.'

Alternatively, he might be thinking, 'Oh bloody hell, there's that complete idiot who tried to play golf with me, that unbelievably dreadful day, using ladies' clubs, who hit his balls into every available stretch of water and sand, and then got heckled on the 18th. I pray with all my heart that he doesn't speak to me now.'

And then there was Tiger, still seemingly unapproachable, not only by the likes of me, but even by the likes of his fellow teammates in the US Ryder Cup team, hence his separate, early morning practice sessions that week and his different clothing from everyone else. Apart from the Open and US Open, this was the closest I had come to him, but still I was no nearer to ever actually meeting him on a one-to-one basis. And time was fast running out.

I had a more immediate concern to deal with, however. David and I used a buggy to drive to the tenth green, where we would start our work. To save time, David had a habit of not actually stopping the buggy as we approached a head-high rope, but slowing down and then asking me to lift the rope above our heads as we drove past. I hadn't foreseen the potential dangers of placing the pins, but a mistimed yank of the rope and we both could have been garrotted.

The famous Brabazon course was virtually empty now, save for a few workers brushing the bunkers and cutting some grass. Thirteen hours later some 40,000 spectators would be swarming around the fairways and greens as the fourballs began the 34th Ryder Cup, but for now all was quiet.

The tenth, of course, is one of the most famous holes in golf. Those confident, brave or stupid enough go for the green, which means a fade over the lake to the right in front of the green. If it works, a birdie is possible. Those more cautious use a mid-iron down the fairway in front of the lake, and then chip on to the green, but this rules out almost any chance of a birdie, and relies on the chip being close enough to the pin to guarantee a par. Suffice to say, all kinds of problems have been witnessed at this hole in the past, although few have copied my experience of playing safe during the pro-am, and then still chipping in to the water with my second shot.

My main responsibility was to act as 'official tester', putting balls across the superb if testing De Vere Belfry greens in order to help Williams decipher the exact lie. Then he, partly on the evidence of my questionable putting, would choose the pin positions best suited to test the players, leaving a small mark with green paint sprayed on to the grass.

'Most people have a set ruling that they make six holes easy, six holes average and six holes difficult,' Williams explained as we drove. 'I tend to go more with my gut feeling on this. We have to be extremely careful today to make each hole a challenge without it being ridiculous.'

So, no pins in the bunkers, then, or on the banks of the lake? 'Funnily enough, sometimes the pins that appear more centrally placed on the greens are the toughest ones to play. If you put a hole a couple of feet from a bunker, no one's going to go for it with an approach shot. Instead, they'll hit the ball on to the centre of the green and then try and hole the putt. But if the pin is eight feet from a bunker the player might just go for it, which then presents the chance of either a fantastic shot or finding a bunker.'

I'd never thought of that. 'I've set pins in the past which have proved too tough and players have complained,' he continued. 'The last thing you want to do is make the players look stupid. When you set a difficult pin, you still make sure there is a way to play it. Besides, everyone in the Ryder Cup teams, having dinner right now, knows we're placing the pins.'

Over the course of the next two and a half hours we found suitable places for the pins for not only the morning fourballs the following day, which Europe would win 3–1, but also the afternoon's foursomes, in which the US would hit back to end the first day's play three and a half to four and a half behind. David also highlighted the likely spots for the singles holes for the crucial Sunday singles.

Some of my putting, as the late afternoon transformed into evening and the West Midlands light faded quickly, was of a surprisingly high standard. Some of it, too, was of a surprisingly desperate nature. On more than one occasion, Williams watched my ball miss the hole by a number of feet and pointed out that it was more likely my putting skills rather than the difficult lie that produced such a wild result.

'The thing is,' he said, as we sped from green to green, 'we'll get blamed if Europe lose and get absolutely none of the credit if they win.'

His walkie-talkie suddenly crackled into life. 'Willy,' a voice was heard. 'We've got the pairings for tomorrow, if you're interested.' We crowded round the walkie-talkie as the names Clarke and Bjorn versus Woods and Azinger were read out, followed by Garcia and Westwood against Duval and Love, Montgomerie and Langer versus Hoch and Furyk, and then, finally, Harrington and Fasth against Mickelson and Toms. 'We'll win that,' Williams announced, as we got back to work. 'Probably 3–1,' he added, which proved to be unerringly correct.

At the 16th, described by Williams as 'smelly' not because of the water in front of it, but because of the degree of difficulty, we had a spot of bother. We had both been chatting so much that neither of us could remember whether we had marked out the pin-placing with the green spray paint that was only slightly a darker tone to the colour of the grass. Although the greenkeepers would find the marked-out hole easily enough in the morning using directions, we could not. Having spent ten minutes trying to find where we had possibly located the hole, we decided we must have forgotten to spray and marked out another hole. This, of course, could have caused all kinds of consternation the following morning if, indeed, we had already marked out a hole before. In fact, it could have lead to two flags fluttering on the small 16th, which would have been a first in the Ryder Cup.

At the 18th, the point where my hitherto abject humiliation during the pro-am with Langer plummeted to the point where I would have liked to have contorted myself into a Basil Fawlty crab position, Williams and I stopped for a moment and gazed at the big leaderboard with all the names of the fourballs now posted up. I told him of the heckle I received at this green, and then the hilarious autograph hunter.

'You did well not to smack a wedge on to his head,' the European PGA tour's tournament director commented.

'Is that allowed in the rules of golf, then?' I asked.

'Well, no,' he replied. 'You would have been thrown out of the pro-am, off the course, and probably out of golf too, and that's even before the police got in on the act. But I wouldn't have blamed you if you had.'

At the 18th, hundreds of ducks and geese were settled, mainly by the side of the huge lake that dominates from the tee to the hole on the green, either sleeping, looking around or, in the case of some, gliding smoothly across the surface of the water. They'd be in for a shock the following morning. In fact, one was almost in for a shock immediately when Williams produced his can of white paint and started marking the out-of-bounds line. The duck – a green mallard for those who prefer looking at them to eating them – refused to budge at first. 'If he doesn't move this instant I'm going to spray the line over his back,' Williams said, which would have resulted in the out-of-bounds line waddling all over the 18th.

It was almost dark when we finally drove back to the rules office close to the first tee. Williams, a player on the European Tour between 1980 and 1996, spent the final few minutes of our time together bemoaning the fact that his golf had gone off the boil.

'There was a time not too long ago when I'd be going round this course in par, no problem,' he explained.

I suggested that now it would be more like ten over. Williams looked horrified at the suggestion.

'Bloody hell, I'm not that bad,' he said. 'More like four over. And on a bog-standard course, whereas it used to be four or five under, now it's par.' He shook his head and added: 'I'm not playing as much as I used to, and it's all going to pot.'

I watched him as he trudged back to the office, this man whose game had gone completely to pot. I hadn't volunteered this information to him, but if I ever recorded a round of five over anywhere I would perform an elaborate victory celebration right by the pin, incorporating a great deal of shouting, waving, dancing and the removal of clothes.

Let's hope, strictly from everyone else's point of view, that this never happens.

24

Grabbed by the goons

My pin-placing, together with Sam Torrance's inspirational leadership, Curtis Strange's questionable tactics and the superior team ethos of the Europeans, led to a Ryder Cup victory for the home team 72 hours later.

After all the shenanigans at Brookline three years before, the tournament was back on track, not only as a magnificent sporting spectacle, but also as a magnificent example of sportsmanlike behaviour. In a sporting world where footballers dive to gain penalties, cricketers claim catches they know they have grounded, and a whole range of others use illegal substances to enhance their performances, it was a timely reminder of one of the true qualities of golf I had once failed to recognise.

Not for the first time the Ryder Cup was a week Tiger would not want to dwell on for too long. Having received mass criticism from the media for his apparent lack of teamwork, his play, by his own extraordinary standards, was decidedly average. When it was all over, and while some of the American team joined the Europeans in celebration, Woods was quick to be heading off for the airport. Once again, it wasn't really the best time to suggest to his advisors a get-together with a guy whose own Belfry experiences were even worse. Time was fast running out to secure my long-cherished dream of an audience with the man.

My wife bought me a green leather-bound book entitled *My Golfing Record* for my birthday. Inside it resembled 'Baby's First Diary', where, instead of having headings such as 'weight, height, time of birth, place' and so on, it bore a series of columns entitled: 'I learned my golf at . . .' or 'My Golfing Equipment . . .' Turning the page, 'My Handicap Record' could be followed and then, a page on 'My Golfing Highlights'. This section was bare and, judging by my exploits so far, could well remain so for a considerable amount of time. After all, I had scored no holes in one in 15 months of playing golf, no albatrosses, no eagles, no sub-80 rounds, and certainly not come close to reaching my first nine over par score. I thought about sticking down my first birdie, my first sub-100 round and first sub-90 round, but felt placing this information under the heading 'A record of my triumphs' was stretching it a bit far. The rest of the book provided a 'Round Report' on each page, encouraging me to spend my evenings after a round, meticulously recording the day's play.

This, then, was the golfer's equivalent of the trainspotter's notebook. The surprise here was that my disenchanted wife, who showed less than no interest whatsoever in my golf, who let it be known that I dressed like 'a 70-year-old' when I donned my golfing wear, and who thought I was referring to the weather when I told her of my 86, was now showering me with golfing gifts. It was akin to presenting me with a Miss Selfridge voucher when discovering I had a sudden penchant for wearing women's clothes.

I met up with David Rennie again at Wentworth for a quick nine holes on the Edinburgh course. I hadn't played with David for a year, not since my third-ever round, and first in England after my return from Australia. He had been present during my nine holes with Fanny Sunesson on the west course a few months back, but acted more as the official photographer on the day, rather than my golfing partner.

We were both in for a pleasant surprise for, if you discount the triple bogey on the 10th and then the double bogey on the 11th, I resembled a golfer. I'm not quite sure what David was expecting, but it clearly wasn't the sight of me dropping four shots on the remaining seven holes. My driving was very acceptable, my putting solid, my chip shots verging on good.

246

'Remember how I described your putting last time?' David asked, after he observed me sink a nine-footer.

'Atrocious, David, was the word.'

'Well, it's perfectly OK now. In fact, I'd go as far as to say I can now class you as a golfer. I'll be honest, a year ago I was wondering what the hell I was doing out on the same golf course as you. You shouldn't really have been allowed to play here at Wentworth at all. But now you can play the game. You can definitely play the game.'

My happy mood improved even more when, during lunch with Rennie in the clubhouse, David Garland, the European PGA Tour's director of tour operations, walked past in a group, stopped, turned round and walked over to our table. 'Just wanted to shake the hand of the man who helped steer Europe to Ryder Cup victory,' he said, with a smile.

The best part of the day was about to come, though. I was taking advantage of the facilities at Wentworth that morning because Ernie Els, the official world number three in terms of rankings at the time, but universally accepted as second only to you-know-who, had invited me to his house on the Wentworth Estate for later in the day. I had been hoping to meet the man dubbed 'the Big Easy' because of his huge, effortless swing since before the summer, but the various delays had worked in my favour because now I would not just be seeing one of the very best golfers in the world, I would be visiting the new Open champion.

A potential problem had been averted by the birth of Ben Els five days previously. Ernie had spent the week before in South Africa, leaving myself and his wife, Liezl, to finalise my visit. Since Ben was supposed to be born around the same day, I had this worrying vision in my head of finding myself with Ernie encouraging Liezl to 'push hard' amid a throng of midwives and nurses.

I was greeted on the Els' doorstep by their huge slobbering Newfoundland, Chloe, and their equally enormous St Bernard, George, who homed in, as all dogs do, on my crotch and backside. Once inside the hall, Liezl, as befitting the mother of a five-day-old baby boy, was in a bit of a flap. Grabbing my bag which contained a Babygro and a bib for

Ben, she explained that not only was Ernie not at home, but she had repeatedly failed to make contact with him.

'I've told him every day this week about you,' she said. 'Every day, except today. He's on a golf course, and there's no way I can get hold of him.' Leading me into their living room, she grabbed a TV remote control, switched on some golf, and suggested I sat down. 'If you're like every other bloody man, you'll be happy with the sport on,' she said, with a slightly resigned smile.

Things were not looking good. After a while I walked round the living room and the adjoining library. The Open was clearly important to the man but, although a Taylor Made driver rested in the corner of the hall, there was little else to suggest that one of the world's greatest golfers lived here. As Loyd Grossman might have said to a mystified panel on *Through the Keyhole*, 'So, David, who lives in a house like this?'

Liezl reappeared, this time with a gurgling Ben in her arms. She looked incredibly well for a woman who had given birth just five days' previously, if a little harassed by the situation. At that moment Ernie rang. My offical time slot with him was supposed to be between three and five o'clock, and here he was having just completed his round at Queenwood Golf Club at 4.45 p.m. Worse still, he wasn't overly keen to come home, either, to meet me. Despite various explanations backwards and forwards between myself, his management company in South Africa, and lately through Liezl, he didn't appear to know much, if anything, of my purpose.

After a brief conversation with Ernie over the phone, he suggested that Liezl and I came over to the club. 'If Mohammed won't come to the mountain . . .' Liezl announced, with another wry grin, before setting off for nearby Ottershaw.

In the plush clubhouse of this new and extremely exclusive golf club sat Ernie with a group of friends and a group of beers. I introduced myself to his merry company – Hennie, Darren and Brian from South Africa, and Lewis, an English professional on the Challenge Tour who seemed to have been taken under the Els wing – before explaining to Ernie what this was all about. He appeared confused until I presented him with a couple of my previous books and watched his expression change from disinterested to incredulous as he gazed at photographs of me in various sporting guises. My experiences training with the South African national rugby team interested him immensely, but what turned out to be the key to what was about to unfold was my time boxing against Roy Jones Junior.

'You fought Roy Jones Junior?' he asked.

'Who's Roy Jones Junior?' asked a couple of his entourage.

'He's only the best, pound for pound, boxer in the world,' Els replied. 'Man, I love watching him. He's awesome.' He looked at me and blinked. 'And you're a fucking madman. You'd better have a drink with us.'

And so began three hours of talking, laughing and predominantly drinking in the clubhouse bar at Queenwood Golf Club, as late afternoon turned into the middle of the evening. After Liezl had returned home with Ben we stayed for another hour, in which time Ernie made me a proposition I could hardly refuse. 'Now that I know you, how about you, me, Brian and Lewis play nine holes after the weekend here at Queenwood?'

The world's number two golfer, and current Open champion, had just invited me to play golf. 'Why not?' I replied, trying desperately to remain cool and hide my excitement.

'Then midday it will be, on Monday,' Ernie announced. 'Now let's have some more Chardonnay.'

My excitement soon began to wear thin, however, when the banter around the table focused on our forthcoming game. 'Do you have a sponsor for this book you're writing,' Ernie inquired.

I replied negatively. 'Excellent,' Ernie declared. 'Then I'll be taking money off you, then.'

Money. Money? No one said anything about money. Ernie was not exactly short of a bob or two, and Brian, sitting opposite with a huge grin on his face, was a retired, millionaire businessman who resided in nearby Sunningdale.

It got worse. When Ernie wasn't referring to me as 'crazy' for fighting Jones he was telling me what he was going to do with me after the weekend. 'I'm going to beat you up,' he said. 'I'm not going to take you on toe to toe because you've fought Jones. And I'm not going to leave your arms loose because I see you've also been a professional wrestler. So you know what I'm gonna do?'

'No, Ernie,' I replied. 'What are you going to do.'

'I'm gonna grab you by the goons,' he answered. 'Goons' is one of those Afrikaaner onomatopoeias. Its translation was never volunteered to me, but it's pretty obvious, isn't it?

Somehow, amid the various 'one more for the road' demands, I had managed to stay below the alcoholic limit for driving. I said farewell at nine o'clock that evening and drove home in a frenzied state.

Just what mess had I allowed myself to get into this time? On previous experiences, every time I had swung my clubs with a top player I had endured a humiliating nightmare. Els, save for Tiger, was the best of the lot.

As if this were not daunting enough, two of the three other people I would be playing with were considerably richer than me, and talking about laying heavy bets on the nine holes. As I approached my house, my own, lovely home I had worked so hard to gain, a sudden fear struck me. Just how much money were we talking about here? And how would my wife react to the news that I had just blown the house on a game of golf?

As I made the return drive back to Queenwood on the Monday morning, after a weekend in which I had thought of little else but this round of golf and the potential disasters that awaited me, I tried to convince myself that my new friend Ernie wouldn't allow such a disaster to befall me. To make certain of this, I decided I would push very hard to partner him in the foursomes we were about to play. This, I reasoned, would be my safety net.

Wrong again! Ernie Els, the three times winner of the World Matchplay (who, incidentally, would be facing Colin Montgomerie four days later in the 2002 Cisco World Matchplay at Wentworth), and noted as being one of the toughest opponents in matchplay golf, had an off day.

When I say an off day this is, of course, comparative. I hardly set the world alight exactly, although my nine over par for nine holes was just about the norm for me after 15 months of golf, and very much better than usual in such vaunted company. Ernie, however, missed a number of gettable putts that would have won or halved the hole.

After seven holes Brian and Lewis had won the match. 'That's £4,000 you owe us, then,' they told Ernie and me. Ernie didn't bat an eyelid. I, in contrast, felt all sorts of movements from around my backside area.

'We'll play double or quits,' Ernie suggested, which left me realising that quits would be good, but double would be totally disastrous.

'Come on pards,' Ernie said imploringly. 'We've got to play as if our lives depended on the next ten minutes' golf.'

Ten minutes later Ernie and I both stood over putts on the 18th green, Ernie for a five and me for a bogey six. If either of us could sink our putts the hole would be halved and all bets would be off. Not for the first time, Ernie's ball seemed destined for the hole until the last few inches when it turned and rolled agonisingly past. It was down to me, then, to save us £8,000, small change for Ernie, but a considerable amount for myself.

I missed the putt. Not by much, say, by four inches, but four inches that looked to have cost me half of the £8,000 Ernie and I would have to fork out back in the clubhouse.

'Whoops,' announced Ernie. 'Sorry about that, pards.'

Brian Mahon took pity on me. 'I'll tell you what,' he said. 'You don't have to pay me cash. I'll give you my address and you can send me a cheque, all right?' Lewis, meanwhile, was struggling to contain his laughter.

It was only as we were making our way back towards the clubhouse that Ernie finally came clean. 'You knew all along we were only having a joke with you, didn't you,' he said, with a grin.

'Yeah, sure, of course,' I said, with a hearty laugh which I hoped disguised my churning guts. 'I don't know. You boys, hey?'

And with that Brian and Lewis went off for some lunch, while Ernie and I found the sitting room inside Queenwood for our long, long-awaited conversation. Seventy-two hours after we were supposed to be talking, a good few Chardonnays later, plus many Afrikaans swearwords, nine holes of golf and the prospect of being fleeced for £4,000, I was finally going to discover what made the Big Easy tick.

25

The importance of being Ernest

Ernie Els used to have a recurring dream. 'I would be playing golf on a beautiful, lush green course, with trees swaying in a slight breeze and firm, firm greens, and I'd be walking up the final fairway on the 18th on the verge of winning a tournament.'

The reality, as experienced before the putt that would either qualify him for the play-off after four rounds of the 2002 Open, or demote him to fourth place, was rather different.

'I was extremely close to vomiting,' Els admitted, with a rather awkward, self-conscious smile.

A few holes back, the South African had what would be his third major triumph in the grasp of his big, bearlike paws. Then he blew his two-shot lead with an inexplicable double bogey and faced a tricky eight-footer just to make what would turn out to be a four-man play-off. In any circumstances this was a pressure putt, but no one watching that day, either beside the 18th at Muirfield, nor back at home in front of their television sets, had any idea just how much was resting on this one stroke.

'I needed to win the Open after the lead I'd built up and then lost,' he explained. 'I couldn't have been beaten in that tournament because, if I had, it could have been career-destroying.'

Really? 'Yes, really. It was not just about a putt, it was about the survival of my inner self. It was way beyond winning the Open. My career depended on it. You could see it in my face, my grip, my whole manner. I've never been so emotional before on a golf course in my life.'

Sinking the putt failed to end his misery. As far as Els was concerned, he had still, stupidly, thrown away his lead. 'I felt terrible before the play-off. I was in the scorer's hut when Sergio Garcia came in. He's a good friend of mine and he was saying: "Come on, you can do it now." But I looked like a man who had just blown the biggest title in the sport. Sergio couldn't understand my attitude at all.

'Then I saw Jos [Vanstiphout, his and my mental coach]. I said to him: "Don't give me any shit now, I know I've fucked up." If he'd got on my case I don't know what I would've done because I was so highly strung. He told me: "Listen, what happened happened. You've now got the four most important holes of your life. Get all the shit out of your head."'

Despite playing what he describes as only 'relatively solid golf', Els came through after Stuart Appleby, Steve Elkington and Thomas Levet all dropped crucial shots. It was the Big Easy's first Open, and third major after two earlier US Open triumphs.

'Afterwards I was pretty low. People must have thought it strange that I wasn't on a real high, but I knew I'd almost lost it. It didn't make it an enjoyable experience at all. In my dreams I'm walking down the fairway with the title in the bag. In reality, I was fighting my heart out just to stay in the competition and make the play-off. Only now, three months later, am I beginning to enjoy being Open champion.'

I stared at the big, blond man sitting opposite me for a while and digested all this information. Like everyone else, I had spent the years looking at golfers and forming the opinion they were nerveless to the point of being automatons. Even listening to someone like Malcolm Mackenzie, who won in his 510th tournament after nearly falling to pieces close to the end, was understandable because Mackenzie was, I had considered, a journeyman.

But this was Ernie Els talking. Arguably the only man capable of giving Tiger a consistent run for his money was close to turning into a wreck in front of the watching world. Golf is capable of doing this to even the best.

Ernie's confession served to provide two rather telling pointers to me. To keep on winning tournaments requires incredible mental strength and an ability to defeat the flood of nerves waiting at any moment to overflow. To do this under the unprecedented spotlight of Tiger Woods makes the job that much harder, and the achievement that much greater.

Yet this reminded me again that these people are only human. Remarkably gifted golfers, yes, and more often than not capable of controlling their minds better than the majority of us, but nevertheless ordinary human beings like you and me. Even Tiger.

Winning majors goes a long way to justifying Ernie's decision as a teenager to become a golfer. It may not seem like the toughest verdict to reach in life, but back home in South Africa it wasn't as easy as it may seem.

'I was a natural, all-round sportsman,' he recalled. 'I was a good 1,500 metres runner, despite my large frame, a decent tennis player, too, and I loved my rugby and cricket. Golf was always a big passion for me, but I had to keep it quiet from the rest of my school.'

I stopped him there. Excuse me? Did he say my drugs' habit, my tendency to wear rubber, my six nipples, or did he just say golf?

Els laughed at my response and explained. 'I grew up in an Afrikaans environment in Johannesburg. Golf wasn't even thought about at school. Everyone wanted to become a Springbok rugby player. People knew I played golf, but they had no idea how much of a passion it was. If they had, they would have looked at me as if something was very wrong.'

Later, at school, Els chose to come out of the closet. 'I'd started to win junior tournaments in South Africa, and then went to America and won the junior world championships, playing with a young boy called Phil Mickelson for two days. Because South Africa was so isolated back then, this became big news in the papers. It kind of justified my reasons for playing golf and by my later teens I knew the other sports had to give.'

So out went the tennis his mother so wanted him to play. 'I'd made the

Eastern Transvaal tennis team and went to tournaments all over South Africa, but there was too much politics and pressure, and I realised I wasn't good enough to become another Wayne Ferrera. Besides, I now live next door to Jim Courier [former world number one and multiple Grand Slam winner] and see how hard he trains. That's not in my make-up.'

Out, too, went the cricket. And, hardest of all, out went the rugby. 'I still trained with the boys, but didn't get involved in contact. It caused a few arguments at the time. You've got to understand that rugby was all part of the Boer macho upbringing most white boys had in those days. So people used to question why I wasn't playing rugby. In fact, I even got asked a few times if I was scared.'

Els had just touched upon the fact that he was a white kid growing up in a South Africa still very much under the abhorrent apartheid regime. It was a potentially tricky area to venture in to but, seeing that he was so worldly-wise now, and such good company too, I was interested to hear how he had come to terms with past history.

'Growing up I had a good life. We weren't rich, but we were by no means poor either, so we had a swimming pool in our garden, I walked to school every day, I practised my golf at Germiston GC and played at Kempton Park at the weekends. It was a perfectly normal and happy childhood. But then again, I had white skin.

'What I'm trying to say is the honest truth. It's not that people like me supported the regime. Don't forget, I was a kid. It was that we had no idea. When I joined the air force for my two years' national service, when I was 20 years old, I was in classes where they showed us what the ANC had done and how they had blown up this and that. The ANC, I was told, was my enemy. Then, five years later, Nelson Mandela was our president and I realised that everything I'd been told before was not correct.

'Look, in many ways, I'm proud to be an Afrikaans-speaking South African, but for the whole of my childhood I didn't know there were other people living in my country too. From the age of 20 onwards, I began to understand the rest of the world and that's when I also saw South Africa in a completely different light. You see, as a youngster, it was all right there in front of me, but I was so far away from it. In America, when I was playing golf in the early days, I'd say I was South African and I'd watch how people would almost back off and behave so negatively. I didn't understand at first why this happened because I was so naive.'

It was around this time that life in golf started to become very good, but not before the usual story of struggle and strife that appears to befall every top golfer at some point in their lives.

'I turned pro in 1989, by which time the expectations in South Africa were that I would become the world number one.' He laughed at this statement and shrugged his shoulders. 'That's how it is in South Africa,' he explained. 'I made 45,000 rand and went straight to America. I thought: "Here we go, go to tour school, get my card, join the PGA Tour circuit, win tournaments." But it didn't quite work out that way. For a start, within a week or so I realised that I wasn't the only good player around. Then I missed the cut for tour school. I returned home and everyone then turned round and said I clearly wasn't going to make it as a golfer.'

So, from becoming the word's best to a no-hoper in one season, then?

'Yeah, that's about right. I went back to America again and this time failed to even make the final stages of tour school. Then I was in big trouble. I'd lost all my confidence and worse, it didn't look as if I was going to make it at all as a professional golfer.'

Then, like a round of golf which suddenly transforms from bad to good in the space of a few holes, everything turned around for Ernie Els. 'I started to win tournaments in South Africa and everything clicked. Finishing fifth in the 1992 Open was a real boost. I also started playing regularly on the European Tour.'

Two years later Els made the considerable leap from promising professional to top player. 'I just felt really confident all season after winning in Dubai and beating Greg Norman in the process. I also won

256

the World Matchplay and, best of all, the US Open.' He laughed again. 'Of course, then I was the king again. I was going to win every single tournament I entered from then on.'

Except, of course, for the minor fact that a golfer named Tiger Woods not only entered the fray, but took a stranglehold on the world game. Els won a few tournaments, including the 1997 US Open for his second major title, but found himself too often finishing runner-up to Woods, including a staggering three times in three separate majors in 2000. To make matters worse, the South African's pronouncements that Woods was the best and too good for the likes of him surprised many who felt Els had adopted a losing attitude.

'This is the total, honest truth. It wasn't that I was scared of him. It wasn't even that I thought he was better than me. I tried reverse psychology on him, and it backfired big time on me.'

How did he mean? 'Well, if you're a foreigner in the US and you're going around saying how you're going to beat Woods, it doesn't look too great, does it? Besides, people like Sergio or Phil Mickelson have kept on saying how they're going to beat him, but they never do when it really matters. So I decided to state how Tiger was the best, and then nail him on the golf course. You see, I've always felt that I could say whatever, but I could always fall back on my golf game. I'd been able to do that for most of my career, at least until Tiger came along. As the results since 1997 will tell you, my policy didn't work.'

At first Els refused to accept Woods held the edge. 'On a couple of occasions he beat me by a single shot, and I could identify many times when I could and possibly should have won the tournament. Early in 2000, however, he beat me in a play-off in Hawaii where he sunk a 40-foot putt to win. That's when it began to really get to me. After that, though, I had just had to hold my hands up. I don't think there's ever been anyone who could have lived with Tiger during 2000. The way he played for the rest of the season was just unbelievable. At the Open at St Andrews, when I finished second again, Tiger really was unbeatable.'

Two years on and Els is the Open champion; Woods won merely two majors in 2002, and some say Tiger's aura is just slipping a little. The South African, however, has come to terms with life at the top of golf. 'Hey, Tiger's still the main man,' he insisted. 'By some distance.'

Is this more reverse psychology? 'No, no, it's the truth. My Open win has solidified my position in the game. I'm a contender, for sure, and I'm one of the best players in the world, but that's as good as it gets.

'Thomas Bjorn lives next door to me in Wentworth. [Doesn't he have any ordinary neighbours?] He's a good friend of mine. We've had this discussion often. We agree that if Tiger hadn't been around there would have been one hell of a battle between ten guys in every single major. As it is, if he's got his "A" game with him, the rest of us are hanging on by his shirt-tails.'

How can the Open champion make such an admission? Els smiled again. 'Listen, you have to make peace with this, otherwise you've got a serious problem. I think I'm getting there now. You have a choice with Tiger. You either switch off the television every time he's on it, refuse to read about him in the newspapers and magazines, and never be prepared to hear a good word said about him. Or, you be truthful to yourself and reality. The reality is that the guy's great, he's a gentleman on the golf course, a nice bloke off it, a hell of a competitor, is more talented than anyone else on the golf course anywhere in the world, and he's the number one.'

So where does that leave the world's number two, and the man most likely to catch Tiger when the best has an off day? 'He's not going to win everything all the time, is he? It's up to me to capitalise on the situation when he doesn't. He's going to make mistakes, after all. I said he's the best, but I didn't say he wasn't human. My goals remain the same. To try and win every time I play. My biggest goal, however, is to win all four majors. I'm now halfway there.'

There really is no escaping Tiger Woods, then, not for me, attempting desperately to conjure up a way of meeting the man, and not for Ernie Els, who tried to beat him, failed, and struggled with it before coming to terms with the reality of the situation and finding peace with himself as a result.

Life away from the golf course plays a significant part in the Ernie Els make-up too, as I had already witnessed three days earlier at the Els' home and then in the Queenwood clubhouse bar. Here the family serves as a helping hand.

'There's no doubt that what drives me on is a fear of failure, or at least a fear of not getting to where I should be. It sticks with me for a while after a bad tournament. People see me as this happy-go-lucky character but I tend to be pretty hard on myself at times.

'This is where my family come in. Now that I have Samantha and Ben, it's difficult to come home and be too het up over a missed putt when I have my children in my arms. And Liezl is just the best for me. There's absolutely no danger of me acting like the superstar in my own home, I can assure you. Liezl wouldn't allow it, although, to be honest, it's not my style in any case.'

Warming to this theme Els explained a little more of his philosophy. 'I think it's important for me to be just one of the guys,' he said. 'I've seen it many times in golf, and I've seen it many times in business. Just because certain people are better at golf than you, or have more money than you, they think it makes them a better person. But it doesn't. It just means I'm a better golfer than you, but there'll be loads of things you're better than me at.'

It was pretty refreshing to hear this, and not a view you hear from too many of the world's better-known sports stars. His easy-going approach to golf and life has not pleased everyone, though.

'Quite a few people have a problem with the fact that I like to have a few beers from time to time, I like to hang out with my friends, and I don't like practising too much. I prefer to play. Some argue that I'm far too relaxed, and I'm just not intense enough. They argue I must be more of a machine.' He didn't say it, but I knew what he was thinking: that his approach should resemble that taken by a certain Mr Woods.

Els, though, is an entirely different animal. 'You have to understand that it wouldn't suit me at all. In fact, if I ate, slept and breathed golf, if I gave up all of my socialising, and if I spent all of my time on the driving range, it would have a detrimental effect on my golf. It's as simple as that.'

As he left he made one final point. 'By the way, anyone who goes in the ring with Roy Jones Junior is a fucking crazy man. I thought that when I first met you on Friday, and I still think that now. But it was fun being partners, and next time we'll win. Right?'

Right, Ernie. Actually, losing a friendly nine holes of foursomes was just fine by me. After all, I could have driven home that night £4,000 down, and worse still, Els could have carried out his promise made in the clubhouse bar. At least the world's number two had forgotten to grab me by my goons.

26

Beaten by a girlie

Later that week the same Ernie Els who lost a matchplay foursomes with me as his partner went on to beat Colin Montgomerie, Vijay Singh and then, in the final, his friend Sergio Garcia, to claim his fourth Cisco World Matchplay title and take home a cheque worth over £250,000. Against Montgomerie, in particular, his game was close to perfection and his putting, so out of sorts when partnering me, was unerringly accurate. It rounded off a quite remarkable year for the South African and served as a launch pad for an impressive start to 2003, too.

If only my game could make such an improvement in the space of just a few days. Instead, I had reached a level of consistency which would continue for a number of weeks. Round after round recorded scores of close to the 90-mark which, on one hand, showed that I was playing half-decent golf but, on the other, suggested I had levelled out on a plateau, and my round of 86 in the summer seemed now like a distant memory.

In spite of my meeting with Mark McCormack, my requests to IMG, to be granted a brief meeting with Tiger, had still not yielded any kind of positive response. My climb up the golfing mountain was drawing to a close and, although so much had happened, with so many differing characters in so many different environments, I was facing the probability that I would fail to reach the summit.

261

I would have been more depressed by this prospect if it wasn't for the fact that I had two invitations to look forward to, a return to St Andrews where, this time, I would be granted the privilege of playing on the Old Course, and a trip to Laura Davies's house in Surrey where one of the best-known women golfers in the world had planned an intriguing day of activity.

A year before, the thought of spending all that money to fly to Edinburgh and back, hire a rental car for a couple of days, and stay overnight in a St Andrews hotel all just for the sake of a round of golf would have appeared both absurd and rather sad. Subsequent trips made across the border to renowned golf courses had always been subsidised by business reasons for making the journey. Now, twelve months later, I was happily dipping into my own pocket.

I arrived just before my allotted tee-off time to meet up again with Peter Mason, my partner on the New Course when we hacked our way round on what would later prove to be such a fateful September day. Before teeing off at the first I met a local celebrity, Stumpy the Crow, named after his one leg. According to the caddy-master, Stumpy hangs around the first tee and the putting green and has been doing so for the past six years. Dennis, one of the better-known local caddies, has Stumpy eating out of his hand, but when tournaments are staged he (or she – nobody quite knows) disappears for a month in protest, before always returning, having made a point. 'According to a visiting American golfer a few months back, crows are monogamous,' the caddy-master informed us, just as we were completing our warm-up swings, a fact neither Peter nor I expected to learn at the first tee at St Andrews, nor anywhere else, for that matter.

Apart from the stunning views and the fact that on this crisp, early winter's day, the sun shone brilliantly throughout, the aspect about playing the Old Course that makes it such an enjoyable occasion is that virtually every hole bears a historical anecdote. Playing with Mason, who refrained from using the word 'buggeration' this time but used plenty of other Anglo-Saxon expletives instead when a shot went awry, meant an incessant string of stories and fables, beginning right at the very start.

After I had sent an acceptable drive down the middle of what is admittedly one of the widest fairways in the world, Mason explained how Ian Baker-Finch, the 1991 Open champion whose game plummeted after some unnecessary tinkering, managed to hook his opening drive out of bounds and close by the Rusacks Hotel. When I followed up with a scuffed eight iron that splashed into the burn, Mason comforted me by explaining how Jack Nicklaus achieved the same unhappy feat once during an Open. 'Jack looked thunderstruck,' Mason added, before following me into the burn with his approach shot. Within two strokes, then, I had fared better than Baker-Finch and matched Nicklaus.

Having followed a triple and double bogey with an unlikely but joyous birdie at the 'Cartgate' third, after rolling in a 30-foot downhill putt, my game that day calmed down to a regular series of pars and bogeys, with the occasional double thrown in for good measure. I managed to avoid the notorious Hill's Bunker in front of the par three 11th, something which Bobby Jones failed to do.

'Jones took at least three shots to get out of it during the 1921 Open and was so incensed by this that he tore up his card,' Peter recalled, before then pointing towards the Admiral's Bunker in the middle of the 12th fairway. 'And that's been given its name after an admiral was walking down the fairway, saw a buxom girl, said to his playing partner: "I wouldn't mind posting a letter in her letter box," fell down into the bunker and broke his leg.'

That particular story has stuck with me for two reasons: first, that there is a clear moral to the tale and, secondly, the phrase the admiral allegedly said to his playing partner, 'posting a letter in her letter box'? I can't see that ever working as a chat-up line, not unless it's uttered at the Royal Mail's Christmas party.

Once I had escaped from the deep Hell's Bunker on the 16th, thanks to Mason hauling me out with his hands, I managed to find the fairway on the famous 'Road' 17th over the corner of the hotel, and complete my round, after the obligatory photograph crossing the 'Swilcan Bridge', with a hugely satisfactory par at the 'Tom Morris' 18th to record a 91. It was yet another score around the 90-mark, but this time I had no complaints. A beautiful day, an acceptable score after my first-ever round at the most famous golf course in the world, even a birdie to boot, and the £300 was, I considered, money very well spent. And all under the watchful eyes of Stumpy the Crow.

I'd mentioned to Peter that I would be calling on Laura Davies the following week and he asked me to pass on an invitation to Laura to play at St Andrews. Despite everything Laura has achieved in the game – 64 tournament wins, four majors, for five years the world's number one, the longest hitter on the women's circuit, still one of the best-known sports personalities in the UK – she had never played at the most prestigious golf course in the world.

'I've never played with Tiger Woods, either,' Laura informed me seven days later, as she led me to her outrageously packed games room, found in a separate building to the large house in Surrey she shares with her mother and stepfather. 'If you can arrange a head to head between me and Tiger at the Old Course I'd be very happy.'

Head to heads was something Laura was palpably into, as I was about to discover. Instead of meeting for a pleasant chat and maybe a couple of hits with a golf club, Laura had devised a heptathlon of sporting events which the two of us would battle out.

I had already gleaned that she liked her sport. Apart from the golf, Laura was a huge Liverpool FC fan and an accomplished football player in her own right, formerly a fine tennis player, a cricketer, and supposedly useful at most sports.

An inspection of her games room merely confirmed this view. Dotted around the walls, the corners, and in every spare piece of space going, was a labyrinth of games, from a dartboard to a three-quarter-sized snooker table, a pool table, a quarter-sized table-tennis table, and a small room sporting hundreds of different golf clubs, bags and balls. Above the snooker table hung a sign that read: 'This is Anfield – Liverpool FC', while in one of the corners stood a 'Who Wants to be a Millionaire' pub game. Add to this a ten-pin bowling ball, a scooter, a collection of signed test cricket bats, a series of photos depicting the Solheim Cup teams, a signed Michael Jackson photograph, plus a framed ticket to one of the star's concerts, and a huge fridge with a glass door revealing hundreds of bottles of beers, sodas and soft drinks, and this truly is the sports addicts' dream pad. Oh, and I almost forgot to mention the large, widescreen TV surrounded by five smaller screens, and the three leather armchairs, complete with footrests and small tables for drinks, all designed for Laura and her chums to watch the horseracing on a Saturday afternoon and place bets.

This infatuation with all things of a sporting nature has been allowed quite happily to invade her golfing career, too, often with interesting results. There was the time, for instance, when she ruined her chances of winning a tournament in Phoenix, after injuring her wrist by tripping over the kerb while attempting a lavish pull shot in a carpark cricket match. 'I missed the cut by a stroke as a result,' she recalled. 'It wasn't surprising. I could hardly hold the club. Still, it was a nice pull shot. Kept it down well. Four runs.'

Well, that's OK, then. Her insistence on following her beloved Liverpool also knows no boundaries. 'Wherever I am in the world, and whatever time it may be, I'll always listen to the commentary if Liverpool are playing,' she said. 'If I'm in Japan I'll set the alarm for four or five in the morning and listen to it on a website if need be. If I happen to be competing in a tournament at the same time as Liverpool are playing, I'll keep on making telephone calls on my mobile to check the score.'

There have been times when I have received homicidal looks from other golfers when I have had to respond to a call, even when my mobile has been on vibrate, and yet one of the most successful women golfers of all time cheerily makes calls during a tournament to receive updates on a football match.

'Actually, it's worse than that,' Laura informed me. 'During the 1996 European football Championships I was playing in a tournament on the

Saturday afternoon when England beat Spain in the quarter-finals. I had a miniature television set in my bag and watched the whole game as I played. I had a five-shot lead and was playing the best golf of my life, so I figured I could take the risk. I was partnering Helen Alfredsson and asked if she'd mind. Helen said go ahead, but afterwards I was fined. Maybe they thought I was taking the mickey, but I wasn't. I went to the Scotland and Germany games, so it meant a lot to me. Anyway, I haven't done it since.'

She led me into the small room where her drivers, irons and putters were housed. This was where the quarter-sized table-tennis table stood and where the first leg of our sporting challenge would take place. I thought it would be a good time to inform Laura that before her stood the Stamford and Rutland League division two doubles champion of 1979, as well as the Hotel Creta Paradise table-tennis champion of the summer of 1998 in Crete.

It has to be said that she appeared unfazed by these notable feats, the more so after I sent shot after shot over the end of her side of the table. Within seemingly a few minutes she had raced to a 21–7 win, punching the air in genuine and disturbing delight as my final effort failed to find its intended target. I couldn't remember the last time anyone had beaten me by such a resounding margin and told her as much. 'Ah, but everyone's the same when they play me on this table,' Laura explained. 'All I have to do is defend and block and watch as my opponent makes all the mistakes.' One-nil to Laura Davies.

She left school at 16 and spent five winters working in supermarkets before turning professional at 21 in 1984. 'Most of my friends hadn't even heard of golf, let alone the fact that women could make a living out of it. I came second in only my second professional tournament and picked up a cheque for £4,500. For a girl who had been used to earning 60 quid a week from Sainsbury's this was a great deal of money. In fact, I remember earning £21,000 at the end of my first professional season which, at the time, made me feel like a millionaire.'

We moved across to the snooker table and fought out, at least initially, a scrappy affair, in which Laura edged into a lead by virtue of the fact that I couldn't seem to pot two balls in a row. When I played a safety shot that snookered Laura, she not only found a hidden red with a perfectly weighted shot off one of the cushions, but then started to make comments designed to throw me off my game. 'It's not looking good for Stafford,' she pronounced. 'But it's looking very good for Davies.' She then promptly cleared up the five remaining colours for a break of 25 and an overall frame win by 63 points to a rather sorry nine. Two-nil down and Laura's assessment was correct. It wasn't looking too good for me at all.

When she discovered that I had come to know Ernie Els, Laura had her own anecdote to share concerning the South African and his two, ridiculously oversized, sloppy and, let's be honest, slobbering dogs. Working for the Golf television channel as a commentator at a Wentworth tournament, Laura was grabbed by the Els' housekeeper on the 16th fairway outside Ernie's house. 'Ernie and Liezl were watching the tournament on TV in America at the time and they wanted to see their dogs on the screen,' she explained. 'I radioed the producer to ask if it was OK, then told the housekeeper to bring out the two dogs. For a minute or so after that, I had to talk live on camera while one of Ernie's dogs attempted to chew the microphone, just so that he and Liezl could see them.'

Round three of the Davies heptathlon focused on table football, a game in which I was confident, despite playing 'away', that I would win. Showing the kind of ruthlessness Laura had revealed at the table tennis and snooker tables, I recorded a resounding 10–2 win to reduce her overall lead to 2–1. A couple of alarming developments took place during this encounter. I was absolutely desperate to win and had long forgotten the reasons for visiting Laura in the first place. And Laura, for once on the wrong end of a thrashing, had started to criticise her defence. 'Come on, you should have blocked that,' she said to a row of four plastic miniature men, joined together by a rod and expressionless throughout the public condemnation. 'Well done,' she said afterwards, shaking my hand vigorously. 'The better player won.' By this stage neither of us realised that any onlooker would have found all this verging on the ridiculous.

It was only a matter of time before the T-word was mentioned. It appeared as Laura was explaining why, unlike many women in sport, she insists it is perfectly right that there is not parity in golf between the men's and women's game when it comes to pay. 'Why should we receive the same when the men are clearly better than us?' she argued. 'And they're getting better, too, because of the Tiger phenomenon. I mean, if I could match Tiger off the same tees over 18 holes, then fine, but if I can't hold a candle to him – and I can't – then why should I earn what he does? On my day I can give anyone a run for their money, partly because I'm long off the tee, but most times the top men will always beat me and when Tiger's playing his best nobody can match him.' Just how long can she actually drive the ball? 'Oh, I'd say around 280 yards,' she replied, matter-of-factly, which is a good 30 yards longer than me at my very best.

I declined to inform her of this as we approached the dartboard for round four of the challenge. 'I expect to win this one,' Laura announced, as she placed a size 22 basketball shoe down to represent the oche. 'I bought the shoe because it looks so stupidly big and I knew everyone would ask me about it,' she said. 'By the way, I reckon this is my second best sport.'

'What, behind golf?' I asked, not unreasonably.

'No, no, behind football,' she answered. 'I totally forgot about golf there for a second.'

On the coffee table in front of the various television screens was placed a rather impressive hardback book with a Latin inscription written in gold on the cover. From afar it looked like a classical novel, at least until Laura opened it up to reveal a box full of darts inside.

We decided to play the best out of five, starting off 301 and finishing with doubles. Laura took the first leg before I replied with two successive wins to need just one more to win the game and draw the overall match-score level. Instead Laura, who had been chiding herself for playing so poorly, responded by clearing up the fourth leg using just nine darts, and then winning a tight fifth leg when both of us had missed previous chances to win. What looked like 2–2 had become 3–1, a point Laura was quick to make. 'It's a big difference to the score, isn't it,' she said, rather gleefully.

As Laura had earlier touched on the Tiger subject, I mentioned his very public pee incident at the US Open, a story that was met with a surprise response. 'I'd love to be Tiger,' Laura exclaimed. 'I really would.'

Even though there is barely a place in the world he can travel where people are not pointing at him, talking about him, and trying to get to him? 'He can handle it. He's the best at what I do. In the future, people will say how one man changed the whole course of a sport because in America, especially, kids now want to emulate him. That means you're getting huge, athletic animals taking up the sport who, before Tiger came along, would have gone into American football and basketball. The courses will become obsolete because all these kids will be driving the ball 400 yards plus. And they will all say it was Tiger they related to.'

On the pool table a series of cards were placed upon the baize with headings such as 'Richard's Runners' and 'Rita's Reckonings'.

'I'm having a caddies' day soon in the games room,' Laura explained, when she saw my questioning expression. 'I've got seven of them coming and we'll be doing a number of sports you and I are playing today, including some betting off the TV screens.'

When the best out of five pool competition got underway, I was confident of reducing the Davies' overall lead again, although it did not begin too well when, in charge of the first frame, I accidentally pocketed the black to forfeit. Laura only needed to clinch the pool to gain an insurmountable lead in the whole challenge, but I managed to bounce back to win the next three frames as Laura provided commentary. 'Stafford's back in it,' she pronounced at the end. 'But I have a feeling his joy will be short-lived.'

Like Ernie Els, Laura's apparent reluctance to eat, sleep and breathe golf has been criticised in the past. Stories such as her cricket injury have only added weight to the accusation that, for all her success, she does not take the sport seriously enough. Laura sees it differently. 'I'm not trying to be clever by not practising or by playing other sports,' she insisted. 'But I do have to be myself. I'm playing five-a-side football tonight, for example, in Guildford. It's part of my make-up and I have to enjoy my life in order to play good golf. I've won 64 times doing it my way so I don't think I've gone too far wrong. Maybe I would have won a hundred times if I'd been more intense. Then again, maybe Tiger would win every tournament he ever entered if he took it easier on himself. All I know is that you have to do what you think is right for yourself.'

All this was said as we ventured out into the garden and down to the small football pitch, complete with two netted goals and floodlights, that she has constructed in her back garden. Trailing 2–3 after the indoor section of the heptathlon, I realised that I not only had to beat her in the penalty competition we had devised but then win the seventh and final discipline, which just happened to be golf. It was a tall order, but at least I would win the football. After all, I was a bloke!

Laura had changed into an England tracksuit top and I into a Flamengo shirt given to me by the Rio de Janeiro based football club when I trained with them a few years back. This, I reckoned, would draw first blood in the pre-competition psychology. After a short warm-up of passing and crossing to each other, I placed the ball on the spot in readiness for the first kick. We agreed on a best out of ten format, with two alternate sets of five penalties each. When I had scored with my first three consecutive penalties, I told myself the sixth leg of this heptathlon was already in the bag. Even when I then failed with my next two, one missing the target and the other hit straight at Laura, the prospect of losing never entered my head.

The alarm bells began to ring, however, after I stood in goal and watched Laura take a ridiculously long run-up and then blast the ball so hard past me that I had barely moved a muscle before it had hit the back of the net. At the halfway stage, the scores stood at 3–3 and I realised I had a scrap on my hands.

At a time like this you need luck to be on your side. Instead, luck deserted me completely. On two occasions my shot beat Laura only for the ball to rebound off the crossbar. Scoring just twice out of my allotted five, my final tally was five successfully converted penalties out of ten. Laura, standing on three, needed to score another three to win, and two to tie the match. Her first penalty was buried so far into the corner that I doubt anyone in the world would have saved it. Her second was sent closer to my body, but so hard that when my hand managed to part-parry the ball it was nearly removed from my wrist. Then, in keeping with the drama, I managed to save her next two attempts, which meant that Laura needed to score with her final penalty to win the game and, indeed, the whole competition.

Taking her longest run-up yet, and looking as intense as I had seen her all day, she smashed the ball past my left-hand side and into the corner of the net. As I picked myself up and scraped the mud off my shirt, Laura began a triumphant lap of honour with both her arms aloft in victory. To make matters worse she was chanting: 'You've been beaten by a girlie, you've been beaten by a girlie.'

Laura's stepfather emerged from the house, having witnessed all this. Riley, their spaniel, had been watching from the window and had been desperate to come out and disrupt the game. 'He probably wanted to bite the ball,' he said. 'He was crying in there.'

Well, I wish he had managed to come out and bite the bloody ball. I would have claimed the win on the grounds of a pitch invasion by the home supporter, to draw the scores level at three-all. Instead I had been beaten and still faced the last discipline in the seven-event challenge, a simple matter of golf.

Laura has a nine-hole pitch-and-putt course, consisting of one green and nine different tees dotted around her six-acre garden. Beside each tee is a description and a name after some of her tournament wins. For example, the first has McDonalds and the Algarve Millennium Skins next to it, as well as its description which, in this case, read: 'Hole 1, 64 yards, par three, stroke index eight'.

The professional lady golfer, Kathy Lunn, holds the course record of three under after nine holes, while Laura's best round stands at two under. We agreed on playing matchplay before Laura raced to two up after two holes. At the 3rd, 'Caesar's Palace', which required you to chip 82 yards over her tennis courts and some bushes to the unsighted green, I managed to halve the hole, and at the 4th, I very nearly holed in one from a mere 41 yards. It was enough to win the hole and reduce Laura's lead to one up but, as had been the case continually throughout the day, she responded immediately and ruthlessly to the setback by winning the 5th hole to regain her lead of two. 'Two down with four to play, it's a long way to come back from there,' Laura told me as we began to play the 80-yard 6th. Two down became three down with three to play. 'He's in big trouble now,' added the on-course commentator. 'I can't see him getting a glimpse of the ninth tee now.'

She was right. Laura won the 7th hole as well, to wrap up the final leg of our epic day of sport and win the heptathlon by five victories to two. I pointed out that this was a home leg as far as she was concerned and that, at my place, on my full-sized table-tennis table, on my pool table, at my dartboard, on my table-football game, and in my garden playing with my football nets, it would be a different story altogether. She would hear none of this, of course. 'You did your best,' she announced. 'It just wasn't good enough on the day.'

As she helped herself to a celebratory drink and served me with a consoling one as well, Laura told me how determined she was to get back from her current world ranking of 12 on the women's circuit to the number one spot she had held between 1993 and 1997.

'If I didn't believe I could do it I'd pack it in right now,' she explained. 'It's not that I'm playing badly at the moment, and I've won a tournament this season as I've done in every year since I turned professional. But I know I can play much better than I have been doing, and that's where the hope comes from.'

We walked out to my car and, as a parting gift, Laura presented me with a putter and two boxes of balls. 'You see,' she added, with an apologetic smile, as I threw my muddy football shirt, trainers, golf shoes and glove into the boot. 'I don't like coming second.' I had just spent the past five hours discovering this for myself.

'Hope you get to meet Tiger,' she added, as she waved and made her way back to the house. 'It's something I'd like to do very much myself.'

She'd probably beat him at penalties, too.

27

'I Believe I Can Fly'

The getting to meet Tiger part of this entire odyssey had proved to be an impossibility. It mattered so much, though. While learning to play golf had been akin to a crash course in maturity, my competitive need for a trophy ending, in the shape of Tiger Woods, still remained.

On every occasion I had observed him from close quarters he had been flanked by so much security, so many flunkies, and such a large number of officials afraid to wander an inch away from their precise orders that I realised I stood very little chance of getting my man.

When my well-argued, very reasonable formal request to meet Tiger was also turned down by his personal agent, I feared my last opportunity had gone. After all, why on earth should Tiger meet me? He didn't meet any other writer and hadn't for five years, at least not in any environment other than an official press conference. Did I have any inkling just how many people in the world would also like to meet him? It was nothing personal. It was just that he didn't do 'meetings' with the likes of me or anyone, he didn't have the time, and he certainly had no need to, either.

I should have just come to terms with this, realised the notion had been unfeasible from the very start, and just been contented with what had happened to me in the past eighteen months. I had embraced the game of golf, I had travelled the world playing my new-found love, I had notched up some dubious but rather novel achievements in the process, and I had spent some memorable moments with a wide and diverse range of characters, some exceedingly famous and successful, in an adventure that I would never forget for the rest of my life.

And yet I couldn't remove the fact that the very force of Tiger had barged its way into every facet of my journey, every golfer I had met, and everybody connected to the sport. Failing to meet Tiger, however far-fetched I realised this notion had been, was like turning back from the summit of a mountain peak with just a hundred feet left to climb.

Then, just when it seemed apparent that the cause was lost, came a glimmer. It was the faintest of glimmers, but a glimmer nonetheless. My friends at Walt Disney World in Florida informed me that Tiger would be staging one of his rare Tiger Woods Foundation teaching days at the resort near his Isleworth home in Orlando. I assumed Tiger would be surrounded by the usual suspects of sharp-suited yes-men but, at worst, it was a late and last chance to see the man away from a golf tournament.

The decision was spontaneous. Was it worth spending a not inconsiderable amount of money to fly to Florida on the off chance that I might, just, be able to grab five minutes with the reason why I had become a born-again golfer? Probably not. But if I stayed at home I would be wondering for the rest of my life.

Three days later I was back on a plane for 11 long hours, cramped up in economy with my knees lodged against the seat in front, chastising myself for throwing away so much money, and likening it to an expensive addiction. Which, of course, is precisely what golf is.

It was a typical Florida day as I checked into my hotel, caught a taxi to Walt Disney World, and then made my way to the Magnolia Golf Course where Tiger would be staging a coaching clinic for 15 children selected from five American cities, before later providing motivational speeches and a brief exhibition of drives in front of three grandstands packed with locals.

I had expected the world's media to be there but, to my amazement, only a small amount of TV crews and representatives from the local

Orlando press seemed to have turned up. Things were beginning to look up.

Tiger was already there, looking resplendent in his yellow shirt, black slacks and shoes, and a Nike cap. It seemed that each of the kids was in complete awe of the man who was holding his or her club and spending a considerable amount of time showing them proper stances, grips and swings. 'I'm never going to wash my hands again,' said one, Charles Pantanto, from Fort Worth, which was either an indication of what Tiger meant to him, or a convenient excuse to his parents. The Tiger Woods Foundation began life seven years ago with a $500,000 donation from the man himself. Since then it has exploded into life, reaching youths who otherwise would never have touched golf.

Not for the first time over the past 18 months I was standing within a few feet of Tiger, wondering how I was going to engineer a conversation. Just for once there seemed to be next to no entourage around him, or even close to him. I knew it would have to be this day or never.

Then I spotted an elderly man holding court in a tent shading the heat of the late morning sun. Earl Woods, Tiger's father and mentor, as well as the president of the Foundation, was watching the proceedings from afar, and waiting to deliver his commitments to the clinic a little later on. He appeared to sport a permanent smile on his patriarchal face.

As Mark McCormack had intimated when we met at his New York offices, Earl Woods is often viewed in the same light as Richard Williams, the father of Venus and Serena. Immensely proud of his son's achievements, Earl has sometimes been too publicly passionate over his belief in Tiger but he is clearly not the crank that some aspects of the media have attempted to portray. And indeed, despite the $1 billion-plus his son has earned from golf, Earl still lives in the small home he bought with his army pension.

It wouldn't have mattered to me if Earl had been the biggest megalomaniac in the world. He was Tiger's father who, together with his estranged wife Kutilda, was one of the two most important people in Tiger's life. He knew his son better than anyone. And I was a desperate man.

Someone rose from beside Earl inside the tent, leaving him sitting there alone, looking around and wiping the sweat from his brow. My legs were moving seemingly before my brain had made the command, and within seconds, my outstretched hand was shaking Earl's.

After I had provided the briefest of explanations Earl seemed happy to discuss his son. 'I always knew Tiger would achieve everything he has,' he admitted, in a slow, rather measured drawl.

'What, everything?' I asked.

'Everything,' came back the reply. 'And from a very early stage as well. I've been proven right, haven't I? And it's far from over, either. I also know what else he can and will achieve. Believe me, there is still so much for him to achieve.'

This may sound like a pushy parent, but Earl could be forgiven for having big plans for his son. After all, considering that Tiger had become the biggest sporting icon in the world, plus a billionaire to boot in his mid-20s, after dropping out of Stanford University to concentrate on his golf, Earl had not gone far wrong.

It turned out that when referring to future achievements Earl was not just talking about golf, either. 'I'm talking way beyond golf,' he said. 'Look around you. This is what we do as well. It's already become so big in so little time, but we're still only at the very beginning.

'The headquarters of the Tiger Woods Foundation may well remain in the United States, but I see the Foundation and its work spreading into Europe, Asia, Africa too. You need to have a starting place for us, and with Tiger, it has to be golf. That triggers everything. But in reality it's not really about golf at all. It's about understanding that everything and anything is attainable. There are no short cuts, of course, and you have to work hard at it, but it's there for you if you reach far enough out to grab it. Every child, no matter how deprived they may be, and from where they may come from, not only has the ability to dream, but the right to dream, and to achieve.'

So where does Tiger fit into this greater picture beyond remaining the greatest golfer and staging various clinics for children? 'Oh, well, towards the end of his career and definitely afterwards he'll become an ambassador at large without portfolio. He'll be influential within governmental circles around the world. And you want to know why? Because everyone in governments plays golf. We've got a global concept because we intend to have a global impact. We want to be at the cutting edge to aid humanity and, especially, children.'

We'd somehow reached a level far beyond my wish to meet his son and explain how I'd only being playing the game for 18 months, had become hooked on what he does best, and felt it necessary to end my journey by his side. Suddenly it all seemed rather irrelevant.

Earl was about to introduce the main event of the day. The event officials were making last-minute checks, and gazing anxiously up at a sky that threatened storms so typical in the sticky, Florida climate. There was time, just, for a couple of personal insights.

'I derive the same pleasure, the same thrill, after every single major Tiger wins,' Earl insisted. 'That's because they are all so very different. Every major, indeed every single tournament, has its own challenges and its own story. It makes me happy that Tiger is fulfilling his potential, and it makes me happy that he has reached the position he has in the game and in the world. But you wanna know the best part of all?'

He paused sufficiently long enough for me to feel compelled to answer.

'Er, well, yes, go on, then.'

'I wasn't present at the last major he won [the 2002 US Open], so the first time I saw Tiger was when he arrived back at Orlando Airport. Tiger walked off the aircraft, came over to me, hugged me and said "Happy Father's Day." That's what makes it all so worthwhile.'

Earl rose to his feet, shook my hand, and wished me luck. Once he had started talking of his passion and dreams in life, I had found it impossible to butt in with a request to meet his son in person. Now he was gone, making his way over to the green in front of the stands where he took hold of a microphone and cleared his throat. I followed him over to one of the stands and managed to find a spare seat.

'How many of you children have been told you're special?' Earl's now booming voice over the tannoy system asked. 'You know, it's not a privilege, but a right to be able to dream. Don't let anyone, ever, take your dreams away from you. I want you now to hold the person's hand to the right and left of you and repeat after me: "I am a person, I am a person, I am a good person, I will love myself, I will love and respect others, my future is mine."'

I had earlier been enraptured by the man's conversation. Now I was cursing Earl Woods. When he asked everyone to hold hands with each other, I looked first to my left, then to my right, to inspect with exactly whom would I be holding hands. In these rare circumstances you always hope it may be someone relatively attractive and, from a male point of view, most definitely a female.

To my left stood a man so tall that when I reached out to hold his hand I felt like his small child. To my right stood a man with a large beard, this time my height but so hairy that his hand, appearing from under his leather sleeve, resembled that of an ape. He looked like a southern redneck and appeared far from pleased to be holding my hand.

The feeling was mutual, believe me. People could make a great deal out of all this. Psychologists could explore the hidden reasons why I felt uncomfortable at this precise moment. I could be in denial. I could have hidden prejudices. Hell, there might even be some deep-seated sexual explanation. All I know is that I don't particularly like holding other men's hands, in public or not, and most certainly not when chanting 'I will love and respect others.'

Earl had not quite finished. 'Now, let's hear it,' he commanded. 'I believe.' We called back: 'I believe.'

'I believe,' Earl said again, this time louder.

'I believe,' we responded.

'I BELIEVE, I BELIEVE,' Earl now shouted, his head looking skywards. 'I BELIEVE,' we bellowed back. I couldn't help but notice that the redneck had tilted his head back at this moment and was close to tears.

At this point, R. Kelly's 'I Believe I Can Fly' blared out of the speakers and people started to sing. My hand to my left started swaying around. I looked up and watched as the tall man closed his eyes and seemed to be mouthing the words, his grip on my hand tightening.

My God! I hadn't come to a Tiger Woods golf clinic at all. I had come to the annual general meeting of some kind of sect. In a moment I was going to be whisked away to a commune in the middle of Texas, to spend my days dressed in turquoise, never to resurface.

Don't get me wrong. The work the Foundation carries out is impressive and important. The effort and the message delivered by Tiger and his father can only be applauded. The results, too, were there for all to witness. It was just that during these particular moments I was thankful nobody I knew could see me.

'I believe I can fly. I believe I can reach the sky . . .'

The music disappeared as quickly as it appeared, to be replaced by noise and colour. Fireworks woke everyone up from their near-religious trance. Explosions lit up the fairway away to my right, and smoke soon covered the area to the extent that visibility across the fairway was down to just a few yards. The sudden guitar chords from Survivor's 'Eye of the Tiger' started to blast out of the speakers' and there, from within the smoke and mist, a golf buggy appeared trundling along the fairway. Inside stood a smiling Tiger, waving to the crowds and resembling the Pope in his Popemobile. Everybody started to scream with delight and wave back at him. I was in the middle of the most extraordinary scenes.

The buggy came to a halt, Tiger stepped out and strode purposefully to the centre of the bright green patch of grass in front of the grandstands. 'Dedication, patience, drive, determination, humbleness, perseverance,' he announced, as he practised a few swings with an iron. 'I've learnt all this and more from being around my father, and being around the game of golf.'

He hit a few balls and explained his warm-up routine. 'When I go out to play I have nothing to worry about because I've taken the time to warm up properly,' he said to a hushed crowd of around 500 people. 'I hit my eight iron, my four iron, my three wood and driver, always visualising the shot I'm going to hit and the conditions I'll be facing. If I don't get it right, I'll hit it again and again. Even if it takes me five attempts I won't leave the range until I've hit the right shot. Then I'll play the exact shot off the tee for my first stroke of the day.'

I made a note of this and decided I would follow suit when I returned to England to complete my half-century of rounds. Tiger then related golf to the bigger picture, as he continued to strike balls down a fairway that had now been cleared of mist.

'Golfers don't go out and cause trouble,' he announced. 'The best way for me to help the kids is to be winning tournaments and then coming out and doing this. We're not trying to find the next best golfer in the world. If it happens then fine, but in reality we're just trying to create a better future.'

He took questions from a couple of small boys sitting in the front row of the grandstand. How old was he when he started out in golf?

'I started playing at nine months old,' Tiger replied. He realised how young this sounded and made a joke. 'Er, actually, I used to practise my swings inside my mother's womb.'

The second child piped up: 'How did you use to practise when you were much younger?'

Tiger made an admission here. 'I used to pretend I'd be partnering Jack Nicklaus and Arnold Palmer,' he said. 'I used to act like them, try to play like them, even speak like them. It's been a dream since then to be able to meet them and, of course, to beat them.'

After a few more hits Tiger completed his act, left the arena and walked over to a waiting caravan where a line of children were assembled in line. The caravan door closed for a few minutes, then reopened to allow the children in, one at a time, to meet Tiger. This resembled Santa's grotto in a departmental store and, if I could have got away with being under ten years of age, I might have joined the queue.

Thirty minutes passed before Tiger reappeared from the caravan. The day was drawing to a close. Many had already left the golf course content, having seen Tiger's clinic and heard the great man in person. I was leaning against a large tree watching all this when the storm that had been threatening all day to break arrived with a vengeance. After just a few seconds of tiny droplets, the rain suddenly gushed down on everyone like a fire hose. Even Tiger, still in his yellow shirt, was hit by the ferocity of the rain. He looked around to find the nearest place to take cover. There, some twenty yards away to his right, was a tree. He jogged towards it, head down, his feet splashing in the puddles that were already appearing. Tiger came to a halt beside the tree stump, shook himself and saw a hand stretched out to take his. He clasped the hand, looked up and saw the face of a smiling, English, obsessed golfer.

There were others standing under that tree, too, but only one was looking Tiger Woods straight in the eye. After a journey that had taken 18 months to complete, I had finally found my man.

28

On top of the golfing world

The moment had come and it was now. Time was short. As soon as the ferocity of the rain had died a little, Tiger would be off again, and this time for good. I had been waiting for this moment for so long, but now, when it had finally arrived so unexpectedly and suddenly, I struggled to select one of a million questions I had wanted to ask.

What's it like being the religious leader of the biggest cult following on the planet? Does he have any disgusting personal habits? Is there life after death? (The definitive answer, please.) What does the future hold for us all? Is there something he's embarassingly bad at doing? And, a personal favourite of mine, does space reach an end and, if so, what do we find beyond space?

That, among a thousand other questions, was what I felt like asking him. Instead, and at breakneck speed, I told him I was a golf nut who, like the vast majority of golfers, was at odds with my mind on the golf course. I wondered if he could tell me how he appeared to overcome any potential mental pitfalls.

I expected him to behave as if he had heard this question many times before and was about to cruise into autopilot but, instead, he became excited and animated in his response.

'Playing golf, especially when it comes to tournament golf, has to be the most important thing in your life at that time,' he explained. 'That's the kind of focus you need in order to play golf. Sure, I get nervous.'

'You do?' I interjected. That was really good to hear. If Tiger Woods gets nervous then it's perfectly OK for me to suffer from nerves, too, even if I'm playing for £5 on a Tuesday morning while he's putting for another major.

'Yes I do,' Tiger continued. 'But when I'm walking up the 18th fairway about to win a major, I say to myself that this is what it's all about. This is the reason why I've run all those miles to get in shape, lifted all those weights, hit all those golf balls on the range. This is why I've busted like hell to get here. This position is where I want to be in life. So, to have that kind of mindset makes it easier for me because I know I'm the champ, I know I've done everything I possibly could have to get myself ready. If I hadn't worked so hard or as hard as I still do, then I wouldn't have enjoyed the success I have.'

That was some answer from the greatest sporting icon in the world to a strange bloke he had met under a tree. The rain was reducing from torrents to a steady but comparatively light stream of drops. I knew I only had a minute or two left of this impromptu audience with the man.

And is everything good about being Tiger Woods? Can he ever just let his hair down and be himself?

He smiled at this, his high, Thai-descended cheekbones in prominence, and his teeth gleaming white. 'I do try to open up and be myself, but it's not that often I find myself in a position to completely do this,' he said. 'My best friends are my best friends for a reason. For a start, they're not going to tell the whole world what I do. There are enough times when I can be myself.'

Despite the rain still falling, the sun appeared from amid the clouds and a sudden burst of heat hit our faces. 'OK?' Tiger asked me, as he started to move away from the tree.

For a man who has had the privilege of spending time with the majority of the greatest global sports stars over the past twenty years, I was now resembling a gibbering groupie. I hadn't been like this with

Jack Nicklaus or Ernie Els. Maybe it was the whole inaccessibility of Woods that had highlighted this moment. I gave an official my camera and asked Tiger if he would mind posing with me.

'How's your golf?' Tiger asked, as we stood next to each other and looked at the camera lens.

Tiger Woods was asking me how my golf was. He probably couldn't care less and was just trying to be pleasant, but who cared. Tiger wanted to know my story. I crammed 18 months into 20 seconds, ending with my intention to break ten over in fifty rounds.

He shook my hand and responded: 'Who knows, carry on like this and we may face each other in a couple of years' time.'

Before I could say: 'Screw the couple of years' time, what are you doing tomorrow?' he was gone, engulfed by a small crowd of WDW officials and TWF representatives. Within 15 minutes he had left the premises completely. The storm resurfaced to put an end to the last remnants of the grey day, in any case. I followed others to the carpark, with my bag over my head to beat off the heavy rain. It was the end of the party. The end of the road.

Midway across the Atlantic the anticlimax began. I had finally met my man, and the decision to risk the long and expensive journey to the Foundation clinic had paid off. Tiger Woods and I had ten minutes talking to each other, and to nobody else. Not only that but I had a photo to prove it.

And yet, as I flicked through the films on show in the back of the seat in front of me, and listened to the heavy breathing of those around me asleep, I began to realise that it wasn't actually the biggest deal in the world, after all. Maybe it was never going to be. Maybe it never could be.

After all, as Boris Becker once said to me during an interview some ten years before, 'We all take a piss first thing in the morning, whether we're the best sportsmen in the world or not.' I thought I would have felt a lot more about finally meeting and talking to Tiger than I did. But there, as I leant back in my seat and closed my eyes, I realised all I had done was talk to someone who happens to be the best golfer in the world. Time moves on very quickly and my time with Tiger had been and gone. His time, too, would go one day. Everything passes.

The next day I had my photos developed.

There stood Tiger Woods and a guy with a large umbrella sprouting out of his head. On second thoughts, it looked like a large umbrella with some bloke looking remarkably like me sticking out of its handle. In all the desperate rush to secure the moment, I hadn't thought to consider the surroundings.

When I told David Rennie my story, ending with the photographic sting in the tale, he threw his head back and laughed and laughed.

I was hoping (in the same way I'd hoped meeting Tiger would gain a whole new world for me) that this would be the day when I would achieve my aim of scoring a round of 81 or nine over par. I arrived at the now-familiar Wentworth unusually, early to prepare myself for the day. Forty minutes down the driving range, following Tiger's routine, of course, was followed by half an hour on the putting green. I performed stretching exercises, I even visualised the round ahead. The sun, that had been so absent over the past few weeks in England, shone sweetly and I began to lose any sense of anxiety.

So . . . what happened? The inexplicable. That's what happened. I scored a triple bogey on the first on the Edinburgh Course, which I dismissed as my usual poor start, but then a triple bogey on the par three second. Not a good start if you're planning to score just nine over. At the third I scored a double bogey as well, which was the last time I could really afford to record such a poor return. At the fourth, a par four, I scored a 12. A 12! This was something I had not achieved since my very early rounds. Various trips to rivers and bunkers, plus a two-stroke penalty for grounding my wedge in the sand by mistake, resulted in this ignominy. Two triple bogeys followed, then a nine at the par three seventh. I felt close, very close, to throwing my whole bag in the river.

David made a tongue-in-cheek suggestion that tempted me sorely. 'Why don't you end your story by leaving your golf clubs in the middle of the fairway and just walking away?' he said. 'It would be the one ending nobody would predict, like *The Italian Job*.'

Respectable bogeys followed at the ninth and tenth but, as a result, David had won our matchplay challenge by taking all of the first ten holes. We decided to play a second game, or a bye, with David giving me two strokes per hole. 'You're playing that badly,' he said. He, in contrast, was playing as well as he could remember. I'd like to say that I was pleased for him. In reality, it was just making my situation worse.

How could this have happened to me? I'd just shot 63 on the outward nine holes. It was as if I'd just been transported back in time 18 months to when I was just starting out.

Then an equally bizarre sequence of events unfolded. I began to play well. Bogey after bogey followed, hole after hole won against David. On the 15th, I even sunk a 30-foot putt from off the green and in the light rough to win the hole. This was more like it. Much more like it.

I won the bye so emphatically that we had time to play what David referred to as the 'bye-bye' over the last three holes. He happened to capture the 'bye-bye' title to add to the initial matchplay challenge, but I was happy as I sunk my final putt in my 50th round to end the quest.

How could I possibly be content with a final round score of 109 when two hours earlier I contemplated, on David's suggestion, walking away from golf for good? The answer was not just in the fact that I had salvaged my pride, played respectable golf in the second half of the round, and even holed a long-distance putt.

The answer, I realised, as I picked my ball out from the cup in the ground, and slung my bag of clubs over my back, was more far-reaching than that. Golf had made a point of highlighting the past 18 months to me in my final round. At the beginning, it grabbed hold of this cocky golfer, who had thought this would be the day when I would achieve my lowest-ever round, and showed him a few harsh truths.

Towards the end, however, the game had teased me back into loving it again, supplied a few treasured moments, and convinced me that was not the end, but just the start. I had no round of nine over to my name. I had no albatrosses or eagles. And I had no holes in one.

But I will. One day. It could take a week, or it could take a lifetime. I will have only a minor say in how the future pans out on the fairways of the world. As my final round had proven, golf will remain the master. Always.

Besides, it is the process, not the outcome, that matters. A year and a half ago I had time for very little of anything because I was too busy, too impatient, probably too self-important, for that matter. Now I had learned to stop and smell the flowers. I had grown to understand how necessary it is not to cut corners. I knew, more than at any time in my life, that rules can be character-building, after all. I had made friends with the most unlikely of people from all over the world. And I had found time, the most precious commodity of all.

As I thanked David for his company and walked back towards my car outside the imposing, cream clubhouse at Wentworth, something else entered my thoughts, something that would have appeared ridiculous and ludicrous to me just a few weeks previously.

In my crazed crusade to reach the golfing summit by meeting the most dominant figure in the game, I had inadvertently stumbled across something more important and bigger even than Tiger Woods, the individual.

And this, to my utter surprise, is you. And me. And him, and her. And everyone else, too, who plays golf. I gazed out over the first fairway on the west course at Wentworth. The sun had gone in by now and it was cold. Bitterly cold.

Out there, with clubs inside heavy bags clinging on to their bent double backs, were four golfers just starting out on their round of golf. It would take them four hours to return, by which time the light would almost have gone for good for the day and the lights inside the Wentworth clubhouse would be shining brightly.

During these four hours those golfers would be happy and sad, at peace with themselves and at other times furious, achieve world-class status for at least one shot, and also play as if they had never picked up a club in their lives.

Whatever the case, they would be back again before too long convinced, like me, that this would be the day when it all just clicks. These four golfers trudging into the distance now were Tigers in their own right, these and every other ordinary golfer too, for that matter.

I had spent 18 months travelling the world and meeting all kinds of golfing figures in order to place myself in a position where I could, with some justification, be able to meet Tiger Woods. Yet the answer had been staring at me all along.

We're all Tigers, yes, even me, now that I have become a total convert to the game. And we always will be, just as long as we continue to head out on to those fairways with our dreams intact and our purpose clear.

You don't have to climb Everest to reach your personal Everest. And you don't have to meet Tiger Woods, after all, to understand that there is a Tiger in all of us.

Now who would have thought that?

Epilogue

Some weeks later the taxi driver, who had implanted the whole idea of discovering golf into my psyche, drove me once more to the airport. He knew I had taken up golf, of course, but it had been a long time since we had last seen each other.

It was another early start to the day and I was tired. His eyes were focused on the road ahead, there were just a few slivers of ice on the edges, and the traffic was busy.

'Peter,' I said, breaking the monotony of the silence. 'You know that story you once told me, of when you were hit by a fork of lightning on the golf course, survived but recorded a poor score as a result?'

'Aha,' he replied, his eyes not diverting from the windscreen ahead.

'Would you mind telling me it again?'

My driver looked across at me sitting next to him for a split-second, before returning his gaze to the road.

'Why?' he asked.

I smiled at him. 'I think I understand where you're coming from now.'

Golf courses

1 Royal Melbourne, Australia, 5 July 2001
Score: 122
Playing partner: Bruce Green (club pro)

2 New South Wales GC, Sydney, Australia, 12 July 2001
Score: 114
Playing partner: Bill Exten (club pro)

3 Wentworth GC (east course), Surrey, England, 6 August 2001
Score: 109
Playing partner: David Rennie (club pro)

4 Sundridge Park (east course), Kent, England, 29 August 2001
Score: 104 (7 bogeys, 2 lost balls)
Playing partner: Archibald Herron (Bromley)

5 Ballybunion (Old Course), County Kerry, Ireland, 3 September 2001
Score: 103 (2 pars, 3 bogeys)
Playing partners: John and Tina Platt (Geneva) and Mark Hoffman
(New York)

6 Chislehurst GC, Kent, England, 9 September 2001
Score: 104 (2 pars, 4 bogeys)
Playing partner: Richard Barratt (Chislehurst)

7 St Andrews GC (New Course), Scotland, 11 September 2001
Score: 112 (1 par, 3 bogeys)
Playing partner: Peter Mason (external relations manager, St Andrews
Links Trust)

8 Carnoustie GC, Championship Course, Scotland, 21 September 2001
Score: 118 (1 bogey)
Playing partner: Michael Ward (student, Michigan, USA)

9 K Club, Straffan, County Kildare, Ireland, 19 October 2001
Score: 104 (first-ever birdie, 1 par, 3 bogeys)
Playing partner: Ernie Jones (club pro)

10 Costa Teguise, Lanzarote, 6 December 2001
Score: 52 after 9 holes
Playing partner: Manuel (club pro)

11 Portmarnock GC, Ireland, 25 January 2002
Score: 104 (no par, numerous bogeys)
Playing partner: nobody

12 Monarch's Course, Gleneagles, Scotland, 2 February 2002
Score: 112 (in a gale)
Playing partner: Simon Crawford (greenkeeper)

13 Championship Course, Muirfield, Scotland, 5 February 2002
Score: 116
Playing partner: Simon Laird (public relations consultant)

14 Purley Downs GC, Surrey, England, 18 February 2002
Score: 104
Playing partner: Ashley Woolfe (sports agent)

15 St-Cloud GC, Paris, France, 1 March 2002
Score: 93 (68 par 'Jaune' course)
Playing partner: Morgan Cailleaux (assistant pro)

16 Richmond GC, Surrey, England, 12 March 2002
Score: 93 (70 par)
Playing partners: Scott Gorham (musician), Nicko McBrain (musician), Glyn Johns (producer)

17 Uummannaq GC, Arctic Ocean, Greenland, 21 March 2002
Score: 90 (70 par)
Playing partners: Roy Wegerle (golf pro, ex-Premiership footballer), Ed Rice (Irish web designer)

18 Ilkley GC, Yorkshire, England, 27 March 2002
Score: 97 (69 par)
Playing partner: Mark James (golf pro, former Ryder Cup European captain)

19 Sundridge Park (west course), Kent, England, 1 April 2002
Score: 98 (69 par)

Playing partners: Gareth Hale (actor/comedian), Anthony Smith (sports shop proprietor)

20 Royal West Norfolk GC, Brancaster, Norfolk, England, 16 April 2002
Score: 98 (71 par, links)
Playing partners: sports writers (*Mail on Sunday*)

21 Cliftonville GC, North Belfast, Northern Ireland, 25 April 2002
Score: 47 (9 holes, 35 par)
Playing partners: Don McElhone, Maurice Harrison, Lee Whiteside (past club captains)

22 The De Vere Belfry, England, 9 May 2002
Score: no idea, and don't care – probably around 106!
Playing partners: Bernhard Langer (twice US Masters champion), Clive Woodward (England rugby manager), Geoff Irvine (owner, Bedford Rugby Club) at Pro-Am Tournament for Benson & Hedges Championships

23 Sundridge Park (east course), Kent, England, 16 May 2002
Score: 86
Playing partner: Archie Herron (retired banker)

24 Pro-Am Tournament for British Masters, Woburn, England (Marquess Course), 29 May 2002
Score: 98
Playing partners: Raphael Jacquelin (France, European Tour professional, 2nd in English Open 2001), PY Gerbeau (former chief executive of Millennium Dome), Peter Gethin (former Formula One racing driver)

25 Pro-Am Tournament for English Open, Forest of Arden, Coventry, England, 5 June 2002
Score: 98
Playing partners: Mark McNulty (Zimbabwe, European Tour professional), Barry Richards (former South African cricketer), G. Wijesuriya

26 Richmond GC, Surrey, England, 10 June 2002
Score: 94, (including 1 birdie)
Playing partners: Scott Gorham, Konrad Bartelski (former GB skier), Andrew Bicknell (actor)

27 Hamlet Wind Watch GC, Long Island, New York, USA, 17 June 2002
Score for 9 holes: 45
Playing partner: Mark Reason (writer)

28 Chart Hills GC, Kent, England, 28 June 2002
    Score for 12 holes: 60
    Playing partner: Simon Crane

29 Hever GC, Kent, England, 11 July 2002
    Score: 105
    Playing partner: Gareth Hale

30 Northwood GC, Hertfordshire, England, 12 August 2002
    Score: 104
    Playing partners: Joe Melling, Malcolm Vallerius (sports journalists)

31 Dale Hill, Ticehurst, Kent, England, 17 August 2002
    Score: 104
    Playing partners: Gareth Hale, Mark Fisher

32 Narita GC, Tokyo, Japan, 29 August 2002
    Score: 93
    Playing partner: Taizo Kawata (Japanese Golf Association, R&A)

33 Sundridge Park, (east course), Kent, England, 6 September 2002
    Score: 89
    Playing partner: Archie Herron (retired banker)

34 Harleyford GC, Marlow, Buckinghamshire, England, 13 September
    2002
    Score: 100
    Playing partner: Sir Steve Redgrave (five times Olympic rowing
    champion)

35 Royal St George's, Sandwich, Kent, England, 20 September 2002
    Score: 101
    Playing partner: Michael Brooks (club pro, former Walker Cup player)

36 Purley Downs GC, Surrey, England, 24 September 2002
    Score: 91
    Playing partner: Ashley Woolfe

37 Sundridge Park, (east course), Kent, England, 2 October 2002
    Score: 90
    Playing partner: Archie Herron (retired banker)

38 Sundridge Park, (east course), Kent, England, 5 October 2002
    Score: 91
    Playing partner: Gareth Hale

39 Wentworth GC (Edinburgh Course), Surrey, England, 11 October 2002
    Back 9 holes only
    Score: 45

Playing partner: David Rennie (club pro)

40 Queenwood GC, Ottershaw, Surrey, England, 14 October 2002
Back 9 only
Score: 47
Playing partners: Ernie Els, Lewis Atkinson (Challenge Tour golf pro),
Brian Mahon (retired businessman)

41 Pedham Place GC, Swanley, Kent, England, 18 October 2002
Score: 92
Playing partner: David Young (teaching pro, World of Golf, Sidcup)

42 Tsada GC, Cyprus, 25 October 2002
Score: 91
Playing partners: Gareth Hale, Mark Fisher, Bob Wilson

43 Sundridge Park, (east course), Kent, England, 7 November 2002
Score: 93
Playing partner: Gareth Hale

44 Pedham Place, Swanley, Kent, 27 November 2002
Score: 91
Playing partners: Archie Herron, John Fenn

45 St Andrews, (Old Course), Scotland, 29 November 2002
Score: 91 (1 birdie, 4 pars)
Playing partner: Peter Mason

46 St Pierre, Chepstow, Wales, 9 December 2002
Score: 92
Playing partners: Malcolm Vallerius, Paul Morgan, Nick Wainwright
(Associated Newspapers)

47 Celtic Manor, Newport, Wales, 14 January 2003
Score: 97
Playing partner: Stuart Evans (sales & marketing department, Celtic
Manor Resort)

48 Pedham Place, Swanley, Kent, 23 January 2003
Score: 91

49 Pedham Place, Swanley, Kent, 25 January 2003
Score: 91

50 Wentworth, (Edinburgh Course), Surrey, England, 29 January 2003
Score: 109
Playing partner: David Rennie